CONDUCTED TOUR

"We all have our fantasies. Ever since I discovered the effect that music could have on me, which was long before I began to write for a living, I have dreamed of being commissioned by some exceptionally understanding magazine or newspaper editor to spend several months going round the music festivals of Europe, provided with tickets for all the performances, a lavish expense account and a beautiful woman, with nothing to do in return but write an article on each of the festival cities visited and the delights found there.

One day, I found myself in the position of the young fellow of Crewe, who dreamt he was eating his shoe; he woke in the night in a terrible fright, *and found it was perfectly true.* Early in 1980, I was approached by Mr George Fisher, Head of Talks for the B.B.C.'s Radio Three, who calmly invited me to live out my fantasy in reality: would I, he asked, care to give a series of broadcasts on a representative selection of European festivals? Yes, I said judiciously, on the whole I rather thought I would . . ."

BERNARD LEVIN

BERNARD LEVIN

"The most remarkable journalist of his kind since
G. K. Chesterton"
Alan Watkins

"The most brilliant columnist in the English language"
Woodrow Wyatt

"The most remarkable journalist of our time"
Philip Toynbee

"The nearest thing to a national institution"
Christopher Booker

BERNARD LEVIN

CONDUCTED TOUR

CORONET BOOKS
Hodder and Stoughton

Copyright © 1981 by Bernard Levin

First published in Great Britain 1982
by Jonathan Cape Ltd

Coronet edition 1983

British Library C.I.P.

Levin, Bernard
    Conducted tour.
    1. Music festivals
    I. Title
    780'.7'924   ML35

ISBN 0 340 32359 0

Printed and bound in Great Britain for
Hodder and Stoughton Paperbacks, a division
of Hodder and Stoughton Ltd, Mill Road,
Dunton Green, Sevenoaks, Kent (Editorial
Office: 47 Bedford Square, London, WC1
3DP) by Richard Clay (The Chaucer Press)
Ltd, Bungay, Suffolk

To the B.B.C., of course

Acknowledgments

The suggestion that I should write this book came from Robin Day; travelling together on a train, we talked of summer plans, and I told him of the B.B.C.'s invitation to me to deliver a series of festival broadcasts. 'While you're about it,' he said, 'why not do a book on the subject as well?' At first, I thought I could use the texts of the broadcasts, with suitable amendment, as the bulk of the book, but this proved quite impracticable, and I have incorporated only a few paragraphs on the talks into the diary I eventually settled on for the form. Anyway, my warmest thanks go to Robin, as also to Beatrix Miller, who solved a problem that had defeated me, the publishers and countless other friends: she thought of the title.

Alan Haydock, the B.B.C. radio producer in charge of the broadcasts, and his secretary Jane Rundle, did much to simplify the inevitably complicated travel and ticket arrangements; even more valuable were Alan's many invariably wise and helpful suggestions over the talks, which stood me in good stead for the book also. Brian Inglis read the proofs with his customary care. The ways in which my secretary, Sally Chichester, helped are as always too many to list. To these, too, my thanks are extended.

A substantial part of the book was written in the beautiful garden in Spain of Tom and Fleur Cowles Meyer, a perfect oasis of peace and harmony; I am very grateful to them.

Once again, Tom Maschler of Jonathan Cape and my literary agent, Graham Watson of Curtis Brown, have been unfailing in their encouragement, as has Sue Freathy of Spokesmen, the broadcasting arm of Curtis Brown; my gratitude is extended to them also.

The index was compiled by Oula Jones of the Society of Indexers. This admirable and essential profession rarely receives its public due, though the work requires a high degree of skill and application; I am most grateful for the care and understanding that Mrs Jones has brought to the task.

Finally, Arianna Stassinopoulos, my companion on most of the tour, provided, in lavish abundance, support and sympathy that never failed, even when Alitalia lost her luggage; no more searching test of a loving and generous spirit could be devised. For that, and for her careful reading of the first draft and the suggestions she made, I am deeply indebted to her.

Contents

Introduction

We all have our fantasies. Ever since I discovered the effect that music could have on me, which was long before I began to write for a living, I have dreamed of being commissioned by some exceptionally understanding magazine or newspaper editor to spend several months going round the music festivals of Europe, provided with tickets for all the performances, a lavish expense account and a beautiful woman, with nothing to do in return but write an article on each of the festival cities visited and the delights found there. (Sometimes the vision ends in marriage to the beautiful woman, who in any case is doing the driving. The perceptive editor is paying for the hire of the car, of course.)

One day, I found myself in the position of the young fellow of Crewe, who dreamt he was eating his shoe; he woke in the night in a terrible fright, *and found it was perfectly true.* Early in 1980, I was approached by Mr George Fisher, Head of Talks for the B.B.C.'s Radio Three, who calmly invited me to live out my fantasy in reality: would I, he asked, care to give a series of broadcasts on a representative selection of European festivals? Yes, I said judiciously, on the whole I rather thought I would.

The idea of writing a book about my summer journey, which in the end stretched from May to November, came later. But I think I am bound to say something first about what came earlier, which was my love of music-going in general and festival-going in particular.

I do not come of a musical family. There was a piano in the

parlour of my infancy, an upright with handsome sconces, and among my earliest memories are those of the regular visits of the tuner, whom I would watch in astonishment and fascination, having no idea what he was doing, or why. But I have only the most fleeting recollection of ever hearing it played; even if I have not imagined the scene altogether, the only possible pianist would have been a favourite aunt who died young. One of my mother's two brothers played the 'cello, though in a dance-band, and the brother-in-law of my other uncle was a violinist in the London Philharmonic Orchestra, and was destined much later to play a significant part in my discovery of music, but apart from these the only other musical theme in my childhood was one which very nearly put me off music altogether for the rest of my life.

When I was born, and I dare say the tradition still persists, it was the custom of every Jewish mother of humble origin and unmoneyed circumstances to be convinced that her son, particularly if he was an only son (as I was), was destined to be the next Kreisler or Heifetz. By the time I was old enough for the theory to be put to the test on me, the currently envisaged destiny was for the child to be the next Menuhin, who was the most recent in the line of prodigies; when Yehudi Menuhin's sensational London début took place I was one year old, and I have no doubt that my mother, reading accounts of the *Wunderkind* in the *News Chronicle*, gazed thoughtfully at my cot and began to think about the pride she would feel as *her* son trotted knickerbockered on to the platform at the Albert Hall and trotted off an hour later with his hair full of rose-petals.

When I was seven, therefore, a miniature violin was bought for me, like the old dancing-master's 'kit'. It came equipped with a bow, a plentiful supply of rosin, a yellow duster, and a fat little black cushion which rested between my left collarbone and the back of the violin; the purpose of this device neither I nor anybody else understood, and indeed it remained obscure to me until ten minutes ago when, embarking on this sentence, it occurred to me to solve the ancient mystery by consultation with Grove, who explained that the cushion was used to prevent the player hunching up his left shoulder in the effort to keep the instrument steady, and thus running the risk of impairing his left-hand technique. I am glad I did not impair my left-hand technique.

All that remained was for a tutor to be engaged. I do not know what was the going rate for violin lessons in the mid-1930s; not very much, I suppose. But however small the fees may have been, I have no doubt that they were a considerable strain on the family finances, particularly since equity demanded that my sister should be taught an instrument too, in her case the piano, though in her case without expectations of the Albert Hall. (In 1980, the educational authorities of one or two of the English counties discontinued, as an economy measure, the provision out of the rates of individual tuition for children whose parents wished them to learn to play an instrument, and a very great fuss was made about it, from which it would have been perfectly possible to deduce that the counties in question had made it illegal, on pain of summary execution, for any child to learn to make music, rather than that they had done no more than decide that one form, and only one, of the learning in question should no longer be paid for by other people. I mention this to show what a long way we have come in a fairly short time; my mother certainly must have found it very difficult to pay for our music lessons, but it would never have occurred to her to ask her neighbours to foot the bill.)

When I think of what now followed, and by what hair's breadth I avoided acquiring a lasting hatred of the very thought of music and an even more intense loathing of its sound, I offer up a *Heilige Dankgesang* to St Cecilia, and beseech her to intervene, as she surely must have done for me, on behalf of I know not how many other children who, with no innate musical aptitude, fall into the hands of teachers who are quite unable to convey to them any sense whatever of what music actually *is*, apart from the notes on the paper and the horrible noises that the unprodigious infant makes in an attempt to reproduce them. Such a teacher was the well-meaning soul who took my musical tuition in hand, and who, for two and a half years, before I finally struck work and refused to spend another minute practising in such torment, left me in complete ignorance even of the fact that there were such things as works of music – sonatas, quartets, concertos, even symphonies – let alone that it was possible to go and listen to them, and derive much enjoyment from doing so. For two and a half years I laboured at this joyless thing they called music without so much as learning the name of a single composer, or indeed discovering that such people existed. Up and down the scales I went, progressing in the end as far as a rendition of 'The Bluebells of Scotland'; I have detested that tune ever since, and it is a mercy I have not grown up with a similar abhorrence of bluebells, or even Scotland.

Of course, there was Sir Robert Mayer, whose Children's Concerts had been going since 1922; but even Sir Robert had to wait until somebody – parent, uncle, teacher, friend – actually brought the child to the hall, and nobody thought to bring me. Some time after my ninth birthday, therefore, I abandoned my violin for ever, and acquired a scooter in its place; I frequently fell off it and skinned my knees, but I never doubted that I had got the better of the bargain.

My boarding-school, Christ's Hospital, though no Bryanston or Dartington, was very musical; there was an orchestra and a choir as well as a brass band, and rooms for practice. But the burnt child shunned the fire, and it was not until my last couple of years, when a group of the more musical boys founded a gramophone society and began to give recitals on Sunday afternoons, that, for the first time in my life, I sat down and listened to music.

I wish I could say that there and then the gates of heaven were flung open for me, but it was a slow business at first. Some years ago, talking to Colin Davis, who had not long since been appointed Musical Director at the Royal Opera House, Covent Garden, I reminded him that we had been at the same school (he, already musical, had played the clarinet in the orchestra) and asked him how *his* early interest in music had been aroused. He could fix the occasion precisely; as a child he had heard Beethoven's Eighth Symphony on the radio, and been pierced through the soul by the revelation it offered him. 'But you make it sound', I said, 'like a religious conversion.' 'Yes,' he replied, 'that's exactly what it *was* like.' No such experience befell me; but without doubt those afternoons in Big Hall ploughed the soil and planted the seed. A little before my eighteenth birthday, I went to a Promenade Concert at the Albert Hall; it must have been the first post-war season of the revived Proms. A few days later, I went to another, and returned the following night for a third. In the end, I went to some thirty concerts in the two months of the Proms, and a month or so later I scrambled up to the gallery of Covent Garden for my first opera. Whatever music was, it had happened to me at last.

There followed a great making up for lost time; for several years, I must have spent an average of fully three evenings a week on music. If it wasn't a concert or an opera it was the gramophone, usually at the home of my cousin Clive, the son of the London Philharmonic violinist; he had discovered music at much the same time as I had, and together we haunted the galleries of the Albert Hall and Covent Garden, the Sunday night chamber-music concerts at Conway Hall (a shilling – sit anywhere – and twopence for a programme), the maiden-auntish Wigmore, little dreaming that in the fullness of the years someone would build an even uglier concert-room, and call it the Queen Elizabeth Hall.

Uncle Alex used to get us tickets for the L.P.O.'s concerts at a reduced price; more, he would often look in on us in Clive's room as we listened, discussed and argued, and join in the musical conversation. He was no theoretician or musicologist, but he conveyed to us a vast amount of musical understanding, from the bee's-eye viewpoint of an orchestral player; if only it had been he who had put that fiddle under my chin, and bade me play 'The Bluebells of Scotland'! He also taught us some of the rhymes that orchestral musicians – a notoriously ribald lot – sing under their breath to familiar tunes, and to this day I cannot hear the waltz from the Serenade for Strings by Tchaikovsky without also hearing a quatrain which begins 'Ha-ave you seen our Nellie make water?'

But to this day, also, I cannot hear Bach's Third Brandenburg Concerto without conjuring up the magical years in which I was making my journey into music. We cannot remember how the practice began, but Clive and I invariably used to end our evenings at the gramophone by playing the Third Brandenburg; its palate-cleansing properties (for who could go to bed on the Eroica or the Brahms Fourth?) provided the perfect coda for such occasions, and left us hungry for more when the next occasion presented itself. I heard it played, with variations, by a busking violinist in a passageway of the Madrid Underground at the beginning of a ten-day intermezzo in this festival summer, and the trick worked instantly; before three bars had gone by, I was drowning in memories.

After the how, the who. At that age, you have to be very odd not to fall without reservation under the spell of Beethoven, and for me, too, he was music's god. As the years go by, I find – this, also, is not an uncommon phenomenon – that Beethoven's hold weakens. Nowadays, a year can easily pass without my hearing the Emperor, whereas at the age of nineteen I was convinced that I would die if I didn't hear it once a fortnight. 'All life', I once wrote, 'is a progress towards Mozart', and what I meant (the remark was widely misunderstood) was that the older we get the more we seek, unless we are incapable of seeking anything, for an answer to those questions which Mozart asks but which Beethoven (the symphonic Beethoven, at any rate) simply buries beneath the molten lava pouring from his volcano of certainty, optimism and joy. Nowadays, I listen far more often to the Beethoven Quartets, particularly the late ones, than to the symphonies,

and to the piano sonatas than to the concertos, and my evenings are far more often spent in the company of Mozart and
Schubert, who were only on the fringes of my young musical
life when Beethoven reigned in glory.

Next came Wagner, which was the *coup de foudre*. I heard the
Tannhäuser Overture on the radio one evening, and can only
describe my feelings in the words attributed to Lesueur at his
first hearing of the Beethoven Fifth: 'I couldn't put on my hat,
because I couldn't find my head'. In those days, Wagner had an
evening a week to himself at the Proms, but the war-long ban
on performances of his music meant that those young people
who were a few years my senior had grown up, musically,
without him, and I have a vivid recollection of vast empty
spaces in the Promenade, where the young usually stood,
while the rest of the Albert Hall was crammed to suffocation
with the older concert-goers who had learned to love Wagner
before they learned that they shared that love with Hitler, and
were getting their first doses of the drug for six years, while I
gulped it down by the bucket with all the enthusiasm of the
newly addicted.

Does his hold weaken too? Yes, it does, though even now,
when I hear the opening bars of the Prelude to *Tristan*, or the
merest growl from Fafner as a snatch of *Siegfried* passes by, or
the shimmering wonder of the Good Friday Spell from *Parsifal*, the passion flares up, and in a few seconds I am once again
drunk beyond breathalyzers. Besides, though I can now conceive of a time when I no longer want, or at least *need*, to hear
the *Ring* or *Tristan*, *Lohengrin* or even *Parsifal*, I cannot see how
life would be possible without *The Mastersingers*. For *The
Mastersingers* is life itself, in all its passing shadows and enduring splendour, and I could no more imagine, or indeed find
tolerable, a world without it than I could think myself into a
world without *The Marriage of Figaro*.

But the shift of emphasis to *The Mastersingers* is a vital clue.
In my early days of Wagner-mania, the four volumes of
Shaw's music criticism were my four gospels; I read them until

I knew huge chunks of them by heart, and I can recite much of them still. It is unwise to assume that the only influence on the development of a musical taste is the music, for the written word can set off explosions of its own; I had read Shaw on Wagner (not only the criticisms but *The Perfect Wagnerite*) well before that first hearing of the *Tannhäuser* Overture, and he had not only awakened my curiosity but in a very real sense injected the fever-agent into my bloodstream, so that I was already in a sufficiently debilitated state to make it certain that I would succumb as soon as I was exposed to the more potent strain of the bacillus in the form of the music itself. It was only many years later, when I began to notice that there were more clergymen in the Royal Opera House on Wagner nights than at performances of any other composer's works, and that most of them were alone, that I also began to wonder what it was in Wagner that appealed to me so much, and what it was that I had in common with the clergymen and Shaw, and for that matter Hitler. We may fear the great emotions, but we need them, and if we cannot allow them into our lives directly, we are under the necessity of bringing them in vicariously, and therefore, we like to think, safely. Whence the clergymen, Hitler, and me. And whence, at last now, the weakening hold.

I came to some composers very late, for purely accidental reasons; when I was setting out on the great journey, Bruckner was hardly known at all in Britain, and his symphonies were therefore very little played; it was years before I began to get to know those vast cathedrals and to realize that their composer can stand comparison with Beethoven himself; there are fashions in music as in everything else, and from fashion grows habit, and habit plays a much greater part in the settlement of our musical and other tastes than we like to think. (I did not get the Sibelius habit early, and the consequence is that I have still not got it, and am conscious whenever I hear one of the symphonies that I am missing a great deal. But I think that I shall never get the habit of Mahler.)

Mozart and Schubert, however, took hold only very gradually. There was plenty of Mozart available, of course, when I was young, though not so much Schubert as there is now, and of course I listened to a lot of it, and of course I had no doubt that here was one of the highest peaks in the whole range. Yet even the symphonies, even the operas themselves, did not touch me as deeply as did Beethoven and Wagner, and every new discovery I made in those formative days served, though I did not then know it, to push further away the moment of true awakening. There was Richard Strauss, for instance, who at first had almost as overwhelming an effect as Wagner; *Rosenkavalier* went straight on to the top shelf of the Pantheon. Nowadays, having more knowledge of what cunning can do, I see through it, and watch it, with one eyebrow up and one down, even while all the young *Rosenkavalier* virgins around me in the darkness are falling in love; but there is no danger of its ever being expelled from its place. There was also Rossini, who is surely the most under-rated genius in all music, much more so even than Haydn, for Haydn is under-rated only by fools, whereas Rossini is dismissed even by many of the understanding.

But Mozart, as I say, stood somewhere where I could only really see him out of the corner of my eye. And here I came up against something puzzling, for Shaw was not only Wagner's champion, but also Mozart's. I can still feel the indignation I experienced when he insisted, as he does throughout his music criticism, that Mozart was a greater artist than Beethoven; Lucifer trying to throw God out of Heaven would not have struck me as of greater impiety. Shaw, obviously, had missed the point (he had to miss it, or rewrite his own life), and analysed Mozart's superiority to Beethoven in terms of greater originality; the pioneer is a more creative figure than the consolidator. The argument is nonsense in itself, and greater nonsense as a substitute for the real argument, but the burr clung to my mind, and eventually, as Mozart grew and grew in my heart (he has not stopped growing yet), I began to realize that Shaw had stumbled accidentally upon the most profound truth of all. So perhaps he prepared my bloodstream for the healing antibody of Mozart, too.

All this took time; at what point did the festival habit start? I went to my first festival in 1947, at Edinburgh. It was the first Edinburgh Festival, too; Rudolf Bing, whose great vision it was, was sufficiently practical to have spotted the fact that with Europe's musical life in ruins amid all the other ruins, the first city to start a truly international festival would have the pick of the best for the asking. Later, other cities woke up to the same truth, and still later others awoke to a newer truth, which was that even if there was now not enough to go round, and the smaller and less lavish festivals could not hope to compete for the greatest musical and dramatic attractions, *any* kind of festival could be relied upon to bring in visitors; the great era of festival tourism had dawned, and soon any town in search of tourists could rub two aldermen against a 'cello and call the resultant wisp of smoke a festival. But in 1947, Edinburgh did indeed have the whole of Europe to pick from, and on that first visit, when Clive and I stayed for the entire three weeks, there was a feast the like of which had probably never been assembled before, not even at Salzburg in the Thirties, and was never to be assembled again. The principal orchestra was the Vienna Philharmonic; it was conducted by Bruno Walter, who was renewing his acquaintance with the orchestra for the first time since he was driven from Austria as the Nazis marched in. They played the Schubert C Major Symphony; they also played for Elizabeth Schumann, and for Kathleen Ferrier, who was to die, tragically, only six years later at the height of her powers. There was a piano quartet assembled *ad hoc* for the Festival; normally, an *ad hoc* quartet would inevitably be unsatisfactory beside those ensembles who had been playing together for years, but this was no normal *ad hoc* quartet, for the 'cellist was Pierre Fournier, the violinist Joseph Szigeti, the violist William Primrose and the pianist Artur Schnabel. The opera was given by the very recently re-formed Glyndebourne company, which had still

not started again in Sussex, and was not to do so for several
more years; they offered *Figaro*, with a cast assembled on the
same ruthless principle that ruled throughout the compilation
of the entire Festival – the point in this case being that with
half Europe's opera houses not yet rebuilt after being destroyed during the war, and with few companies operating
even where there were buildings to house them, singers were
happy to come to a city the very existence of which can hardly
have been suspected previously by most of them. Anyway,
Italo Tajo remains, after a third of a century, the finest Figaro I
have ever heard, and the young Giulietta Simionato the finest
Cherubino, just as, in the other Glyndebourne production of
that first Edinburgh, Verdi's *Macbeth*, Margherita Grandi
remains the finest Lady Macbeth. Meanwhile, down the road
at the Empire Theatre (a venue even more unsuitable for ballet
than the King's Theatre for opera) the Sadlers Wells Ballet – it
had not yet acquired the 'Royal' – were giving *The Sleeping
Beauty* with a cast which included Margot Fonteyn, Beryl
Grey and Frederick Ashton. Even the theatre, which lost its
hold in the official programme at Edinburgh very early, and
has rarely regained it, the official drama having long since been
overshadowed by the gargantuan Fringe, provided productions to excite a growing love of the drama, and help to fix the
festival habit as it did so. Louis Jouvet's company had come
from Paris with Molière's *L'Ecole des Femmes* and Giraudoux's
Ondine, and the Old Vic company, which had been re-
assembled towards the end of the war on the same principle
that governed Edinburgh (at one time the company included
Olivier, Richardson, Guinness, Sybil Thorndike, Margaret
Leighton and Pamela Brown all at once) came from London
with *Richard II*, in which the young Guinness as Richard faced
the young Harry Andrews as Bolingbroke.

Next year, Clive and I went to Salzburg, where we heard
Fidelio, conducted by Furtwängler, with Kirsten Flagstad as
Leonore, Julius Patzak as Florestan and Paul Schöffler as
Pizarro. That settled it.

All music-lovers, it is true, dwell in a golden age of the past, and this naturally coincides, more often than not, with the years in which they were making their own discovery of music. Even as I searched the heavens of memory for that catalogue of musical stars in the preceding paragraphs, I was aware that most of the names would mean little or nothing to many readers younger than I, their heads understandably full of Mehta and Muti, Barenboim and Brendel, Zukerman and Perlman, Domingo, Pavarotti, Vickers, Caballé, Cotrubas, te Kanawa. But then, when I was young my galaxy could not compare with those of my elders, and I would listen unbelieving as I was told how my heroes and heroines could not hold a candle to Melchior and Leider, Ponselle and Lehmann, Caruso and Chaliapin, Kreisler, Paderewski, Casals, Rachmaninoff, Ysaye. I didn't believe my elders, and do not expect my juniors to believe me, for if every generation is right then either there has been a consistent decline in musical standards from the day that music was born, or distance lends enchantment to the hearing. Or perhaps not; perhaps the Second World War, a watershed for so much in our world, and the end of so much that was precious and irreplaceable, swept away something from the arts too, and left behind only something lesser. Perhaps a musical golden age did close in September 1939, and perhaps my generation did have the good fortune to hear its very last echoes immediately after the war ended, before those echoes faded for ever.

But my habit of festival-going, once acquired, has been almost as difficult to divest myself of as the habit of music itself. On the other hand, why should I divest myself of it? For even if the giants who once roamed the land at festival-time no longer do so, and in so far as they do are never now assembled in the kind of profusion that was once available, the habit of festival-going is an exceptionally rewarding one. To begin with, many of Europe's festivals are set in outstandingly pleasant places. Salzburg, Florence, Edinburgh, Aix-en-Provence, Lucerne, Bath, Verona, Aldeburgh, Bregenz,

Granada – all these are well worth visiting out of festival-time, and many of them did not have to wait for someone to found a festival on the premises to become attractive to visitors; Florence, after all, had been on every civilized European's itinerary for some centuries. The ideal festival town, I have noticed, is of a size big enough to accommodate all those who want to come, but small enough to be dominated, at festival-time, by its festival function. Thus, Edinburgh is the biggest city that can have a festival within the meaning of the act; there is one in London, but it has to be called the *City* of London Festival, and in any case nobody has ever heard of it. There are festivals in Berlin and Vienna, too, but although good work is done at both, they cannot be taken seriously as festivals; the cities are too big and too full of their own business to bow for two or three weeks in the year to the visiting muses. But if the festival town is small enough, the visitor is struck at once by the festival atmosphere, which at its best seems to seep from the very walls. The truth (which is never told) about the banners that fly all along both sides of Edinburgh's Princes Street at festival-time is that they are almost invariably hideous; but behind that truth lies a far more important one, which is that it doesn't matter. Edinburgh's banners are not there as an exhibition of paintings; they are there to announce, like a peal of visual trumpets, however eldritch the tune, that this splendid city is *en fête* once more.

But there must be more to it than that. After Edinburgh and Salzburg, I went to Aldeburgh. After that came Glyndebourne, then Florence, then Bayreuth, then Aix, then Wexford; the most recently acquired festival in my quiver, which is also the youngest of any note in Europe, is Hohenems. And it cannot be an accident that festival-going has become so pleasant a habit for so many people. Some return year after year to the same place, some choose a different festival each year, some, and I am one of them, have a regular rendezvous with an occasional visit elsewhere. What is the special attraction of a festival for visitors who have access all year round to good music, good theatre, beautiful scenery, handsome buildings, fine food?

It is not an easy question to answer, but I could hardly have written this book without coming to some conclusions on the subject. First, and most obvious, the festival visitor is normally on holiday; how much sweeter music sounds at the end of a day of walking, bathing, sunning, sipping, than of a day of working! Music, of course, *is* a holiday in one crucial sense; a holiday from the mind. We cannot take in any artistic experience through the mind, and music least of all; art enters only through the feelings, and if music should ever need to justify its existence it can claim to provide a means of quietening the mind so that not only can its own strains be heard, but that, when they have died away, the heart and soul have been made more receptive to those silent harmonies the hearing of which is the goal of life. With the cares of daily life left behind, the claims of eternal life can be heard; no wonder music seems more intense at a festival, where music-making, for those weeks out of time, is the whole purpose of the place in which it is being made.

In addition, though perhaps it is only an extension of the same point, the grace of such festival centres as Salzburg or Florence reinforces these feelings; the harmonies of Fischer von Erlach's architecture in the first, and of Brunelleschi's and Michelangelo's masterpieces in the second, make the visitor's soul vibrate in tune even before a note of music has sounded. I even wonder whether it is entirely a coincidence that Wagner's festival, which offers the most deeply disturbing music, belying, at least in the *Ring*, *Tristan* and *Lohengrin*, the claims of the festival spirit to provide celestial harmony, is housed in the least attractive town of them all.

Then again, the performers are likely to be striving to get closer to perfection; festival performances, in which more often than not there has been insufficient rehearsal time, are generally of an exceptionally high standard. It is not just that the performers are trying harder, either; the festival atmosphere has a quality that gives them something extra with which to strive, and I have often heard singers and instrumentalists perform better at a festival than I have ever heard them do in the course of ordinary music-going. And such feelings provide a two-way traffic; audiences tend to take more trouble at festivals (with the prices of the tickets at some of them, it is not surprising), not only dressing better but behaving better, even listening better. How can they fail to feel that a festival is something greater than the sum of its parts?

Festival towns tend to be furnished with better food than the average; festival weather tends to be sunny; the countryside around festival centres tends to be beautiful, and easy of access; if the Festival Director knows his business, the programmes are balanced with special care, and if the town's Director of Tourism knows his, there are always plenty of extra-curricular activities available. The total credit, totted up, is impressive; so many tens of thousands of festival-lovers bear eloquent witness to the attraction of the habit.

And the profusion of festivals in Europe is testimony no less convincing to the widespread incidence of the habit among European lovers of the arts. There are literally too many to count; but the total must be well into four figures. This, as may be imagined, made the selection of festivals for my tour extraordinarily difficult. A few, of course, chose themselves; I could not leave out Salzburg, Edinburgh or Bayreuth, the Big Three, nor did I feel I could omit Aldeburgh. To Wexford and Hohenems I would have gone anyway, as also to Glyndebourne. I was abruptly invited to Adelaide. But that still left an almost infinite variety of permutations available. There were geographical considerations; the list had to take in as many countries as possible. There had to be variety in the kinds of programme to be found at the festivals included, from the huge eclectic choice offered at Edinburgh to the fortnight of a single composer provided at Hohenems. Moreover, the selection had to take in festivals with different atmospheres;

the dedication and sausages of Bayreuth would contrast well with the gaiety and champagne of Wexford, the charm and innocence of Aldeburgh with the sophistication and over-charging of Salzburg, the Verdi of Florence with the Schubert of Hohenems, the unfailing warmth of Provence at Aix with the howling gales and pitiless rain of Edinburgh. And there was chronology to be considered, too, from Florence in May to Wexford at the end of October.

In the end, the selection was made, though I was very conscious that it could have been made with countless different combinatons. But that was not the end of the matter, for the next thing I had to decide was how much knowledge of, or interest in, the subject of festivals, and the music heard at them, I could assume for this book. On this at any rate I came to a firm conclusion; I hope the right one. Bernard Shaw, when he became a music critic as 'Corno di Bassetto', vowed to make 'musical criticism readable by the deaf'. That was a fairly audacious claim (though, incidentally, he made it good); my own ambition goes no further than to make this book of interest, and I hope of pleasure, to readers who have never been to a music festival and have no great desire to do so, as well as to those who are familiar with one or more of the musical gatherings described in the following pages.

This is, after all, a travel book, not a work of musical analysis or instruction. The unmusical reader need not fear that he will be regaled with tales of second subjects modulating into the remote key of B flat minor or of slurred semi-quavers in the soprano's *cabaletta*; the musically knowledgeable can likewise be reassured that they are not going to be told that Parsifal is the hero of the opera of that name or that Mozart was an Austrian composer of the late eighteenth century. Anatole France defined his literary criticism as 'the adventures of my soul among masterpieces'. This book does indeed describe the adventures of my soul among the musical and other masterpieces which I had the good fortune to hear, but it also describes my adventures among cities and hotels and trains, and the adventures of my eyes among sights, of my mind among thoughts prompted by my journeyings, of my memory among reminiscences of earlier travellings for the same purpose, of my palate among the varying cuisines of Europe.

No morals will be drawn, and none therefore need be sought; no axe will be ground, and no neck therefore need quiver; no villains or heroes, other than operatic ones, will be encountered. This book is the result of the fact that I visited twelve music festivals in the space of some eight months, and had a very enjoyable time in doing so.

That is hardly surprising. For it remains abundantly true that listening to beautiful music, well played and sung, in one of the more charming festival centres of Europe, is an experience to be compared with the very best that life can offer. To look across the hurrying river at the Cathedral of Salzburg from the windows of a room at the Österreichischer Hof, its sill alive with window-boxes full of geraniums; to leave that room and stroll over to Tomaselli's, there to consume a cup of chocolate and a pastry of diabolically deceptive lightness, accompanied by an immense amount of whipped cream; to go from there, at the same leisured pace, into the Festspielhaus, and there hear Mozart sung by a fine cast and played by the Vienna Philharmonic under one of the world's leading conductors; to dine after the performance in a simple wine-house; to emerge into a balmy evening, and to wander for an hour, before going to bed, through the streets of the old town; to return to the hotel with head and heart and soul full of the Countess's '*Perdona, perdona*', and the chorus of benediction and joy which follows it; this is to pass a day at a level of pleasure and fulfilment that is not easily surpassed.

And if that seems too grand, and something simpler is sought, try this. Leave a less luxurious hotel in Aldeburgh and stroll up the High Street to the Festival Office in its handsome Georgian building; catch the bus outside, full of music-goers, friendliness and expectation; travel through the lanes to Snape; hear there a recital of songs, carefully balanced between the familiar and unfamiliar, by one of England's loveliest voices; eat simply but well, of fresh natural food; return to the hotel, there to be lulled to sleep by the sound of a gentle sea; the experience will be very different from the one in Salzburg, but the peace and satisfaction at the end of it will be of a like quality. If I have succeeded in conveying something of that peace and satisfaction in the book which you now have in your hands I shall be well content.

1 ADELAIDE

The White Queen

Landing in Adelaide, with all my northern-hemisphere pre-judices and concomitant guilt-feelings intact, I feel horribly like Mr Micawber contemplating *his* first visit to Australia:

> This country I am come to conquer! Have you honours? Have you riches? Have you posts of profitable pecuniary emolument? Let them be brought forward. They are mine!

Christopher Hunt, the Festival Director, who had invited me, meets me at the airport; he is a lean and leathery man, whom it would be no use trying to eat in a siege. He warns me that Adelaide is a city of a million inhabitants with the outlook of a town of 25,000; a somewhat daunting introduction. I console myself; even if I don't like this country, I have planned to stop in India on my way home, and I know I like India.

I am given a brisk tour of the city; and the first surprise is a big one: the place is beautiful. The centre square mile is a very square mile indeed, its squareness emphasized by the fact that it is laid out in a regular grid without curves. This square is surrounded by parks; you could walk right round the whole thing without leaving grass or losing sight of the spire of St Peter's Cathedral. The square is Adelaide's downtown; it contains almost all the city's important public buildings, including a Town Hall that looks like a railway station, a railway station that looks like Parliament, and a Parliament that looks like a copy of the Parthenon made to the designs of a man with a bad memory.

The streets are astonishingly clean; they might be swept every morning with a crumb-brush for all the litter that is visible. I can see no modern building of any architectural distinction within the magic square, but the unbroken sunshine makes the whole place glitter, providing an optical illusion which suggests that the entire city is made of white stone.

Outside the square and its encircling green girdle are the suburban hillsides, confettily bestrewn with the villas of this obviously prosperous city's inhabitants. That they are bungalows presumably reflects, like the immense width of the streets, the fact that Australia can afford to be profligate with space; but what is betokened by the fact that no two are alike? The white-painted wood or metal filigree that breaks the line of the eaves and porches strongly suggests something consciously English, a hint of lace curtains in the old country overlooking those billiard-table lawns, shining in the abundant sun; there is no reason at all to suppose that the people who live in these villas are eager to come to terms with the new world of haste and productivity in Sydney (there can be few Western cities of a million people that contain so little industry), let alone in Europe, the United States and Japan.

WEDNESDAY, MARCH 19TH

Adelaide women wear hats. For that matter, they carry parasols, and must be the last on earth to do so. I notice this on my way to the Festival Centre.

This is a remarkable building; it stands just outside the square mile, stark white against the green of the park. More than white now, for the plaza in front of it has been turned into a fairground, alive with colour and noise; there are booths selling everything from apples to cobwebs, the latter designed to make your brashest Barossa Valley *vin de l'année* look like an ancient and immeasurably valuable Mouton Rothschild; there is a stand from which you can hire bicycles (though nothing in central Adelaide is far enough from anything else to be worth the extravagance); there is a popcorn-dispenser, roasting as it sells; a miniature stage on which something – clowns, folk-dancers, Punch-and-Judy, jazz groups – is happening from morning till far into the night; there is a children's playground, a bar, a café, a souvenir-stall, an Information Bureau, there are poets reciting their works, conjurers prestidigitating, lovers holding hands, and a gloomy gentleman with a placard intent upon assuring the passers-by that they would do well to repent, for the end of the world is at hand. I can see no sign of his claim coming true as I push my way through this uproar to the Festival Centre.

Australia's cultural inferiority complex (I put it as baldly as that because almost everybody I speak to raises the subject – indeed, it has an official name, 'The Australian Cringe', taken from the title of a book about it) is such that I expect to learn that the design of the building had been entrusted to an architect from abroad, as was the Sydney Opera House. But no; the building was designed by a local firm, Hassell and Partners, who had never built a theatre before, and in building three in this complex seem to have justified the city's trust. The unifying force of the building, which looks like two huge angular cheeses, the larger with a wedge taken out of the middle, is unmistakable, and the dazzling whiteness of the exterior is set off by the brown-tinted glass that separates the sloping shell from the ground like a row of teeth. The main auditorium, a 2,000-seater that can be used as opera house, theatre or concert hall, is finished in warm, dark wood, and the seats are faultlessly sprung, a phenomenon sufficiently rare nowadays to be worth noting; even more so, because even more rare, is the fact that the distance between the rows has clearly been calculated on the assumption that the patrons might well wish to bring their knees with them. Outside, there is a combination of balconies, grass and water, the last provided by the River Torrens, which runs by just beyond the Festival area, placidly belying its fierce name; it is weired off into a lake in its middle stretch, and the whole scene sparkles irresistibly in the sunshine, reminiscent of both Britain's Stratford and Canada's. I immediately promise to bring them a dozen swans on my next visit.

In the evening, I go to the Town Hall, pressed into service as a theatre, for Tom Stoppard's *Every Good Boy Deserves Favour*. I had never had any doubts about this play from its first, single performance at the Royal Festival Hall; it is a masterpiece for our time, born out of our time and its cruelty, and fashioned in a mind of genius as a lance for the army of truth and humanity. Other great satirists have used humour to deadly didactic effect; Swift, Voltaire, Jonson. But Stoppard fills the pool with a flood of laughter apparently conceived for its own sake, and only when his audience has drowned in the pool, weak with a total surrender to joy, does he permit the hideous creatures from the deep to come crawling to the surface. Freezing an audience's laughter with a stroke of horror is a familiar playwright's device, and not a particularly difficult one for a technically accomplished writer to handle, but Stoppard goes further; he shifts the whole structure bodily into the horror, and so deftly that we do not even realize that we are moving until we are there. And he goes even further than *that*; he plaits the horror and the laughter together until they are making the same point simultaneously, and we laugh ourselves helpless at the horror itself, the better to cry with rage. The first time I wrote about *Every Good Boy Deserves Favour* I said that Stoppard could write a comedy about Auschwitz if he set his mind to it, and seeing his play in Adelaide, its universal quality emphasized rather than diminished by the unfamiliarity of the surroundings and my Eurocentric feelings of incongruity at the Australian accents, I am more than ever convinced that it is literally true.

THURSDAY, MARCH 20TH

A morning matinée by a company from abroad, for schoolchildren; a very soppy story, in French: *Les Lions de*

Sable. The din before curtain-rise is at brain-damage level; I station myself on an aisle and take careful note of the position of the exits, for riot, possibly including murder and arson, is surely inevitable. Stupefaction follows; my British preconceptions simply do not hold good here, for from the moment the performance begins, it is watched in unbroken and attentive silence by the children, mostly ten to twelve years old. Abruptly, I understand the explanation of a feeling I have had since I arrived, like a corner-of-the-eye glimpse too brief and too incomplete to register on the mind; a feeling that there is something missing from the visual aspect of this city. There is: I have seen no graffiti of any kind.

In the evening, the children's older siblings, and indeed their parents, are on show at the concert in the Festival Centre by the Warsaw Philharmonic. Not an outstanding orchestra, though its chances are not improved by the decision to put it on the stage, where it is stifled by a rigid proscenium; the woodwind, at the back, may as well have stayed at home. But the brothers Paratore give a scintillating account of the Mozart two-piano concerto, and offer as an encore their own arrangement, for four hands at one keyboard, of the finale of *The Carnival of the Animals*, played in the manner of Chico Marx, though one of the brothers is the living image of Harpo.

'The show is not the show, but those who go'; there are no sumptuary regulations, but the sight of the audience is as instructive as the silence of those children, except perhaps for the gentleman in the front row of the dress circle who arrives in T-shirt and shorts and then takes his shoes and socks off the better to waggle his toes in time to the music. But the girls are as trim as the lawns of the villas, in laundered dresses and brushed hair, and their mothers, though tragically indebted to Norman Hartnell, the Annigoni of dress design, are no less faultlessly pleated and coiffed. I recall Christopher's remark about the city of a million with the outlook of a town of 25,000, and am struck by the realization that Adelaide would take it as a compliment. Adelaide is clearly behind the times. But what times, Adelaide would say, to be behind!

FRIDAY, MARCH 21ST

I discover, not altogether to my surprise, that I am able to walk on water. On the bank of the river there is a huge transparent plastic tube, a hundred yards long and some ten feet in diameter; it is tethered at both ends and projects on to the water in two short legs joined by a long cross-bar. The point, however, is that it floats freely in the river; you pay a trifling fee at the entry end, go through an air-lock, and find yourself literally walking on the water. This is very difficult at first, but after a few falls I get the hang of it and soon find myself not only walking but running. I have an uneasy moment, on emerging at the far end into the waiting crowd, in case there should be a general clamour for loaves and fishes, but the danger passes.

In the evening I discover, with little joy, what *Norman Lindsay and his Push in Bohemia* is about. Lindsay was an Australian painter; 'push' is Australian dialect for a gang or coterie; Lindsay and his push led a bohemian life. But the play is prim rather than raffish, and so is the performance.

SATURDAY, MARCH 22ND

The day begins well, with a letter in the local newspaper complaining that too few of the items in the Festival are suitable for heterosexuals. It gets better with a lunchtime concert by our own Gabrieli Quartet; Haydn (C major, Op. 54) and Richard Blackford, an interesting, and appallingly young, English composer. This, his first quartet, was written for the Gabrieli, which gave its first performance in Britain last year; I got to know him soon afterwards. He is a man of an exceptionally strong inner vision, influenced by an even stronger spiritual questing; the music is spare, bright, reflective, gradually shifting in a circle, even more impressive on a second hearing. 'All things change, but nothing dies'; the quotation is from Ovid's *Metamorphoses*, and Richard found his original inspiration in the passage.

SUNDAY, MARCH 23RD

A concert in St Peter's Cathedral; one of the nice things about the interior is that the exterior is invisible from it (I have always believed that Selfridge's Christmas decorations look the way they do because the designers are instructed to produce something that will compel at least the more sensitive of Oxford Street shoppers to duck into the store in order to get away from them). It is Rossini's Petite Messe Solenelle, though Rossini could no more be solemn than he could stop breathing, and the work sparkles along in a scandalously delightful manner. The performance, however, includes an unscheduled, indeed aleatoric, element; towards the end of the Gloria, Myer Fredman, the conductor, is suddenly joined on the podium, much to the audience's surprise and no doubt even more to his, by a lady who had until then been sitting quietly on the floor near the front, and who now, fascinated by the sight of a man waving his arms about in time to the music, has decided to practise this sport herself. Her beat strikes me as positively Furtwänglerian in its uncertainty, yet not without a certain liveliness amid its disorder, and I watch the musical forces closely to see which of the singers or players will be the first to panic and start to follow the insurgent beat instead of the loyalist version. Before it happens, however, the lady is led gently away by an attendant, and the back of Mr Fredman's head is wonderfully expressive of relief.

MONDAY, MARCH 24TH

A day for approaching the central cultural problem of Adelaide and Australia. How can Australia hope to deploy the kind of festival forces that in Europe can be drawn from a huge reservoir of cultural endeavour and experience? (Of course, Australia's population is hardly a twentieth of Western Europe's; still, it is twice Austria's, and the Vienna Philharmonic need not fear just yet the competition from the Adelaide Symphony Orchestra.) Obviously, she cannot. But that would matter less if it were not for the other prong of this cultural Morton's Fork. High artistic standards cannot be developed and maintained unless there is *regular* acess to the best. The Warsaw Philharmonic is far from being one of the world's leading orchestras; its level is that of, say, the London Symphony on a poor day, or any French orchestra on a good one. And the warmth of Adelaide's reception for it, and indeed for the feeble *Norman Lindsay*, was more than politeness; it was an indication that, in the literal sense rather than the colloquially rude, *Adelaide knows no better*. In London alone, to say nothing of the rest of Europe, I see the world's best theatre and hear the world's best conductors, orchestras, instrumentalists and singers, regularly and often; that, and that alone, explains the fact that I was less impressed than were the rest of the audience.

What can be done for people with neither absolute, nor relative standards? Tonight Adelaide gets the answer. Peter Brook and his company give, in a disused quarry and amid conditions of frightful cold, the first performance in English of *Conference of the Birds*, a play in speech and movement, based on an ancient Persian poem. The birds go to seek their mysterious king, the Simorg; their journey is beset by terrible hardship, amid which some die, some desert, some turn back, some lose heart. When the survivors reach their goal, it is to learn the world's most profound and vital truth: they are told that they have carried the Simorg with them all the time, and they realize that the treasure which we believe lies across cruel wastes, boundless oceans, towering mountains and dreadful valleys really lies always within our own hearts.

The audience reels out as men and women dazed, stunned, overturned. I am talking to Peter a few yards beyond the gate in the direction away from the route back into town, when suddenly, the stream, some six or eight spectators wide, which has been pouring out and turning straight down the hill, develops a kink, formed by the wish of hundreds of members of the audience to thank Peter before they leave, or even simply to touch him. And *there* is the solution; the absolute standards, the fructifying life that will sow seeds in Australia (Brook and company are going on to Sydney and Melbourne), to flower in a hundred unforeseeable ways for years to come, annihilating the miles between Europe and Australia by setting a-quiver that secret string of today's world, so perfectly symbolized in the play.

Peter and Natasha Brook and I have dinner together afterwards. I wonder she survived her performance in the play, dressed as she was in nothing but a thin shift whipped by arctic winds; but her laughter fills the room. A couple of lovely, relaxed hours, Peter tired but happy (as a matter of fact he is only really happy when he is tired, as it is the only proof he will accept that he has been working properly), doing his usual trick of crinkling his eyes against the light, which makes him look even more like a bear woken up from hibernation, and full of wary enthusiasm for the mighty project that now fills his horizon; an ancient Indian saga to be re-worked in Europe and then taken back to India.

He is also full of his experience of the Australian aborigines. One of his company has some connection with aboriginal life, and on arrival in Adelaide has made contact with them. Peter's theatre must have been ideal for talking across an impenetrable language barrier; after *The Ik*, with its considerable speechless content, and his extraordinary journey to Africa with a series of mime-plays, and indeed after the now-legendary *Orghast*, a play written in a language entirely devised for the purpose of writing it, and finally *The Conference of the Birds* itself, not to mention *Ubu*, there can be no man better equipped to communicate without words and without any overlapping cultural references.

That is an understatement. The Australian aborigines have a direct, orally transmitted tradition which goes back for 40,000 years. The extermination of a large part of the indigenous Australian inhabitants (the entire population of them in Tasmania) by the early settlers, and the well-meant modern efforts to assimilate them into white Australian society, have frayed that extraordinary rope until only a few strands are left. The aborigines' champions today are engaged in the struggle for land rights, for the restoration of what was taken from them; but keeping that rope from breaking is even more important. Peter has been discovering something about the nature of the rope, and now it comes bubbling out; he had invited a group of aborigines to the performance of *The Conference of the Birds*, and sat me among them, which gave me two fascinating evenings at the same time, for their reaction to the play was scarcely less interesting than the play itself. Few spoke any English (I was introduced in pidgin – 'He writes [with a mime of writing], far away [a mime of a bird, wings flapping]; he may write about *you* [more writing-mime, and pointing]' – and within minutes they were offering me their blankets against the appalling cold), but since Brook's aim is to create a universally intelligible drama he could not have happened upon a better test. I watched them surreptitiously, their extraordinary round, protuberant faces, unlike any other of the peoples of the earth, showing laughter, pity, even fear. Peter explains what he has learnt about their geographical legends, which are not simply prehistoric stories located in particular places, but stories made out of the places themselves; the land itself – valleys, peaks, rocks – is the language of the tale, so that if you stamp your foot at one of their sacred sites you are literally treading on a book which is at once their scripture, their myth and their anthropology. (It is also, they insist, their land.)

This amazing man, when he and his company finish their Australian tour, is staying on to explore the aboriginal world more thoroughly, going deep into the outback. There is a verse of Flecker's *Golden Journey* that sums up Peter Brook; it is the pilgrims speaking:

> We travel not for trafficking alone:
> By hotter winds our fiery hearts are fanned:
> For lust of knowing what should not be known
> We make the Golden Journey to Samarkand.

TUESDAY, MARCH 25TH

Why has nobody told me that Sydney is made of hills? But the hills provide the materials for a remarkable game of hide-and-seek; every time we come round one, there below is a new combination, as magical as all the others, of Sydney's four-ply masterpiece of a view: the harbour, the bridge, the Opera House and the open sea behind.

My first words at my first sight of the Opera House, jerked from me without thought, are a startled 'But it isn't white!' I have used those words before, in exactly the same circumstances, at the first shock of another building I have seen in photographs a thousand times: the Taj Mahal. The Taj Mahal is almost every colour *except* white, though the shades of pink and blue and grey are very pale, which is why it looks white even in colour photographs. (At only one time of day is it truly white; the moment just after the sun dips below the horizon, when the colour drains out of it and leaves it looking like a ghost. Then, slowly, it puts on its evening garb, and the colour comes back into its cheeks.) The Sydney Opera House, unless it, too, is rife with optical illusion, is the palest yellow-brown imaginable, which is perhaps why it fits so well with the brown glass with which the shells are fronted.

Whatever else this building is, it is undoubtedly the most operatic opera house in the world. And just as Neuschwanstein, poor mad Ludwig's eyrie among the Bavarian hills, is a two-dimensional picture translated into three dimensions (he drew it with the aid of a theatre-designer, then gave it to his architect and told him to build it), so Joern Utzon's master-piece was conceived not as architecture but sculpture. He then found that there was no way of actually building it until certain engineering problems of stress and dynamics had been solved – problems which had never been solved before.

Well, there it stands, to witness that the questions were eventually answered, and as it changes position below me every time I catch sight of the view from yet another angle (it is huge, incidentally, and holds its own comfortably even against the mighty proportions of the bridge), I reflect that the comparison with the Taj Mahal is not so absurd as it might seem.

It is inconceivable that Utzon did not have consciously in mind the array of sails with which the water around and beyond the Opera House site is so lavishly dotted; his building picks up and flings back the spinnaker shape that the visitor can see almost wherever he looks round the harbour. Yet this is not a copy or imitation of a ship; it is an echo of one, so that one senses the analogy rather than seeing it directly. All the same, the sensation is enough to give the whole building a feeling of motion, of the wind filling the shells and causing the mighty vessel to go scudding across the placid waters of the sheltered harbour; for so massive a building it is astonishingly light on its feet, and it really seems ready to catch the wind full-on and go sailing up to the sky.

It also is, or seems, not quite symmetrical. From photographs it looks as though the shells unfold with absolute regularity, proportionately spaced, but this is not how it strikes a visitor. After my tour of the city, I am given a tour of the Opera House itself, and again and again we come round a corner to be greeted by what certainly strikes me as a slight asymmetry in the angle.

This aspect, even if it is another optical illusion, gives the building an extra air of movement, and the combination of the dynamic quality with the setting, material (the shells are glass-fronted), colour and shape results in a feeling of exhilaration that grows continuously throughout a visit, and that is exactly complementary to the feeling of serenity and peace that the Taj Mahal provides.

There is a paradox here. The chief note sounded in the immense harmony of the Taj Mahal is serenity; that of the Sydney Opera House, exhilaration. But there is a sphere where the two become one; the Taj Mahal I leave with an almost overpowering tearing of the heart, the Sydney Opera House with a heart leaping with joy. Yet the two feelings seem to well up from a common source, and leave me with the reflection that the two men who carved so memorably in stone must have drunk side by side from the water of that same spring.

WEDNESDAY, MARCH 26TH

A final glimpse of the Opera House from the aircraft as it banks over the harbour. And I am on my way to see the Taj Mahal again.

2 FLORENCE

The Case of the Disappearing Pavement

This is good weather in which to leave London, amid the echoes from the siege of the Iranian Embassy, for the Maggio Musicale (why *Maggio* when it goes on well into July?) in Florence. It is viciously cold and drizzling – impossible to believe that there is a sun anywhere behind the impenetrable clouds. Lo! Italy is even worse; the rain far heavier, the prospect of relief even more remote. Still, I am bound for Florence, which I have not visited seriously for years. And there is a reason for this omission; every year, in the early spring, I have a few days in Italy, but every year I go to Venice.

I had forgotten that from the road between Pisa airport and Florence the Leaning Tower can be seen. First, it is glimpsed among buildings; then the road curves round and the buildings thin out; finally, for a few seconds, the weird wedding-cake is clear, the Baptistery standing guard and the rest of the city acting as a back-drop. It was on the Leaning Tower that I first discovered I suffered from vertigo. I went up to the highest permitted level, where there was no guard-rail, and found myself on the edge, convinced that there was a giant hand in the small of my back, trying to push me over. Falling off the Leaning Tower of Pisa would, no doubt, be a most distinguished way to die, particularly if there were somebody at the edge of one of the lower levels to hear and note my last words, which, in view of the famous investigation into the relation between mass and speed in falling bodies conducted by Galileo from the very spot where I was now standing, would certainly have had to be '*Eppur si muove*', but these merrier reflections only occurred to me afterwards; at the time, I was consumed with a phobic terror that precluded rational thought altogether, and afterwards I had no recollection at all of getting down. (There are photographers at the bottom who, for a trifling fee, will arrange the customer with arm outstretched and palm at right angles to the wrist, then crouch down and take the picture from such a position that it shows the modern Hercules or Amazon singlehandedly preventing the Tower from falling down; but I was too far gone to cheer myself up in this fashion.)

When I get to Florence, it has stopped raining, though the streets are swamped, and a fitful sun is doing its best to convince passers-by that it is shining. (Somewhere in Proust – and it must be in the first seventy pages, as I have never been able to get further – there is a wonderfully evocative phrase: 'The wintry sun had crept in to warm itself by the fire'.) A homely trattoria swims into view; the waiter makes exhausted signs expressive of lateness, shutness, finishedness, and for a moment I might be in Britain, and provincial Britain at that. Only for a moment, though; the chef, emerging from the kitchen and removing his apron, takes in the scene, abuses the waiter, puts his apron back on and goes back into the kitchen. The waiter produces the menu; he smiles, bearing me no ill-will.

The first time I ever went to Florence I arrived badly in need of a haircut. The morning after my arrival, therefore, I set forth in search of one, only to realize that I did not know the Italian for a hairdresser. However, though I might not be able to speak Rossini's language, at least I knew what his best-known opera was called. I approached a policeman; but I paused. To ask for '*un barbiere*' would be simple; but I calculated that a Florentine policeman's pay would hardly run to more than a modest establishment in a back street, where they would probably cut my ears off. How was I to make known that I wanted a high-class barber, a de luxe barber, a veritable Figaro among barbers? Then I recollected what Figaro, in the *Largo al factotum*, actually calls himself: he insists that he leads the life '*D'un barbiere – di qualità, di qualità*'.

I got my barber of quality, and my haircut, and the episode set me wondering just how far round Europe an opera-loving traveller could get, using nothing but the Italian, German and French that he knew from the operatic stage. Even a moderately assiduous opera-goer would have at his disposal a wide variety of ways in which to swear undying love to ladies, or to announce that he has just been fatally stabbed, shot or poisoned. The briefest study of *Die Walküre* will tell you what to do should you happen to fall in love with your long-lost sister, and from *Siegfried* you may learn the proper etiquette for conducting an affair with your aunt. And from the last scene of *Falstaff* you can learn, as the fat man tells the chimes of midnight, how to count in Italian from one to twelve. But all that would still leave some crucial gaps. Nobody in opera buys a railway ticket or a pair of shoes, let alone a ticket for the opera; nobody asks the way to the Town Hall, the nearest bus-stop or the lavatory; nobody books a room at a hotel; nobody tries to explain to a policeman why he has parked his car where no car may be parked; indeed, I know of only one opera in which anybody is even offered a normal drink, and in that, *Madam Butterfly*, the choice that Pinkerton offers Sharpless is restricted to milk-punch, whatever that might be, and whisky.

THURSDAY, MAY 8TH

The sun's out, and Florence is herself again. But not entirely as I remember her. To start with, the noise is much worse. On the north bank of the Arno, from the Lungarno Vespucci on the western side of the city to the Lungarno Colombo on the eastern, the cars roar and rev throughout the morning and afternoon as though they have discovered the perfect practice circuit for the Mille Miglia, and in the middle of the day they sit immobile in an immense traffic-jam, hooting like so many demented owls. The crowds are larger, too, and there is less room for them to rush; the pavements of Florence are continually shrinking, and in many places they are down to nine inches, the rest of the space between the buildings being given over entirely to *la macchina*. Sooner or later, all tolerance of pedestrians will finally vanish; perhaps, in vindication of Darwin, the Florentines will by then have developed suckers on the palms of their hands and the soles of their feet, so that they will be able to get along by adhering to the walls. Such a means of progress will at any rate spare them any more suffering from the Fourth Plague of Florence, its ravages being at present no less dreadful than those of the noise, the crowds and the motor-cars. In Italian law, dogs must be muzzled; but alas, only at one end. Florence is no city in which to walk with one's eyes permanently turned towards the ground, but he who walks with his head erect will be sorry ere long, and ere long I am sorry; when I find myself in the Via dei Malcontenti, I am not in the least surprised. But soon the glory of this city makes itself felt, and I am even less surprised when I stumble across the Via delle Belle Donne. Italian cities, like the cities of other lands, vary, and the response they awaken in their visitors likewise; you can be melancholy in Venice, horrified in Naples, exhausted in Rome and shot in the legs in Milan, but in Florence none but an incurable malcontent can be cross for long, even at the horrible dogs. (There is a dog show advertised on posters throughout the city; I am seized by a wild dream of going there and poisoning the lot.)

It is easy, in Florence, to get up to a vantage point from which the whole city may be seen: the Piazza Michelangelo, the Belvedere, Fiesole, San Miniato, even some of the buildings in the city offer a bird's eye view. I make for the Piazza Michelangelo, and look down on those red roofs and ochre walls that have been soaking up the sun for five hundred years. In the middle, Florence is fixed to the ground by the brick-red drawing pin of Brunelleschi's dome.

Peace descends. *Domani* is another day; if I wander down and find myself in the Piazza della repubblica or the Piazza della Signoria, it will be agreeable to sip a glass of wine as the horse-drawn cabs clop lazily by. Presumably, people who live in Florence work for their living, some men quarrel with their wives, some women are unhappy with their lot, some of both are late for important appointments. But there never seems to be any evidence of this; most of my fellow-sippers, for instance, are clearly Florentines, and it is a weekday, yet they are as carefree as I.

It is no accident that it was the Medicis who dominated this city for so long, and whose spirit dominates it still. The pleasures of the senses, the pleasures of learning, of beauty, of music, of argument, of exploration and discovery, of battle and victory and power, of adventure and art, imagination and ideas, jewellery and jesters – these are the qualities that the Medici courts cultivated, these the threads that colour the tapestry of the Renaissance to which Medicean Florence was so central, these, in their modern forms – diluted, changed, adulterated, yet never altogether lost – the clues to the spirit that animates Florence still.

No city in the world, not Venice herself, has had a more dramatic history; well, perhaps Rome. In none, not even Rome, does that history so permeate its bones and bricks to this very day. Florence has had many choices to make, over the centuries, surviving again and again by making the right one. Guelph and Ghibelline, Dante and Petrarch, Mussolini and the Allies; Florentine history is built on pairs. And no choice has been so dramatic as that between the spirit of the Medicis and the dark angel of Savonarola, between the family that inspired works of art and the man who made bonfires of them, the princes who loved poetry and the monk who hated it, the people who welcomed life, with all its variety, flaws and splendour, and the fanatic, full of holiness and anger, who rejected it. Florence has done many notable deeds in her time, good and bad, but she never did anything more *characteristic* than when she burned Savonarola at the stake, marking with a plaque the spot outside the Palazzo Vecchio where she did so, as a warning to others who would seek to stop Florence enjoying herself. No one has risked it since.

I finish my glass and my reflections, and go off to collect the catalogues for the Exhibition. It is already clear that Florence is taking it seriously; across every street is strung a blue banner, proudly announcing that Florence and the Medicis are on show together. The Council of Europe organizes these shows once every three years or so; I went to the last one, in 1977, in Berlin, on the art, design, architecture and life of the 1920s, and a rich experience it was. This one is called 'Florence and the Tuscany of the Medicis in the Sixteenth Century'.

The title begs the question immediately. Cosimo the Elder, 'the Father of his Country', died in 1464, and Lorenzo the Magnificent in the year that Columbus discovered America. So the Medici sun was already going down when the new century opened. Still, though Lorenzo represented them at their apogee, and the sceptre was now slipping from their grasp, the Medici rulers continued to be among history's most understanding patrons of the arts and sciences, and this exhibition is really of the effect this astonishing family had, from first to last, on Europe. And they had their own effect, too; they were no *nouveaux riches* tycoons or newspaper proprietors with Duveens or Berensons, Sotheby's or Christie's, to advise them, but a family which had so profound, formative and enduring an influence that the fifth century B.C. in Athens is the only period in history that can be compared to theirs in creative richness.

The catalogues make it clear at once that I am in for a spell of most un-Florentine hard work. To start with, a wheelbarrow would be required to take them away in comfort (I weigh them later, and find they come to ten pounds ten and a half ounces); I stagger to the nearest pavement café and drop them on the table. A fortifying glass or two later, I begin to examine them. The exhibition is divided into nine sections, and a brief computation reveals that it must comprise something like eight thousand items. Florence, it is clear, is determined not to be accused of niggardliness; she has assembled paintings, drawings, etchings, sculpture, books, letters, scientific apparatus, architectural plans, jewellery, pottery, glass, tapestries, armour, guns, swords, furniture, carpets, costumes, maps, stage-designs, manuscripts, tools, musical instruments, genealogical tables, death-masks, mosaics, astrological calculations, alchemists' equipment, machinery, papal Bulls, seals, coins – in fact all of art and most of history – in such stupendous and variegated profusion that a month would not suffice to look at it all, nor six to take it in properly. I have a week, and had better get started.

I allow half an hour for 'The Rebirth of Science'. Several times as long, it turns out, would be insufficient for the building alone; the Laurentian Library, itself a summation of the Renaissance, with its cloisters laid out by Brunelleschi, monumental staircase completed by Vasari and main hall designed by Michelangelo, deserves a full day's study. Inside, Medici science proves as absorbing as 1920s' architecture.

Why is it so inexpressibly moving to look upon Galileo's compasses, a map of Tuscany by Leonardo, first editions of the *Principia Mathematica*, Vespucci's *Mundus novus* and the rediscovered Aristotle? And what exactly is the feeling of harmony that comes from gazing up at the magnificent ceiling, or indeed at the Cathedral, visible over the roof of the cloister? Or the lovingly detailed coloured drawings of birds and animals, which to us are beautiful pictures that would look well on our walls, but to the artists and the princes who commissioned them an exercise in the scientific recording of fauna? But they must, artist and prince alike, have been conscious of beauty, too.

As I leave, a tourist-party flock is arriving. The guide goes ahead, holding up the tour agency's symbol on a pole for them to keep in view, lest they should stray and get lost; the comparison with a shepherd and his crook is irresistible. They wear labels on their lapels with the agency's name in large letters, and another analogy suggests itself: the ranch brand-mark on American cattle. Are there tourist-rustlers, driving off another agency's beasts in the middle of the night and changing their labels at dawn?

Next, to the Belvedere, for 'Power and Space'. Last time I was up here it was for the huge Henry Moore exhibition in 1972, which included the enchanting sight of visitors eating their sandwiches while sitting *inside* the holes in the larger pieces on the lawns. Now it is Medici architecture, but the exhibition is useless; elaborate explanations and commentaries are provided on virtually every exhibit, but they are in Italian only, and it is impossible to make sense of the plans and photographs and models without such information. Still, a visitor from implacably monoglot England is in no position to complain. In my flight, I am stopped by a case of mason's tools from the seventeenth century; again, that deep feeling of touching hands with one long dead, a feeling impossible to get from paintings, even portraits.

I lunch at Mamma Gina, behind the Ponte Vecchio. Amid the mad bustle, I share a table with a gaunt, elderly American, long resident in Florence. He starts with a notable conversation-freezer: have I been to the dog show? But there is more to it than conversation-freezing: his Cairn terriers are in it. Then, 'You from Britain?' I am. 'I like Thatcher better than that guy Heath.' Yes? 'Yes. And *he* was a lot better than the guy he succeeded. What was his name?' Wilson. 'Yeah, Wilson.' And without words he rolls his eyes expressively to the ceiling. But he recommends the *tortelloni verdi*, and is right to do so.

The last exhibition of the day: astrology, magic and alchemy. Books of spells abound, weird alembics, pages of astrological calculations that look like bits from Einstein's *Special Theory*. In front of a case full of cheiromantic aids, a young girl has stopped at a book open at a picture of a palm with all the lines and marks to look for. She glances quickly from side to side, then shyly puts out her hand alongside the drawing and compares. Can she see good fortune in her palm, according to the printed instructions? Marriage? Riches? Is she about to scream in terror at some terrible impending fate she has seen? No reaction; clearly, the signs do not even tell her that there is a dark stranger standing behind her.

Last time I went to the Maggio Musicale (it was my first visit to Florence, too, the one with the haircut, and I stayed in a hotel from the breakfast-room of which I could see the very spot where Lucy Honeychurch, in *A Room with a View*, found the blood from a stabbed man on her picture-postcards, and was sustained by young Mr Emerson), the opera started an hour and forty minutes late, and nobody seemed to mind at all.

First surprise: tonight, the opera does start on time, and I am in my seat, reflecting on the remarkably low prices, not just by international festival standards, that Florence charges for the tickets. The highest price at the opera, excluding the gala opening night, is 15,000 lire, which is about £7·50, and the bottom price is under £2. The best seat for Giulini and the Los Angeles Philharmonic is £10, and for some of the recitals (Brendel, Richter, Rostropovich, Vickers) you can get a seat for the equivalent of £1·30, and the best in the house for little more than £3. Studying these details, I also contemplate gratefully the inexplicable and infinite mercy of God, by which I am to find myself elsewhere in Europe on all three of the evenings devoted here to the music of Stockhausen.

Second surprise, in the form of a grim reminder: the handsome, modern auditorium of the Teatro Comunale, its ceiling charmingly decorated with glittering stars, is steeply raked, so that the distance from the floor of the stalls to the rim of the stalls circle at the front of the house must be something like twice the distance at the back. On that rim, at the front end, is a line, accompanied by an inscription; the line, as the inscription relates, marks the level reached by the waters of the Arno in the floods of November 1966. At the front of the house, the line is ten feet from the floor.

Otello is by no means my favourite opera. The second act is not as good as the first, the third as the second, the fourth as the third; left to myself, I think I would always leave at the end of Act II, and certainly not later than the end of Act III, for I would give much to be spared the Willow Song. A few weeks ago, London heard an *Otello* that for once moved me from beginning to end; but that one had Placido Domingo in it, the finest and most convincing singer of the role alive today. In his youth, Domingo tried bull-fighting; when he first took up singing seriously, he was a baritone; if he had remained one, we could have had a *Carmen* in which the last act is set *inside* the Plaza de Toros instead of outside, and the Escamillo, for the first time in the opera's history, could have fought a real bull. There are too many ifs in that dream, but there was none in the *Carmen* that Domingo sang at the Edinburgh Festival in 1977 with Teresa Berganza, and Claudio Abbado conducting. That was not only the finest performance of the opera that any of us had ever seen or heard; it occurred to me a day or two later that it may well have been the best performance the work had received since it was written.

Anyway, Florence has Carlo Cossuta; he has the bright ring the part needs, but he is drowned deeper than the Florence flood in the memory that Domingo left so recently. Muti and the orchestra are doing fine work in the pit, but the action is hampered by a massive fixed set, three-quarters of it looking like a toast-rack that has fallen on its side, toast towards the audience, and the other quarter being the only space available for the opera to happen in. The chorus, though it can stand comparison with any I have heard, moves like something out of the last days of the Carl Rosa, or even the present days of the D'Oyly Carte; the lighting appears to be the fruit of an alliance between St Dunstan and St Vitus; the wine in Act I is the nastiest-looking rosé I have ever seen, and gallons of it would be needed to make Cassio drunk. But Miklos Jancsó, in his first opera production, has emphasized the real personal tragedy, too often forgotten in loftier productions of both the opera and the play. 'When beggars die, there are no comets seen; the heavens themselves blaze forth the death of princes.' Perhaps; but the death is the same, for all that, and so is jealousy and murder, and it is this that Jancsó has got right, though he goes too far in denying Desdemona a bed in the last act. Next day, talking to him, I learn that the idea was to prevent the drama becoming too domestic, too cosy. I also learn something about the amount of rehearsal time at Jancsó's disposal, which goes far towards explaining not only the bedlam lighting but also the low price of the tickets.

A very well-behaved audience; they never come in with postlude-ruining applause, even at the end of '*Si pel ciel*', where premature cheers are almost obligatory, and certainly irresistible. All *Guardian* writers – I was one myself in my youth, and am no exception to the rule – claim that the worst misprints happened to them. Neville Cardus has a better claim than most, including mine; he said that he had once referred to the 'banal duet' at the end of Act II, and the paper obligingly printed it as 'canal duel'. (Philip Hope-Wallace told me that his review of the first production of *Idomeneo* at Glyndebourne was published in the *Guardian* under the headline 'Sierra Leone to try self-government', but it is only fair to add that I did not, much as I would have liked to, believe him, so Cardus must carry off the palm.)

I walk back along the Lungarno in the warmth of a beautiful mild Florentine night, made abruptly less pleasant by the fact that half-way home I crock my knee, and am obliged to hobble the rest of the way in such agony that before I reach the Ponte Vecchio I am contemplating a do-it-yourself amputation with my penknife.

FRIDAY, MAY 9TH

Third surprise: no more music for days. Florence has the barest calendar of all the festivals I know. In the week I am spending (the opening week, too) there are only two items, and in the nine weeks it lasts there are only fifty-one altogether. To one used to the crowded timetables of Salzburg or Edinburgh, where there can be half a dozen performances going on simultaneously, this is delightfully relaxed; well, there is no better city to be delightfully relaxed in. For the moment, however, there are more exhibitions to be seen. And my knee has uncrocked itself in the night.

In the Laurentian Library, with Kepler, Galileo and Leonardo, we can see where the modern world was born; in the Orsanmichele, where the theme is 'The Court, the Sea and the Merchants', we see how it worked. Here are the relations between Medici Florence and the rest of Europe; portraits of the nobles who directed their affairs, letters patent of the ambassadors who went between them, records of the travelling and trade they indulged in, the coins they paid in, the letters they sent to one another. Emperors, kings, princes, dukes, crowd the walls and the showcases; half the cast of Don Carlos are portrayed; every now and again, I bump into Machiavelli, and shiver at the sight of the man who has worked his name into practically every language, as a symbol and definition of cunning, duplicity and ruthlessness. He achieved his almost lexicographical fame with astonishing speed, too; in *Henry VI*, Shakespeare's apprentice work, the future Richard III, cataloguing his own villainy, claims the right to 'set the murderous Machiavel to school'.

Two *trouvailles* leap out at the eye and the imagination. Here, amid the business and the diplomacy, is a letter, to Ferdinando de Medici, from Boris Godunov. And here, carefully dated August 15th, 1584, is a letter from Philip II of Spain, 'King of England', which must be one of history's most notable examples of hubris duly punished. Austin Dobson had a word for it; I have loved his cheerful and rollicking essay in retrospective patriotism since I was a boy:

> King Philip had vaunted his claims;
> He had sworn for a year he would sack us,

With an army of heathenish names
　He was coming to fagot and stack us;
　Like the thieves of the sea he would track us,
And shatter our ships on the main;
　But we had bold Neptune to back us, –
And where are the galleons of Spain?

His carackes were christened of dames
　To the kirtles whereof he would tack us;
With his saints and his gilded stern-frames,
　He had thought like an egg-shell to crack us;
　Now Howard may get to his Flaccus,
And Drake to his Devon again,
　And Hawkins bowl rubbers to Bacchus, –
For where are the galleons of Spain?

Let his Majesty hang to St James
　The axe that he whetted to hack us;
He must play at some lustier games
　Or at sea he can hope to out-thwack us;
　To his mines of Peru he would pack us
To tug at his bullet and chain;
　Alas! that his Greatness should lack us! –
But where are the galleons of Spain?

GLORIANA! the Don may attack us
　Whenever his stomach be fain;
　He must reach us before he can rack us,
And where are the galleons of Spain?

Later, I think I have discovered the Florentine for 'Bloody
Roman driver, why don't you go back where you came
from?', though I am unfortunately unable to reproduce it. But
the episode serves to remind me of how centralized Britain is,
compared to so many of our European neighbours. No bright
Milanese or Torinese or Bolognese lawyer or journalist or
businessman or artist needs to go to Rome to make his name,
any more than his peers in Munich and Frankfurt, Düsseldorf

or Hamburg, need to go anywhere (not that there would be anywhere in particular for them to go) to make theirs. Nor does a Marsellais or Lyonnais feel any such pull towards Paris. Only London is the all-powerful magnet, not because of its attractions but because it is still far more difficult for talent in any field to be recognized and to flower elsewhere. All talk of decentralization in Britain invariably ends in increasing the weight and power of the centre, and the only architect to achieve fame in Britain outside London in recent years is John Poulson of Pontefract.

The next exhibition is *hors concours*: 'The Return of the Kings', thirty stone heads, hacked from Notre Dame at the Revolution and only recently rediscovered. They are exhibited on columns in a hall in total darkness except for a spotlight illuminating each head. In the glittering gloom, a line of Chesterton's swims into the mind: 'Your foul dead kings, all laughing in their graves'. But there is no laughter here, and not many whole noses.

At the main exhibition my response collapses under the assault of such quantity, and I cling to a few landmarks. A Piero di Cosimo 'Andromeda' with, for once, a really terrifying dragon; Cellini busts – Cosimo I, Perseus, Ganymede; Dante by Bronzino, in profile with his boxer's nose; a bust of Boccaccio by Rustici, looking like a rather sly nun; Medici portraits in scores, not one showing the sitter as anything but noble and handsome (the lightning-artists under the arches of the Uffizi, sketching tourists at 5,000 lire a time, are squarely in the tradition); a startlingly modern-looking St Paul by Pontormo; a marvellous pair of Ghirlandaios; wonderful glass; verses in Michelangelo's own hand; a letter from the Archbishop of Florence to Cosimo I, dated August 1561, saying that he is off to the Council of Trent, and another from Cosimo's Ambassador a little later, asking pardon on behalf of the Archbishop for taking the anti-Medici line.

Dinner with Alan and Peggy Haydock; only a few doors from Mamma Gina I have discovered Camillo, which is as good in its way. I still cannot keep out of my voice the note of hilarious incredulity at the summer-long enterprise on which I am embarked, and I beg Alan not to give me away to his superiors when he gets home. He solemnly promises not to.

SATURDAY, MAY 10TH

A day with the Florence that is always there, even when the Maggio Musicale and the Council of Europe are not. The Uffizi first, before indigestion sets in at the remaining exhibitions. The Botticelli room is the revelation it always is, though I am more than ever convinced that the 'Primavera' needs cleaning; surely it ought to be as bright as 'The Birth of Venus'. Between them, though, they constitute an allegory of the Renaissance so vivid and unmistakable that it seems almost impossible to believe that Botticelli did not consciously intend them as such. This is yet another pathetic fallacy; Wycherley, filling in forms, did not give his profession as 'Restoration dramatist', and a Roman shopkeeper out of lentils did not excuse the shortage to an irritated customer by saying 'It's the Decline, Sir'. All the same, there are enough examples in history of thinkers or artists who knew, even if unconsciously, that the trembling of the earth they could feel was not caused by thunder. 'Hello, Botticelli, what are you doing these days?' 'I'm ushering in the Renaissance.' No; not quite. But I am sure he scented something utterly new in the air around him, as clearly as did Dostoevsky or Voltaire, Erasmus or de Tocqueville.

There is another kind of knowledge waiting in another room: the Leonardo 'Annunciation'. She has been interrupted while reading; with her finger she marks the place in the book, so that she may return to it as soon as her visitor has stated his business. Such meticulousness is born of more than an interesting book, and her face tells us plainly just how much more: *she knows already what the Angel has come to tell her.* This smile is not the fatuous self-confidence of the Mona Lisa; it comes from the inner peace that has followed the understanding of the most momentous news any woman has ever heard. Perhaps she really will go back to her book, where she left off, when he has gone.

The Piazza della Signoria: the Michelangelo Problem. The Michelangelo Problem is that I find most of the sculpture hideous beyond endurance: no small problem, you must agree. The Pietà in St Peter's (the one a madman assaulted with a hammer, now hidden behind a glass screen apparently designed to reflect the light in such a way as to make it always invisible) has a power to move; the unfinished Rondonini Pietà in the Castello Sforzesco moves overwhelmingly. But there I stop, and the David only makes me want to set Mark Twain to music:

In this connection I wish to say one word about Michael Angelo Buonarotti. I used to worship the mighty genius of Michael Angelo – that man who was great in poetry, painting, sculpture, architecture – great in everything he undertook. But I do not want Michael Angelo for breakfast – for luncheon – for dinner – for tea – for supper – for between meals. I like a change occasionally. In Genoa, he designed every thing; in Milan he or his pupils designed every thing; he designed the Lake of Como; in Padua, Verona, Venice, Bologna, who did we ever hear of, from guides, but Michael Angelo? In Florence, he painted every thing, designed every thing, nearly, and what he did not design he used to sit on a favorite stone and look at, and they showed us the stone. In Pisa he designed every thing but the old shot-tower, and they would have attributed that to him if it had not been so awfully out of the perpendicular. He designed the piers of Leghorn and the custom house regulations of Civita Vecchia. But, here – here it is frightful. He designed St. Peter's; he designed the Pope; he designed the Pantheon, the uniform of the Pope's soldiers, the Tiber, the Vatican, the Coliseum, the Capitol, the Tarpeian Rock, the Barberini Palace, St. John Lateran, the Campagna, the Appian Way, the Seven Hills, the Baths of Caracalla, the Claudian Aqueduct, the Cloaca Maxima – the eternal bore designed the Eternal City, and unless all men and books do lie, he painted everything in it! Dan said the other day to the guide, 'Enough, enough, enough! Say no more! Lump the whole thing! say that the Creator made Italy from designs by Michael Angelo!'

Alarmed by my own heresy, I seek reconciliation with the faith in the Ghiberti doors at the Baptistery. One panel is missing; being restored. The rest, and the doors themselves, are filthy and unkept, the pavement beneath encrusted with bird-droppings and deep in litter.

SUNDAY, MAY 11TH

A day for nothing at all, a view clearly shared by the fishermen on the embankment by the Uffizi; their lines are out, but unless the fish, when hooked, are going to call out to tell their captor to reel in, they will never know, for they all have their backs to the river and are discussing life, politics, the weather and other grave matters that from the earliest times have occupied the thoughts of fishermen to the exclusion of fish.

I pass a cinema, advertising 'Sexy Movies'. Beneath, in Italian, the promoters are more specific, though not much more; the film consists, if my translation is correct, of 'particularly erotic moments'. I try to envisage myself, or for that matter a skilled Medici ambassador, explaining that to Lorenzo the Magnificent. I fail, utterly; there is no way in which anybody could induce the leap of the imagination required by a Renaissance prince, or for that matter a Renaissance dustman, to comprehend the particular form of human deterioration demonstrated by such films, or to mend the divorce between feelings and the personality implied by them. Renaissance Man and Sexy Movies; the *uomo universale* and *particularly erotic moments*; imagination, straining till it threatens to crack, gives up.

MONDAY, MAY 12TH

A visit to Fiesole, where young Mr Emerson first kisses Lucy Honeychurch and is observed by Miss Bartlett. An excellent lunch served by a waiter ebullient to the point of lunacy; neither of us can understand a word the other is saying, but I guess that he is recommending the speciality of the house, and I conclude that I cannot go far wrong with it. It is lamb roasted with rosemary, and I don't.

From the terrace of the little church, inside which I can hear the Franciscan monks at their devotions, I can see the whole of Florence spread out like a map, Brunelleschi's drawing pin more glorious than ever. Behind me, a gnarled and ancient olive offers a little shade; I am tempted to stay beneath it until nightfall, but there is music waiting for me down there. The taxi-driver announces the fare in advance; when I try to tip him on top of it, he refuses. Where am I?

The shade of the olive had been most inviting, but I am glad I abandoned it. Murray Perahia, with his Beatle-mop, is one of that extraordinary group of younger musicians today – Barenboim, Perlman, Ashkenazy, Zukerman are others – who give the appearance of making music for fun. They attend each other's concerts, which is a clue; the fun is shared. This is much rarer than any but a regular concert-goer would suppose; Wilhelm Kempff is a very great pianist indeed, but no one who heard him would suppose that he played for *fun*, or would even know what playing for fun might consist of. Such players serve a different power, and serve it with a devotion beyond the understanding of mere spectators; but there are other muses, and the younger players serve them with a light heart, though with scrupulous musicianship, and the result is that they provide, because they feel, a lightness of heart that is very different from the exaltation derived from the graver elders. Brendel is the only player who seems to follow both paths, playing for fun and serving God at the same time.

Perahia plays the great Chopin Fantasia in F minor, and ends his programme with the D959 Sonata of Schubert. The glory of Schubertian song is less in evidence in this work than in most Schubert; at least in the first three movements. But in the last there comes pouring out that noble glowing tune in the right hand and the major key – pouring out into the listener's heart – and Perahia gives it its full measure of richness and farewell. The crowded house recalls him for two encores.

TUESDAY, MAY 13TH

There is time, before leaving for the airport, to slip once more into the Uffizi, and sit once more in the Botticelli room; the effect is the same. As I leave, the cars seem less angry, the noise less intense, the crowds less frenzied; even the dogs less foul. Beneath the Uffizi arches, a rally of the Agricultural Workers' Union, on strike, is holding a singularly relaxed demonstration. The main speaker, on the platform, *reads* his speech; his followers, ground beneath the iron heel of capitalism, happily ignore him and read newspapers or chat to one another in the cheerful sunshine. Florence abides.

3 BATH

Candlelight

I first went to Bath for the very first reason that anybody ever went to Bath; to recuperate after an illness. It was a very weird illness; all my red corpuscles, or possibly my white ones, suddenly fled from my veins, no man could say whither, leaving nothing but the white, or, as it might be, the red, to carry on. This they found difficult, even impossible, and I presently discovered that I was dying. Or rather, I did not discover that I was dying until, in hospital, the progress of my affliction had been first halted and then reversed, so that I had sufficiently emerged from danger to be told what danger I had been in. At this I was extremely sad, and every time I have thought about it since, and it was more than twenty years ago, the sadness has returned. The reason for it is a certain kind of curiosity: had I been told that I was very likely to die quite soon, how would I have responded to the news? No doubt one day I shall hear the news again, but the likelihood is that it will remain true; what I wanted, and still want retrospectively, is to know that I am dying *but not in fact to die*. This boon is granted to few; the spontaneous remission of incurable disease is not something that can be taken for granted. How, before my own remission was announced, would I have felt, how behaved?

Of course, it is more than mere curiosity. Very many of those who have technically 'died' – whose hearts, say, have stopped during a surgical operation – have subsequently found their lives transformed when the implications were borne in upon them, and they, naturally, knew nothing of their strange condition while they were actually in it. To make one's reckoning, if not one's peace, and then to have the I.O.U. torn up by the creditors, would be an experience that could hardly fail to have a profound, and probably lasting, effect. But what effect? That, it seems, I shall never know, and ever since that episode I have been firmly in the camp which argues that a doctor should tell his patient everything.

Armed with my recovery and my disappointment, I took a fortnight's holiday and, not feeling up to going abroad, decided that what was good enough for the eighteenth century, and for that matter the Romans, was good enough for me. I went to Bath.

It is a strange city. Possessing, as is well known, the highest proportion of Georgian buildings of any town in Britain, it has been plagued by a succession of freely elected municipal authorities apparently determined to pull down most of these and to build motorways through, round and over the rest; one of the books written about Bath's penchant for official vandalism, by Adam Ferguson, was called *The Sack of Bath*,* and that was by no means coming it too strong. When I first visited the city, however, the work of destruction and spoliation had not progressed very far, and the exhilaration provided by its grace and elegance, the cunningly variegated uniformity of its architecture, the handsome proportions of its streets and their layout, the cleanliness of its stonework, which at once struck a visitor from London in the days before the Clean Air Act, was immediately reminiscent of that which Edinburgh, for me at least, has always provided.

In those days, too, it had – one within the city limits and one a few miles outside – two of the best restaurants in Britain. The Hole in the Wall, founded and run by George Perry-Smith (who gave up the restaurant and the restaurateur's life, but found the virus inextricably entrenched in his blood, and after a few years opened a new one at Helford, in Devon,

* Published by Compton Russell, Salisbury, 1973.

where he flourishes still), has been often, and rightly, celebrated, in guide-books, cookery books, restaurant books and countless newspaper and magazine articles. The Vineyard, however, run by George Fuller, seemed never to get the full acclaim that it deserved; its great days were somewhat before the widespread improvement in the standards of British restaurants had led to a concomitant increase in the keenness of the public to learn about, and pass on the news of, exceptionally good tables.

The first day after my arrival in Bath, I went to the Pump Room to take the waters; that, I reasoned, was what Beau Brummel and Beau Nash had done, and I would follow in their footsteps to the end. A bitter end, too; with the single exception of the waters of Tunbridge Wells, which I was one day tricked into drinking by two old friends, Sidney Bernstein and Gerald Barry, no more revolting liquid has ever passed between my teeth than that of which I drank half a glass from Bath's spring before transferring my mid-morning allegiance to gin and tonic. They say that Bath water is good for you, and if the shock doesn't kill you I suppose it may well be, though I think that a moderate degree of ill-health would be preferable to a regular regimen of the stuff.

Anyway, for the next fortnight I commuted between the Vineyard and The Hole in the Wall, lunching at one and dining at the other; that in itself dates it for me, for it is some years since I have been able to eat five courses, accompanied by three wines and followed by a brandy, twice in a day, at any rate for many days at a stretch. Among the many fine specialities of the Vineyard was a dish similar to the *timbale Rothschild* served at the Grand Véfour; a cube of bread, hollowed out and toasted all round, then filled with crevettes in a cream sauce. I had to restrain myself from eating it at every meal there, for there were so many other good things to try, but it was certainly one of the best of the good things in question. The restaurant also remains in my mind for one of the most charming examples of perfect service in my experience; my last Vineyard meal during my stay was lunch, and I decided to do the thing in style, eating the *specialités de la maison*, marked in the menu with a red asterisk, from the beginning to the end of the meal, like a champion jockey 'going through the card' at a race-meeting. I began, as I recall, soon after noon, with half a bottle of champagne as an aperitif; I emerged a little before five in the afternoon, feeling extremely pleased with life. But as the afternoon shadows lengthened, I concluded the meal with coffee, armagnac and a cigar: this was before the *Good Food Guide* had turned into a tract for anti-smoking fanatics. The waiter brought me the boxes of cigars; I made my choice; he inclined his head and murmured, 'Piercer or cutter, sir?'

And here I am again. The Vineyard is long since dust, and the Hole in the Wall, though it still exists, and under the same name, casts only a shadow of its former glory. Bath is not, however, without resources to gladden the heart of the serious eater, for Popjoy's, named for Juliana Popjoy, Beau Nash's mistress, is run by Mr and Mrs Stephen Ross, who were of the school of Kenneth Bell of Thornbury, where they learned their lessons so well that at times I think the pupils have surpassed the teacher.

FRIDAY, MAY 23RD

On the other hand, I am not here to eat, or at least only to eat, but to attend the Bath Festival. This is another of those founded in the decade of festival growth that followed the Second World War; it is three years younger than Edinburgh, and the gentle hand of Yehudi Menuhin, for so long the inspiration behind it, can still be discerned, though he no longer directs it, in the beautifully balanced programmes, the careful choice of new works, the feeling that audience and performers are united in friendship as well as music.

It begins with Schubert. I am to hear a lot of Schubert next month at Hohenems, but who can have too much Schubert? Moreover, it is played by the Melos Quartet from Stuttgart, whom I first heard at Hohenems and have been seeking to hear ever since. In the Assembly Rooms, which has five chandeliers to the Guildhall's three, though the Guildhall makes up for it with its gold fluted Corinthian columns, they play the *Quartettsatz* and two complete quartets, in B flat and G respectively. I put it like that because they are identified in the programme as 'Op. 168' and 'Op. 161' respectively, and it is a long time since I have seen Schubert counted in Ops rather than D-numbers. The great and good Herr Deutsch, who did for Schubert what the great, good and pioneering Herr Köchel did for Mozart – that is, sort out, identify, classify and catalogue the huge and confused body of work he left – has established his numbering so firmly that opus numbers for Schubert now look positively strange, like the old, replaced, numbering of the Dvorak symphonies. But whatever these works should be called, apart from indescribably beautiful, the Melos play them with a sweetness of tone and eloquence of shaping that confirm my original high opinion of this ensemble, and confirm also my view that the Amadeus, commanding though they still are, and immense though our debt to them is, had better look to their laurels. But I shall always love the Amadeus for reasons outside their music-making, too. Some years ago, I proposed, only half in jest, the canonization of Mozart under the name (for a St Wolfgang already exists) of St Amadeus. A brisk correspondence ensued in the columns of *The Times*, where my suggestion had appeared, which was concluded with admirable brevity, by the Amadeus Quartet. Their joint letter read simply 'What a good idea'.

After the performance, Bath's very special illuminations are on show. In a continuous chain of splendid Georgian streets – the Circus with its five gigantic planes, Brook Street, Royal Crescent and Marlborough Buildings – the windows of virtually every house are candlelit. The candles have been distributed free; thus encouraged, the householders have provided their own matches and lit up the town in the most charming way. I am reminded, walking through this display in the dusk, of Willy Brandt's appeal to the citizens of West Berlin, when the news of President Kennedy's assassination came through, to put lighted candles in their windows, in tribute to the man who had said '*Wir sind alle Berliner*', and how, all over the city, the candles of memory, salutation and gratitude had flickered into life.

I remember also one of the most striking and beautiful *coups de théâtre* I have ever seen, in an otherwise unremarkable pantomime of twenty years ago. It was *Aladdin*, and although Aladdin had won the love of his Princess, he had not won her father's consent to the marriage, and he was not likely to, for he had rashly promised to build the King a new palace, made of light, before the clock struck twelve, and now midnight was approaching and he had to make good his vow. Aladdin – the part was played by Bob Monkhouse – came down to the footlights of the Coliseum (this was long before it became the home of the English National Opera), and appealed, as pantomime heroes and heroines have done since the art was invented, to the audience. He instructed the parents, and enlisted the aid of the children to ensure that the parents complied, to take out matches or cigarette-lighters, to hold them up as the clock began to chime, and on the count of seven to strike fire, dousing the flames as the twelfth note struck. He began to count; by 'three' all the children in the theatre had joined in the counting, and by 'five' so had the parents. At 'seven' he cried 'Now!' and instantly the vast shell of the Coliseum's auditorium was alive with a thousand tiny points of light. Aladdin counted on, accompanied now by the whole audience with one voice, to a final triumphant 'Twelve!' The little flames went out, and at the back of the stage, the promised palace of light rose into view amid rapturous cheers. It was pure magic and pure theatre, made out of a multitude of single, tiny flames, as the tributes to Kennedy were paid and as here the beauty of Bath is glittering and glowing all round me. A lighted candle is a mysteriously powerful sight; it is no wonder that candles figure so prominently in the practices of so many religions, from the votive candles of supplication and gratitude that Catholics light for their saints, to the candles that, for the Jews, usher in the Sabbath or mark the anniversary of a loved one's death. 'There is not enough darkness in all the world', says an ancient proverb, 'to put out the light of one small candle.' In the dark streets of Bath, amid the needlepoints of fire, I can well believe it.

SATURDAY, MAY 24TH

I stroll through Bath in the sunshine, among the Saturday morning shoppers. I am rewarded almost at once; the Morris men have arrived, and are performing in the middle of one of Bath's pedestrian precincts. They dance to the band with the curious tone of penny-whistles, fiddles, concertinas, tambourines and small side drum; the maidens are bonneted and beribboned, and wave handkerchiefs in time to the music; the men are cross-suspendered and have bells on their knees. The miniature fiddles – they remind me of the one I so hated as a child – strike up syncopated versions of 'Johnny So Long at the Fair' and 'The British Grenadiers', and the dancers whirl and leap, thread the needle and link arms, come together in the centre and retire to their corners, until the girls are apple-cheeked with effort and pleasure, and the spectators are a-quiver from their own tapping feet. It is very easy indeed, looking round the crowd, to spot the foreigners, indeed to sort them into their respective nationalities. The ones taking photographs in such hysterical haste and excitement are the Americans; the ones paralysed and open-mouthed with a total inability to believe their eyes are the Germans; that bewildered family who are clearly not quite sure whether this is a religious ceremony, a revolution or a compulsory national rite in which they are expected to join, can be nothing but French. For my part I feel like rushing home to look at my passport, to reassure myself that I, too, am part of this unique and splendid nation, and that I do not in the least mind the rest of the world believing that we are all mad, even if the rest of the world is right.

A tea-time concert in the Guildhall; Christopher Hogwood and his Academy of Ancient Music. I shall never cease, whenever I hear such ensembles exploring the apparently inexhaustible riches of pre-polyphonal music, to mourn the dreadful death of David Munrow, founder and inspiration of the Early Music Consort. Hogwood worked with Munrow, and to a large extent has carried on his work; but the large extent, however large, can never be complete. The concert is entirely of early English music – Purcell, Blow, Jeremiah Clarke. Poor Clarke; he only wrote one piece of music that achieved widespread and lasting fame and popularity, and he has had to suffer the perpetual indignity of seeing that one – his Prince of Denmark's March, better known as the Trumpet Voluntary – invariably attributed to Purcell. (Clarke shot himself; not from chagrin, however, but from unrequited love.)

In the evening, back in the Assembly Rooms, Vlado Perlemuter plays Ravel's Gaspard de la Nuit. This veteran, whose giant playing tonight belies his years, studied with Ravel; perhaps that is why, to my astonishment, I find myself really enjoying Ravel for once. The *petits maîtres* of French nineteenth- and twentieth-century music – Fauré, Debussy, Ravel, D'Indy, Poulenc – have always sounded very thin in my ears, and even those of rather more substantial quality – Gounod, Saint-Saëns, Massenet – have never seemed to me in any way indispensable. There is Bizet, of course, but even he is surely not in the first or even the second rank; and there is Berlioz, who was certainly a genius, but who did write a great deal of the musical equivalent of expanded polystyrene, and also wrote quite a lot of music which, though beautiful or stirring or both, really does not justify the praise heaped upon it, the most notable example in this category being the Symphonie Fantastique. Berlioz, I fear, has suffered at the hands of his posthumous admirers even more than he did at the hands of his contemporary critics; if a man tells you, as many Berlioz boomers do, that the Symphonie Fantastique is worthy to be ranked with the symphonies of Beethoven, Mozart and Brahms and the operas of Wagner, you are less inclined to believe him – for the claim is obviously untenable, the work in truth taking its place at the level of Rossini or middleweight Verdi – when he tells you that the best of *The Trojans* really can be compared with the best of anybody at all, though in truth it can.

I dined at Popjoy's; an outstanding meal, the more so for seeing the Rosses again, their enthusiasm undimmed and their perfectionism undiminished. But times are hard, and getting harder, for those who will not compromise on quality. By London standards Popjoys, and Thornbury Castle, too, are not at all expensive; but in provincial Britain, even in a city as sophisticated as Bath, the pool of diners willing to pay a reasonable sum for an excellent meal is simply not big enough to keep such places full every night.

SUNDAY, MAY 25TH

A last walk through the still sleepy city, testing Bath's claim, which I have never yet been able to contradict, that there is only one thoroughfare in the place from which no greensward can be seen, and that, most neatly, is Green Street. But Quiet Street lives up to its name this morning.

Then once more to the Assembly Rooms, to hear The Trout (but who can ever have enough of The Trout?) and a new work, Firewhirl, by John Casken. This festival tour is not going to offer very much new music, indeed not a lot that is even unfamiliar, and I am glad of this piece, an extended *scena* for soprano (Teresa Cahill) and a chamber ensemble. The words, by George Macbeth, tell a Rossetti-like tale of a strange demon-haunted girl and her fire-dance. An impressive piece, not least because the composer clearly does not scorn melody; presumably because he is capable of creating it. It is good to see

Michael Tippett in the audience, enthusiastically applauding the young composer; creative artists have never been noted for the extravagance of their generosity towards their fellow-artists, but Tippett, a strange and fascinating mixture of the withdrawn and the outgoing, is a notable exception. I have just done an extended television interview with him, in which he has talked about artistic creation, the hardest thing to define in words, with the possible exception of God. It is the second such television conversation I have had with him, whereby hangs a tale, for the first time, a good many years ago, he used the fee the television company paid him to buy a washing-machine, and felt that it was only right to name the device after the benefactor who was, at least indirectly, responsible for his being able to afford it, whence the odd but pleasing fact – pleasing to me, anyway – that there is a washing-machine in Wiltshire called Bernard Levin.

4   ALDEBURGH

The Sea Around Us

Is it possible for a festival centre to be too small? If Edinburgh, with half a million population, is the biggest festival city in which the festival idea works, what is the smallest? Aldeburgh, without a doubt; its population is only about 2,500, and the visitor can walk from one end of it to the other in ten minutes. But is it *too* small? Does its Festival swamp its identity altogether, leaving the town invisible under the programmes and the visitors? That is one of the questions I am here to ask.

In truth, I am not here at all yet, and shall not be for some time. Well within living memory, Aldeburgh and its surrounding area was visited by hordes of savage Beechings who, disembarking from their fast battlecraft, the blunt-nosed *rollsroyce*, laid waste the railway lines with fearsome axes, against which the peaceful tribes of East Anglia had no defence. When the barbarian invaders retired, driving before them their booty – herds of ticket offices, porter's barrows and signal-boxes – the inhabitants crept out of the cellars and lofts in which they had hidden while the sack was going on and surveyed the damage.

It was extensive. Aldeburgh is almost the most easterly point in the British Isles, standing on the bulge of the East Anglian coast. It used to extend a good deal farther east, but the sea has eaten away at it over the years, and buildings which once stood in the centre of the town now find themselves on the shore; the coastal railway line has gone, however, and the nearest station is now Saxmundham, seven miles away. But to get from Saxmundham to Aldeburgh it is first necessary to be at Saxmundham. Trains start from Liverpool Street, but it is no use expecting them to go to Saxmundham themselves; the drivers have doubtless heard of the ancient raiders, and are taking no chances. You change at Ipswich, or, as it might be, Colchester; the tribes there are clearly hardier, and willing to go closer to the danger area for a substantial fee.

I think I have changed at both today. At all events, here I am at Saxmundham, but something strange is happening. I got off the train, which was more like a tram, with a couple of dozen other passengers, but they have all instantly vanished, and I am quite alone; the station itself is unmanned (tickets are sold on the trains themselves) and there is not a human being in sight from whom to enquire about the means of getting to Aldeburgh. I drop my suitcase and go exploring, being soon rewarded by an encouraging sign on the wall of the only building there seems to be in the vicinity, which may be a pub from the look of it: the sign reads 'For Taxi, Enquire Within'. Things are looking up; or rather, they would be if it were not for the fact that the place in which I am to enquire is locked, dark and silent, and no amount of knocking will raise a reply.

Baffled, I retire to my suitcase, if necessary to sit on it while considering my next move, and – as abruptly as my fellow-passengers vanished on leaving the train – a bus materializes beside me. It is a large red double-decker, and has 'Aldeburgh' encouragingly displayed on the front. It may be a ghost bus, as the train may have been filled with ghost travellers, but a ghost bus going to the right destination is better than nothing, and I clamber aboard.

The driver-conductor, who has nothing spectre-like about him, asks a trifling sum in reply to my cautious question as to whether he is really going to Aldeburgh, and we set off. Along the way passengers are added as well as subtracted; I am reminded that in the country people know one another, for every new arrival is greeted by name, and asks in turn after the relatives of those already on board. At least, I think they do; they speak, however, in the dark, mellifluous but incomprehensible accents of Suffolk, so it is impossible to be sure. Plucking up courage, I ask the driver if the bus, when it gets to Aldeburgh, goes anywhere near the Brudenell Hotel. 'Stay on to the end,' he says, 'and it's just round the corner.'

They have wide corners in Aldeburgh, but eventually I have dragged my suitcase across the doorstep, and have arrived, for the first time in more than twenty years, in Aldeburgh. I hurry out into the afternoon sunshine to remind myself of this lovely little village and of what I remembered with the most intense pleasure, its almost absurdly complete Englishness. Clearly, it is early closing day, because the High Street is bare of human life; I speedily discover that it is *not* early closing day, and the High Street is deserted because it so chances that at that moment nobody in Aldeburgh is going shopping. I have a long conversation with the only living creature in sight, a cat, which looks as surprised to see me as I am relieved to see it; passing on, I find myself opposite the municipal noticeboard.

This is worth studying; Aldeburgh is even more English than I had remembered. Indeed, by the time I have finished reading the minutes of the Town Meeting for May, I am convinced that if the rest of the country were to vanish down some celestial Black Plughole, leaving nothing but a deserted Aldeburgh, the essence of England could be recovered and reconstructed, *ex pede Herculem*, by Martian archaeologists, down to the last detail.

The Council balance-sheet is most instructive. It records that £23·45 had been paid to Carter's Garage for petrol and a new inner tube, doubtless for the mayoral motor-car; £22 had gone to Pegg and Son, ungrudgingly I dare say, for repairing the slide and swing in the children's playground. Estimates for the repair of the municipal typewriter had been considered, but no final decision had been taken. Are there other countries in which the elected representatives of the people get estimates for the repair of a typewriter, and discuss them so thoroughly that the meeting runs out of time before they decide which to accept? I like to think not, and if I am right, Aldeburgh is indeed a perfect microcosm of the country. Alexander Woollcott once offered, as a definition of democracy, a country where the Archer-Shee case, better known as *The Winslow Boy*, could happen, where redress of a wrong that affected only a single family could be obtained through the use of the mightiest engines of the law and the constitution. There is something in the municipal balance-sheet of Aldeburgh that brings the definition to mind.

Not that the Town Meeting for May had been confined to matters of finance. The heady wine of municipal politics had also been quaffed. Councillor Studd had proposed, and Councillor Mrs Gifford seconded, the motion for the election of Councillor Mrs Brook as Mayor. Looking up and down the placid street, still as empty as it was when I began my walk, I feel that a bitter fight for the office, with allegations and accusations and writs flying about, and the good guys winning in the last reel, is most unlikely, a conclusion much strengthened by the fact that there had been no other candidate, so that Councillor Mrs Brook was elected unopposed, doubtless with acclamation. I wish her a tranquil term of office, confident that she will have it, and pass on. In the window of the newsagent-cum-sweetshop there is another noticeboard, as characteristically English as that recording the affairs of the Town Council. There are motor-cars offered for sale, sewing machines, dinghies, a 'lovely litter of Cairn terriers'; I think of my American table-companion in Florence. The shop window also contains a large and daft-looking stuffed rabbit, with Bugs Bunny teeth; passers-by are invited to guess its name, at twenty pence a time, the proceeds to go to a worthy charitable cause and the rabbit to go to the winner as his prize.

Further down the High Street there is a dog fountain, long since disused, by the look of it, over which is inscribed, in stone, this poignant verse:

Drink, doggie, drink, man is your debtor,
And you never present the bill;
But faithful serve, for worse, for better,
Drink, doggie, drink your fill.

In the circumstances, it is hardly surprising that the fountain is described on a tablet as having been erected 'in grateful memory of John Shaw Sheldrick and his doggerel'.

The next landmark is the town cinema. There are no 'particularly erotic moments' to be seen here (a poster glimpsed at the other end of the street suggested hideous depravity with a film called *Sex with a Smile*, but closer inspection revealed that this was taking place in godless Leiston, a full four miles away); instead, the forthcoming attractions are a three-part documentary on Tibet and Walt Disney's *Fantasia*.

I know the worst that can be said about this film, and I have frequently said it myself. Its vulgarity, its superficiality, its reduction of the pantheism and profundity of the Pastoral Symphony to the gambolling of Bambis and of the slight but dramatic Night on Bald Mountain to a comic-strip horror-story – all this is true, and the mind which conceived it understood nothing about art. But there are two arguments for the defence, and the second of them carries the day.

The first thing to be said in *Fantasia*'s favour is that it does contain one pure and perfect masterpiece: Mickey Mouse as the Sorcerer's Apprentice. Dukas' tone-poem is, after all, true programme music; it depicts exactly, bar by bar, what we see happening on the screen. And Mickey Mouse might have been created to play the role; all his notorious clumsiness, lack of foresight and innocent precipitation of catastrophe are exactly what the Sorcerer's Apprentice is made of. The result is a blend of image, sound and story that is a new work of art in its own right, and an enduring – and endearing – one.

Not enough; very well, now for the main defence. Disney succeeded in spite of the limitations of his commonplace mind. The popularity of *Fantasia* is inexhaustible; it reappears, in cinemas all over the country (including London), year after year. And, through almost four decades now, it has introduced countless children to music, easily and painlessly, and without doubt successfully. The child does not notice the grotesque bad taste, the ugliness, the cheapness, any more than he does at the pantomime, which is an exciting, funny story, full of surprises; and this film is, in its way, exactly the same. But in the case of the film, seeds are sown, and in an immeasurable but significant proportion of instances, they fall on fertile ground. It is probable that *Fantasia* has done more to enable children to love music than any other force for musical good, with the single exception of Robert Mayer. Let that be put in the balance, and it tips the scale on the side of righteousness.

Outside the cinema there is a ledge on which rests a loose-leaf book; in it, intending patrons are invited to inscribe their names in order to reserve seats for future visits. First Aldeburgh surprise: the book is still there. How long would it have lasted in London? But I am not in London, and I am reminded sharply that England is not only its big cities, and that in its villages the inhabitants still do not trouble to lock their front doors when they go out, nor see any London-like need to.

The heart of England is here, not in the capital, and the map of the Aldeburgh countryside shows how long that heart has been beating, and how strongly it beats still. The place-names of England have no equal in the world for history, resonance and vigour, and nowhere in England are they more evocative than in Suffolk of the spirit of the country, or for that matter of its poetry. Indeed, given the slightest encouragement, they will turn into verse of their own accord:

Aldeburgh, Blythburgh, Rumburgh, Mettingham,
Kettleburgh, Grundisburgh, Dickleburgh, Cretingham,
Worlingham, Helmingham, Framlingham, Badingham,
Coddenham, Debenham, Tibenham, Gisleham,
Pulham and Needham and Wrentham and Mendham,

Denham and Horham and Barsham and Darsham,
Burston and Starston and Leiston and Friston,
Dallinghoo, Ashbocking, Chickering, Mutford,
Theberton, Ilketshall, Yoxford and Snape –

to say nothing of the sinister Bloodmoor Hill and Savage Wood, or the doubtless rigidly teetotal Sotterley and the scandal-free Cuckold's Green, though Ipswich to the south seems to be regarded in these parts as a combination of Megalopolis and Sodom. At any rate, when a friend of mine who has a cottage in Aldeburgh had a hanging flower-basket stolen from outside her front door, the town's general opinion was that those who took it must have been Ipswich folk, and the verdict was delivered with a distinct feeling that nothing else was to be expected of such a place.

FRIDAY, JUNE 6TH

Aldeburgh and its hinterland are not just delightfully and absurdly English; they are also beautiful. Exploring further, I am delighted and astonished to find how untouched the place is. True, I had not expected to find that a thirty-two-storey Hilton had been erected next door to the Parish Church, nor has it. I did not suppose, on my way here, that the nights would be made hideous by the din from amplified disco-theques vibrating until dawn; nor are they. But it is not only these more obvious signs of the decline of civilization that are missing from Aldeburgh; every stone of the place is just as I remember it, and just as enchanting, and I begin to suspect that when an inhabitant of Aldeburgh paints his house, he invariably paints it exactly the same colour as it was before, and would look askance at his neighbour, or even take him for an Ipswich man, if his neighbour were to do otherwise. The geographical isolation from which Aldeburgh suffers should really be called the geographical isolation which Aldeburgh *enjoys*: it is not much easier to get here by road than by rail, so that the only simple and popular access is by sea, which is why the summer influx is largely of yachting folk. But the result has been that Aldeburgh retains its character unspoilt, its appearance unchanged, its attitude unadapted to the needs of the modern world. Long may it remain so.

The first time I came to the Aldeburgh Festival I arrived in a mighty storm, and from the windows of my room I watched as, amid driving rain and fleeing black clouds, the lifeboat was launched for a ship in trouble off-shore. That lifeboat has been replaced by a more modern and better-equipped one, which now stands high and dry upon the beach, while the sea is as still as a duckpond; all the same, the ubiquitous leaflets and collecting-boxes for the Aldeburgh Lifeboat Appeal remind anyone with imagination of the grim truth that when this placid sea is provoked, it is among the most savage and implacable of all Britain's waters.

Today, that is difficult to believe, and a walk makes it more difficult still. Around Aldeburgh the countryside, with its crowded wheatfields just beginning to turn to gold, is laid out in gentle ripples of earth, for although Suffolk is not quite as flat as it's painted, there is nothing much in these parts that can seriously be described as a hill. The sky really does seem to stretch on for ever, the horizon so far away that it is a relief to the eye, scanning it, to look in a little and see the huge porcupine of masts that denotes the habour where Aldeburgh parks its fishing-boats, its yachts and its dinghies, sport rubbing gunwales with business, both knowing that in the precarious balance of the economic life of such places neither can survive without the other.

Unchanging Aldeburgh, where the harbour is still a harbour, not a marina; and the Festival, though it has constantly developed, and indeed grown, in the thirty-three years of its existence, does not change in essentials either. This year is the fourth since the death of Benjamin Britten, its inspiration and its *genius loci* (it is said that Britten and Peter Pears were returning from a visit to the Lucerne Festival, when the composer turned to the singer and said, 'Why do we have to go to other people's festivals – why can't we have one of our own?'), and of course his music continues to hold a central place in the programmes. But his influence on Aldeburgh, its Festival and its spirit goes much wider and deeper. The Red House, his home with Peter Pears for more than two decades, is a local landmark, quite apart from its function in housing the Britten-Pears Music Library; the Britten-Pears School for Advanced Musical Studies, housed near by, is in effect his memorial – a living one, its function not to preserve the cause of music, but to advance it; his private life was a model of devotion and integrity – it is not at all an exaggeration to say that the example set by Britten and Pears went far to instil throughout this country a sympathetic understanding, so long and so brutally denied, of homosexual love.

It is most fitting that Britten found early and formative inspiration in the work of Aldeburgh's other great claim on the attention of the muses, George Crabbe. Crabbe's poetry is dark, and *Peter Grimes* seeks out the darkness of a hard, unyielding world in which a living must be dragged by force from reluctant earth and cruel water. Crabbe's world has gone, though it can still be conjured up here when the wind gets behind that sea and the breakers begin to pound, but Britten captured it in all its savage beauty. Yet though there is darkness elsewhere in Britten's music, his genius was essentially sunlit – his masterpiece, surely, is the Spring Symphony – and this evening I am in the Parish Church of St Peter and St Paul to see his genius fittingly symbolized not in marble but in glass.

This is the service that traditionally marks the opening of the Aldeburgh Festival, and today it includes a ceremony of dedication. John Piper, a lifelong friend of Britten's, and designer of many of his operas, has made a memorial window in the form of a triptych showing scenes from his three 'Church Operas' – *The Prodigal Son*, *Curlew River* and *The Burning Fiery Furnace* – and the Bishop is to unveil it.

So indeed he does, but not before the Englishness of Aldeburgh has asserted itself in the interlude of John Piper reading the lesson. Something, it is clear, is wrong; either the light on the lectern doesn't work, or the artist cannot find the switch, or he has brought the wrong spectacles. Whatever the cause, the result is wonderfully comic: Mr Piper cannot get his head at the right distance from the words, or his neck at the right angle for reading them, and he gives a most engaging impersonation of the bewilderment felt by a short-sighted chicken pecking at what it thinks is a grain of corn but which turns out to be only a mark on the floor.

Afterwards I linger to look at the window, the evening sun glowing through its golds and reds and greens. It reminds me of a verse from a hymn I sang at school, and understood only years later:

> A man who looks on glass
> On it may stay his eye;
> Or, if he pleaseth, through it pass,
> And then the Heavens espy.

After the benediction comes, alas, a powerful temptation to curse; later in the evening, the English amateur spirit is on show at its worst. In the Jubilee Hall, which for years was the only hall available for operas and concerts (the audience still walks straight from the street into the auditorium), John Amis and Donald Swann, with 'help from Anna Dawson', present 'An Unusual Evening'. It is all too usual; unprepared bumbling by Mr Amis, weak music from Mr Swann, little help from Miss Dawson. Champagne is promised in the interval, but the night air seems preferable to the promise, and anything at all to the second half of the programme. Surely it will get better tomorrow?

SATURDAY, JUNE 7TH

Temporarily, yes. When the Aldeburgh Festival started, with nothing but the Jubilee Hall to house the music, the churches of the surrounding countryside were pressed into use for recitals and chamber music, and this admirable and delightful practice has continued ever since, in Orford, Framlingham and Blythburgh. The first concert is in Blythburgh Church, where the vicar welcomes us with the very English news that the work on the roof has at last been completed. It has indeed, and the work has been done with care and discretion; even Sir John Betjeman ('Look up! and oh how glorious / He has restored the roof!') would admire it. There is the usual English worry about whether to applaud in a church, but after a good deal of swivelling the eyes to left and right to see what their neighbours are doing, the audience in general decides that applause is permissible, provided of course that it does not include any unseemly cheers, let alone whistles, and the Fitz-william Quartet's performance of the unfinished Haydn Quartet in B flat, followed by a new work by Colin Matthews, a protégé of Britten's, and indeed his amanuensis, is warmly received. The new quartet is accessible, its roots in recogniz-able influences (including that of Britten), but emphasizes again the problem (Richard Blackford's Quartet posed it for me at Adelaide) of new music in our restless time; a work like that cannot be fully taken in at a single hearing, not because its sound is in itself so strange but because our ears are so dominated by other sounds that they refuse to assimilate those which are different, though they are no more than different. How and when shall we have a chance to hear this work again? It must be a very thankless life, that of a composer today, as I dare say both Colin Matthews and Richard Blackford would say if they were to discuss the matter. Oddly enough, though, Mr Matthews, when he appears to take his bow, looks singu-larly cheerful, as indeed Richard always does whenever I meet him; do they know something, the artists, that the rest of us do not know?

Arianna arrives and in the evening we take the bus to Snape, and to one of the most magical concert-rooms in the world. The Snape Maltings Hall, built in time for the 1967 Festival, and unanimously agreed to have virtually perfect acoustics, or as John Christie of Glyndebourne used to insist, *acow*stics, was burned to the ground exactly two years later (thou canst not say I did it, never shake thy gory locks at me), and rebuilt within a year, just in time for the Festival of 1970. Now although many learned men make their living from the science of acoustics, some of them, indeed, holding professorial chairs in it, there is in fact no such thing, and the aural properties of theatres, opera houses and concert halls, though untold sums of money are spent on getting them right, are always a matter of chance. Great, therefore, was the astonishment of those in the secret when the rebuilt Snape proved to have acoustics as good as, or even better than, the one it had replaced. But Snape is more than an acoustic masterpiece; in its combination of noble proportions, warm, light-coloured wood, rich brick facings, gleaming brass and faint smell of good quality furniture polish, it is one of the most inviting halls I have ever been in. Performers, I suspect, love it because it offers them a challenge; though it does not have the clinical quality of so many modern concert halls, it nevertheless leaves a performer nowhere to hide, picking out and holding in its vibrating warmth every nuance of every sound.

This, as it happens, is just as well, for the performance of Britten's *A Midsummer Night's Dream* needs all the musical excellence available, production and design alike being disastrous in their ugliness and inappropriateness. Indeed, director and designer show little evidence of having noticed what the opera is called, let alone what it is about. In place of midsummer's warmth and greenery, we are given a surround of Stygian darkness, only the central action being lit. Would that it, too, had been veiled in the decent obscurity of night, for then we would be spared the set, a collection of metal fire-escapes in front of which panels of what are presumably meant to represent trees or clouds, but in fact resemble nothing so much as the wire mesh of an old-fashioned meat safe, jerk convulsively across the stage. Titania's bower is a kind of raspberry gâteau; the fairies are bald, and clad in body-stockings painted to suggest that they are in the last throes of some multi-coloured skin-disease; behind it all there gleams fitfully a kind of curtain, in strips, which seems to have been made out of those black plastic sacks that thoughtful borough councils distribute free to the ratepayers whenever the dustmen are on strike.

The producer points out in a programme note that the work is, after all, set in a forest. True; but a cure for that sort of attitude is, surely, to listen to the music, which contradicts it in almost every bar. There *is* a sinister element in the score, of course; but Britten's music, though it does not forget how ancient and how deep in the human psyche are the roots of myth, does not forget, either, that the words it sets here are by Shakespeare, and include some of his most beautiful and verdant lines; the lyricism in the score is not confined to the quartet of lovers, but breathes the poetry of nature as well as of art.

This truth has at any rate been seized on by the cast, the orchestra and the conductor, Steuart Bedford. The King and Queen of Fairyland are particularly impressive; David James's Oberon has majesty and mystery, and the inevitably ghostly timbre of a counter-tenor is complemented by a richness that does not by any means always accompany it. The Titania (Marie McLaughlin), too, is a fitting consort for this imposing figure; the part lies cruelly high, but there is nothing shrill or forced about her singing. On the contrary, she soars through the music as the gulls by the shore float and swoop with that languid ease of theirs.

SUNDAY, JUNE 8TH

Back to Snape for an afternoon recital. The view over the marshes from the bar-restaurant is so extensive, and so beguiling, that it is usually very difficult to leave it for the second half of a concert; not today, though. A friend, contemplating the lamentable state of the world, and in particular the likelihood of its coming abruptly and unpleasantly to an end, remarked to me a year or two ago that all men of sense owe it to themselves to lose no opportunity of hearing Janet Baker sing. This glorious artist, as beautiful, serene and English as Suffolk, sums up the spirit of Aldeburgh and its Festival, at which she has been singing for nearly twenty years, and she makes a programme of Duparc, Ravel, Brahms, Fauré and Spohr as uplifting, as transporting, as a couple of hours of Mozart and Schubert. It is not just the dark loveliness of her voice, the infallibility of her instinctive musicianship, the infinitely flexible expressiveness; there is something in her personality that includes all these and something less definable besides, and it is that last quality that is most apparent when we are sitting talking together next day.

MONDAY, JUNE 9TH

It is the devil's own job to find any flowers in Aldeburgh. But how can I approach this English rose empty-handed? Eventually I find a pot of brisk-looking geraniums and off I go. She talks of the change in the Festival now Britten is dead. 'We performed for love of Ben,' she says, 'but what happens when most of the people who come never knew him? It must be just another job for them.'

'But what about you?' For an hour and a half I persuade her to talk about herself – not her career, her triumphs, her forthcoming appearances, but her deepest beliefs, her progress on her spiritual path, her search for harmony and truth. I emerge as a man drunk, and in a sense I am; this great artist, talking about the most important things in the world, pours her enthusiasm and understanding straight into my bloodstream, where it has a potency greater than any alcohol. Leaving, I tell her that that is the effect she has on me whenever we meet, be it for only a few minutes, and she laughs loudly, without affectation or embarrassment. In the sunshine, the High Street is even more dazzling, the colours brighter, the smiles of the passers-by surely more genial. This seems as good a moment as any to carry out the ritual that for me is essential whenever I am by the sea – any sea – for I claim to be one of the world's leading experts at Ducks and Drakes, and on the beach I arm myself with a heap of flat pebbles. The sea is stiller than ever, and I score some immense leaps between wavelets.

In the afternoon I hear Shura Cherkassky; the immediate reason for my hearing him is that Richter, who was to give today's recital, has cancelled yet again. One of these days I am going to arrange a Grand Cancelling Championship, so that the three leaders in this field, Richter, Michelangeli and Peter Schreier, may finally decide the question: which is the greatest Canceller of them all? It will, I predict, be a very exciting finish, and no one but a fool would bet a penny on the final placings.

Substitutes carry an extra burden, but there is no sign that Cherkassky is apprehensive as he goes to the piano with his neat, short steps. There is even less sign of perturbation in his playing, which dissolves any disappointment the audience might have been feeling, and the fire and conviction that he brings to Brahms's Variations and Fugue on a Theme of Handel could not have been bettered by Richter, or indeed anyone else.

My visit ends in the evening with a treat that is now rarer than it once was; a performance of the César Franck Violin Sonata. An alarming sight, though; the violinist, Nigel Kennedy, and the pianist, Yitkin Seow, both look as though the 8.30 performance should be long past their bedtime. Do we know we are getting old when the musicians look young? Where is Arthur Rubinstein to make me feel young again? (Unfortunately, he always makes me feel even older.)

TUESDAY, JUNE 10TH

A last stroll through the town before leaving. The High Street is astir; in the middle of it, whom should I meet but Eric

Crozier, the librettist of *Let's Make an Opera*, doing his shopping. I feel at home here after less than a week; another couple of days and my encounter would have given me no surprise at all. The sea-scented air is like crisp white wine, and the fresh flowers on Benjamin Britten's grave shine in the sunlight before the simple black basalt slab that is his headstone. The atmosphere of happiness mingled with music has seeped into the very stones of this lovely unspoilt village; in leaving it I feel as though I have lost my passport. And I am bound for London, too, where we do lock our doors, and our cars, and our hearts. Aldeburgh is a place to leave looking over your shoulder, and so looking I fancy I can detect – and take away with me – something of the essence and spirit of this Festival and the things that make it what it is: history, and the vast sky, and those floral tributes to its musical begetter, and the ripening cornfields, and the mewing gulls, and the radiance of Janet Baker, and the uncontested election for Mayor, and the rabbit without a name, and the young fiddler playing the César Franck Sonata, and the roof of Blythburgh Church, and the lapping sea; and the Englishness of England.

A Nightingale Sang

'How would you like to hear all the works of Schubert in chronological order?' This startling question was suddenly put to me down the telephone one day by Robert Muller. It sounded like a riddle, though Robert is not much given to word-play, but since I certainly would like to hear all the works of Schubert in chronological order, I said as much, and waited for the joke. There was no joke; Robert had discovered, in a bulletin of forthcoming national attractions put out by the Austrian Embassy in London, something called 'the Schubertiade'. It was to take place in June, which was a few months off, at a place called Hohenems, of which neither of us had ever heard, and the only other information about it on the sheet was the extraordinary claim embedded in Robert's question. The words were clear, though abbreviated: however many times we translated them, they still suggested that in June, at Hohenems, all the works of Schubert were to be played in chronological order.

This seemed extremely unlikely to both of us. Schubert was an exceptionally prolific composer; not quite so fecund as Bach or Mozart, but much more so than most other composers. He wrote more than six hundred songs, for a start, which would take something like fifty hours to perform, together with very large quantities of chamber music, sonatas, masses, symphonies, overtures, operatic fragments and miscellanea. Thirty days hath September, April, June . . . it could just about be done with a regime of some twelve hours of Schubert a day, but nobody in his right mind or out of it would stage such a marathon, and even if someone did, nobody could

possibly listen to it all. What is more, the chronological order
of many of Schubert's works is largely beyond anything but
conjecture, and scholars will argue about it to the end of time.
That, it is true, was a small point beside the general incredulity
provoked by the bald announcement we had seen, but it made
the whole idea even more bizarre.

The first thing to do, clearly, was to find out more. First,
where was Hohenems? The answer was: not on any map of
Austria that Robert or I possessed. Perhaps, we thought, there
was no such place, and 'Hohenems' was a recondite Austrian
word meaning 'Wouldn't it be lovely'. Eventually, however,
the mysterious village was discovered on a more detailed map,
lurking at the extreme left-hand end of Austria, just south of
Bregenz. Warily, we approached the Austrian Tourist Office
in London; could we have details of the forthcoming
Schubertiade in Hohenems? Unfortunately, the Austrian
Tourist Office had never heard of the Schubertiade, or for that
matter Hohenems. But enquiries would be made in the appropriate quarter, and an answer elicited. Enquiries *were*
made, but no information could be elicited; the Austrian
Tourist Office in Austria hadn't heard of it either. Don't
worry, said the head of the London office; he was himself
about to pay a visit, in the course of his duties, to Vienna, and
would return bearing all the information required. He went;
he returned empty-handed; even in Vienna nobody had heard
of the Hohenems Schubertiade.

Robert and I retired to take stock. It was alleged, in an
official publication of the Austrian Embassy, though the Embassy, and in particular its cultural attaché, knew nothing
about it, that in June 1978 all the works of Schubert were going
to be played in a tiny and quite unknown spot in western
Austria; unfortunately, the details clearly constituted a state
secret of the most important and dangerous kind, akin to the
dispositions of the Austrian army, the whereabouts of the
country's strategic reserves of refined petroleum and the pre-
cise details of the recipe for *Sachertorte* at Demel's. That very

special blend of inefficiency and bewilderment called *Schlamperei*, which is Austria's most characteristic national product, had achieved much in its time, but this was its finest hour.

I cannot reveal how, in the end, we cracked the code; lives are at stake. Suffice it that a copy of the programme, together with a booking form, was finally obtained. It was not true, after all, that the entire contents of the good Herr Deutsch's comprehensive Schubert catalogue were being played in June; but the truth was, in its way, even more extraordinary. It seemed that Hermann Prey, the German baritone, had suddenly decided, two years before, to start a Schubert festival at Hohenems, though neither he nor Schubert had any connection with the place. The family who owned the only building of any distinction in Hohenems, the late sixteenth-century Palace or Castle (it answers willingly to both names, but is neither grand nor warlike), had made it available for the purpose, and Prey had decided to call his enterprise a Schubertiade rather than a Festival to emphasize the intimacy of the music-making and of the place in which it was to be made, for 'Schubertiade' was what informal concerts of Schubert's music were called in his lifetime – and few enough of them the poor devil had a chance to hear before his butterfly's span came to an end.

That much we discovered, along with details of the concerts, which lasted for just under a fortnight. But the idea of performing Schubert's complete works was not entirely chimerical; Prey's aim was to play them all over a period of ten years, and after the first two or three years (when, if the chronological idea were rigidly adhered to, there would be too high a concentration of *juvenilia*)* to perform them in the

---

* This is less of a deterrent in Schubert's case than it would be with most other composers; indeed, it could be said of him, even more truly than of Mozart, that he didn't write any *juvenilia*, as his earliest compositions are fully mature works. Is there anything childish, or even precocious for that matter, about his setting of the *Erlkönig*? He was seventeen when he wrote it.

order in which they were written, so far as scholarship and guesswork could ascertain it.

The Schubertiade of 1978, then, was the third; Robert and I could find no suitable accommodation in Hohenems itself, and decided to stay in Dornbirn, only a couple of miles away, for which an even more detailed map was required. We also discovered that the best way to get there was to fly to Zürich and take a train, though we would have to change twice. On the way to London airport, however, Robert proposed that we abandon the idea of getting to Hohenems by rail from Zürich and hire a car to take us there. He regretted the suggestion as soon as the words were out of his mouth, but I agreed so enthusiastically that he could not very well go back on it; he regretted it a great deal more later, for the car that met us in Zürich was a Mercedes so vast that it could have accommodated a four-poster bed in the back, with bathroom *en suite*, and he spent much of the journey rocking back and forth, moaning in a piteous manner, as he contemplated his impending bankruptcy. But twelve days of Schubert cheered him up no end, as indeed they did me. More to the point, they persuaded me that a week or two of Schubert at Hohenems every June from now on was advisable for my soul's health, and I therefore returned in 1979: and in 1980.

WEDNESDAY, JUNE 11TH

I start at Zürich, where I discover, at the airport, that the ingenuity of the Swiss does indeed, as we in Britain are always telling one another in the hope of being plausibly contradicted, know no bounds. At the arrival gate there are luggage trolleys, at first sight indistinguishable from other luggage trolleys; I put my hand baggage, a good deal heavier than usual, on one, and wheel it through the passport check. I make for the baggage-reclaim area, only to find that it is at the bottom of an escalator. Grumbling that I might as well be at London airport after all, I am about to heave my case off the trolley when I catch sight of a large notice, with diagram, at the head of the moving stairs. It seems that what I have under my hand is very far from being a luggage trolley like any other, for the notice says, in four languages one of which is English, that it can safely be taken on to the escalator; what is more, it seems to make no difference whether the escalator is going up or down. My first reaction is one of disbelief; even the Swiss . . . But the notice is explicit, and the diagram clear; very cautiously, I wheel my trolley on to the down escalator, heroically stationing myself below it, convinced that I am about to be swept down the stairs to end in a heap of mangled flesh at the bottom, and unwilling to include strangers, particularly women and children, in the holocaust. To my astonishment, the trolley stands patiently and docilely where I put it. I take my hands off it; it doesn't move. At the bottom I draw it gently off, and temptation overcomes me; I spend the next quarter of an hour going up and down the escalators with my magic trolley. After a few goes, I discover something even more amazing: *it wheels itself off.* The rolling action of the escalator, up or down, simply starts the trolley's wheels moving when it gets to the grid at the end, and off it trundles. I devise, and put into practice, the Grand Coup; I push my trolley on to the up-going escalator, bidding it *au revoir* as I do so, then sprint to the nearby fixed stairs, gallop up them, and arrive at the top of the moving ones to greet my faithful trolley as it lands. By now I am expecting to be apprehended as a madman, but the Swiss take no notice, and the reason becomes clear when a porter nonchalantly pushes on to the escalator a supermarket-like line of more than a dozen trolleys, nose to tail, and walks away without even looking back to see them travel up unaccompanied and wheel themselves off in convoy at the top.

Spending the night in Zürich, I dine at the Veltliner Keller, where on our 1978 visit Robert and I had broken our journey, bidding the Mercedes wait if the driver could find a parking place big enough; he had telephoned for a table reservation for us from the car itself, and I had great pleasure in pointing out to

Robert that the cost of the call would certainly be added to our bill. But the Veltliner Keller has stuck in my mind for a reason much older, and much stranger. Friedelind Wagner, the composer's grand-daughter, left Nazi Germany in 1940, in revulsion at what was happening; she eventually got to the United States, and spent the rest of the war working for an Allied victory. But she went first to Switzerland, and her mother, Winifred, was sent by Hitler to persuade her erring daughter to return; Winifred's friendship with the Führer, for whom she never ceased, to the end of her life in 1980, to proclaim her unabated admiration and affection, and the cultural importance of Bayreuth in the Third Reich, were such as to make possible almost any indulgence for the head of the Royal Family of Bayreuth (the phrase used by Winifred as the title of her book about life at Wahnfried under the Nazis).

Friedelind recounts the conversation that followed lunch at the Veltliner Keller. Winifred first pleaded with Friedelind to return, saying that she had Hitler's personal assurance that there would be no recriminations, and that Friedelind, provided she kept quiet, could continue to live freely in Germany. When the daughter proved obdurate, the mother began to threaten her; it culminated in Winifred's assurance that if Friedelind went so far as to work against the Nazis, she would be '*ausgetilget und ausgerottet*' (destroyed and exterminated).

A charming scene to flavour my *Züriches geschnetzeltes*. I wonder what Winifred and Friedelind ate?

THURSDAY, JUNE 12TH

Robert and I, on a walk during our 1978 visit, had discovered a charming hotel, the Rickatschwende, in the hills above Dornbirn; I stayed there in 1979, and liked it so much that I have booked a room there again this year. On my 1979 visit, elaborate roadworks were going on just below the hotel, and a year later they still are; *Schlamperei*, thy name is Austria.

The Rickatschwende is real treasure trove; my beautifully

appointed room has five wardrobes and fifteen shelves. From my balcony I can see Lake Constance. The map says that the Rhine goes in at one end and comes out at the other, but I have always felt that this is cheating; how do they know it is the same water? I prefer to think that the Rhine rises in the Bodensee itself before setting off on its haunted, legend-strewn, castle-bedecked, Lorelei-dangerous journey to the sea. The lake is shining in the sun, which bodes well; this part of Europe has notoriously treacherous summer weather, and it can rain without cease for days on end. The hills are lush, a shimmering green; herds of the velvety brown cows of Austria and Germany are munching their way up and down the hill-sides, immediately raising again one of the great mysteries of life in German-speaking Europe. Austria and Germany between them seem to have about half the continent's total supply of cows, yet not only do they make practically no cheese, and none at all that is any good; it is almost impossible to find milk, and German and Austrian hotel breakfasts, which are the world's most delicious, are marred only by the fact that they serve with the coffee not milk but the world's nastiest condensed cream, tasting largely of metal polish. (Later in this magical-musical-mystery tour I am to challenge this problem head on, and demand milk with my breakfast at my Bayreuth hotel. The waitress is willing but puzzled; is not that milk beside your plate? No, it isn't, my dear young lady, it is some ghastly alternative which makes the coffee unendurable. I want *milk*. Light dawns; you mean *drinking* milk? I do not know of any other kind of milk, but I say yes out of curiosity, and lo! a jug of what I call milk arrives, fresh, sweet and suitable for coffee. From now on I shall always ask for *Trink-milch* with my breakfast in Germanophone countries, and shall no doubt acquire a reputation for eccentricity by doing so. But the mystery remains; what happens to all the milk those brown cows produce?)

When we arrive at Hohenems, the haymaking is going on within a few yards of the Palace; now that's a sight you don't see outside the Royal Festival Hall, or for that matter in the Haymarket.

No *Schlamperei* here; there are efficiently manned traffic barriers on both sides of the little square, and police making parking effortless at both. The yellow façade of the Palace, light and delicate with its two uniform storeys and its square towers, belies its date; it might be anything up to two centuries younger. The Palace stands before a noble backdrop, a massive spur of rock that towers over it and indeed over the town. There are concerts, *hors concours*, up there in fine weather, but it is difficult to see where the musicians, let alone the audience, would perch on this beetling crag, and it is even more difficult to see how either would get up there in the first place. Surely Schubert, of all composers, should be approached without such exertions? I decide to miss the '*Musik im Grünen*'.

A green carpet has been laid over the cobblestones to the massive wooden gate; inside, the courtyard brings to mind a mightier *Hof* in Salzburg – not surprisingly, for it was built by the brother of Marcus Sitticus, the Prince-Bishop who built Salzburg's Residenz. The Hohenems Palasthof, too, is open to the sky, but the Austrians' notorious terror of being struck by even a single drop of rain has been taken into account, as I discovered on my first visit here, when rain began to fall during a concert in the *Hof*; before the audience could run, shrieking, for cover, a canvas roof slid soundlessly over them. *Schlamperei* was not to be denied on that occasion, however; somebody had forgotten to turn off the little fountain at the back of the *Hof*, and the interval was spent emptying the piano.

Standing in the doorway, I recognize many of those arriving for the concert as regulars who were here last year and the year before; I am not the only one to have caught the Schubertiade habit. Presently, however, I see two smiling friends from London: Kenneth and Sallie Snowman. They have arrived earlier in the day, and already explored Hohenems, making as by instinct for the *Schloss* café.

The *Schloss* café, which Kenneth and Sallie have christened the House of Sin, lies cruelly close to the music; just across the road, in fact, and in it you can get a reasonable light meal. But soup and sausages can be had anywhere; the House of Sin specializes in gâteaux, accompanied by mounds of whipped cream the size of the rock above the Palace. There is *Erdbeertorte*, which is strawberry gâteau, and *Nusstorte*, which is walnut gâteau, and *Himbeertorte*, which is raspberry gâteau, and *Schokoladetorte*, which is chocolate gâteau, and *Mochatorte*, which is coffee gâteau, and *Schwarzwäldertorte*, which is more or less everything gâteau. Arriving with half an hour in hand before the concert, it has become my invariable practice to enter the House of Sin; on leaving it my invariable resolve is never to enter it again. Alas for resolution, weak enough already; Kenneth and Sallie, useless for stiffening the resolve, are fit only to increase temptation. Thank God the intervals are not quite long enough to make another daily visit possible.

We salve our consciences with the thought that Schubert had a sweet tooth, too, and a waistline to match, and make for his music. The opening concert is in the Rittersaal, on the first floor; Rittersaal means 'Hall of the Knights', but anyone expecting something on a Wagnerian scale will be pleasantly disappointed, for the Rittersaal is a tiny, square room with a lofty decorated ceiling, a minstrel's gallery at back and front, the one at the back being pressed into use for an overflow audience when the seats below are full, plain windows letting in the evening sun to light up the performers in silhouette; and seats for only 300.

That is why it has to be a Schubertiade; 'Festival' is altogether too grand a word for such a room; and even the *Hof* downstairs holds only 700. But there is nothing casual or amateur about the music-making.

I first heard Gidon Kremer, and must have been one of the very first in the West *to* hear him, at the Ansbach Festival in 1977. In those days he still lived in East Germany; he looked thin, white and ill, but he had played hardly a dozen bars of unaccompanied Bach before it was apparent that here was one of the most remarkable violinists in the world. Later, I heard him in London, and a little later still twice more, by which time I was convinced, as I still am, that this is the man to ascend the vacant throne of Heifetz. Both his technical accomplishment (how easy it all seems for him!) and the depth of musicianship and meaning he reaches seem to me comparable to Heifetz's – and he is still twenty years younger than Heifetz was when I haunted the gallery of the Albert Hall to hear him.

Since then, Kremer and his wife Elena, who is his accompanist, have made their home in the West, and as he walks on to the platform at Hohenems he appears at least a stone heavier and has lost the characteristic haunted look of those who have got out temporarily, but have to return. He plays the Fantasy in C, hitherto unknown to me, which is built on a full symphonic scale, with such fire and beauty that it has the audience gasping; truly, the king's throne is no longer vacant. I wish Heifetz, retired but reported to be in good health and spirits, could hear his heir apparent.

FRIDAY, JUNE 13TH

There is beautiful walking country all round the Rickatschwende, and starting from it has the additional advantage of dispensing with the preliminary ascent from the village; fifty yards from the hotel and I am in open country.

Striking off across the fields, I am happily lost in less than half an hour. There is always a path or track, though, and since I am not going anywhere in particular, and will no doubt eventually come to a road, from which I can ask my way home, I am not alarmed. I have not brought my walking stick, a magnificent staff that I bought many years ago in the shadow of poor mad Ludwig's Neuschwanstein Castle, but I soon come upon a tree with an inviting stout twig growing out of its trunk only a few feet from the ground, and I pluck it. I lay about me vigorously; a dozen brigands bite the dust, and another score flee in terror; several mad dogs are despatched; a beautiful maiden is rescued from a bull, and another from a dragon. Enough of this; awakening, I come to a farmhouse, where they seat me at a rough table out of doors and sell me bread, butter, cheese and beer; the sun is high. I go my way, and once out of earshot of the farmhouse I start to sing. Schubert, of course.

Hermann Prey has written that he conceived the idea of the Hohenems Schubertiade in conversation with Marc Chagall, whom he quotes as saying: 'Beethoven and Mozart are geniuses, but Schubert – Schubert is a miracle!' There are times, particularly at Hohenems, when I think that Schubert is the greatest mystery of all, greater even than his brother-in-God Mozart. For Schubert seems even more conscious of his function as a channel from the divine to the human. I don't mean conscious literally; I do not imagine that Schubert sat thinking of himself in any such terms. But conscious in the sense of understanding his own feelings, and the way they were translated into music. The world is full of fools who insist on explaining art in terms of biography; for them, Shakespeare could not have known how sharper than a serpent's tooth it is to have a thankless child unless he had had one himself, and could not have invented Malvolio and treated him so cruelly unless he had been snubbed by a presumptuous steward in some great house. These people hear '*Der Musensohn*', and declare that Schubert must have written it when he was happy in love; then they hear '*Der Leiermann*', and insist that it was written in a week when Schubert couldn't pay his rent; then they hear '*Kennst du das Land*', and come to the conclusion that he wrote it as he was packing for his annual holiday by the seaside.

There are two fallacies in this attitude, not one. The first is the belief that a great artist draws as crassly as that on his experiences, but the other mistake is more significant; it is the belief that it is possible to allocate the various aspects of an artist's work among his various feelings, so that Schubert, for instance, wrote some 'happy' songs and some 'unhappy'. Genius, however, is indivisible; indeed, that is yet another definition of it. Schubert's music, as anyone with ears and feelings of his own can tell, is both happy and sad at the same time; or rather, it is neither happy nor sad, because it moves at a level where such considerations do not apply. The greatest miracle of Schubert is his realization that joy and pain are inseparable, that the latter is the inevitable shadow cast by the sun of the former, and that they are Janus twins because they reflect a Janus mystery, the mystery of creation itself. And the next best thing to finding a solution to the mystery is to contemplate it.

If we listen to '*Der Musensohn*' with this in mind, we can hear its understanding of sorrow; if we listen to '*Der Leiermann*', we can hear the joy, even if it is nothing but a faint echo, behind the grief. I do not believe that there is any other way of explaining the fact that if we listen to a melody that is neither 'happy' nor 'unhappy', but pure beauty all through, like the violins ushering in the second subject in the *adagio* of the Choral Symphony, it brings us close to tears. The tears are the measure of the distance that separates us from heaven, and that is the secret that Schubert knew. Chagall was right.

But here is the road, and it is time to ask my way home.

SATURDAY, JUNE 14TH

I arrive at the Palace, via the *Schloss* café, to be greeted by the Administrative Director of the Schubertiade, Gerd Nachbauer, who has that tendency to jump at slighter sounds than most of us which is the most noticeable characteristic of festival directors. Rossini said that all impresarios in his day were bald before they were thirty, because of their habit of tearing their hair out in desperation at the latest disaster, and indeed there does seem to be a strand or two missing from

Herr Nachbauer's immaculately brushed crown; it seems that the first cancellation of the 1980 Schubertiade has just taken place, Edita Gruberova having been taken ill. 'Now for ze good news . . .' Her place is being taken by Christa Ludwig. That is all very well, but both Richter and Peter Schreier are due to perform here; if Miss Gruberova, who is not even an entrant in the Grand Cancelling Championship, has fallen out thus early, what chance have we that either of the co-favourites will turn up, let alone both?

Ludwig is still a beauty. I heard her, in that unforgettable Salzburg *Figaro* in the early 1950s, as Cherubino, when she was a girl, and a newcomer to stardom; now she is moving towards the end of her career, and stardom has been part of her life for more than two decades. I have heard her many times in those decades, in the opera house, as a notable Carmen, among other roles, and on the recital platform; she has husbanded her voice carefully, and in any case this composer is not for beginners. Ludwig sings like a woman of the world in love with Schubert, which I suppose is exactly what she is. She has not given out the details of her programme in advance, and may well be deciding on it as she goes along; at any rate, she announces one group of songs at a time from the platform. She includes some of my favourites: '*Du bist die Ruh*', '*Frühlingstraum*' and '*Nur wer die Sehnsucht kennt*' reveal a profound understanding of Schubert, an understanding that is not nearly so widespread as is sometimes supposed. Many singers can show the beauty of Schubert, make his melodies soar, touch the heart with his feelings, but there is something more in Schubert than all of those qualities, and only the very finest of his interpreters know what it is.

SUNDAY, JUNE 15TH

Once, years ago, when I thought I might learn to drive, a friend, experienced in the rule of the road, gave me some advice which I have not needed, for better judgment prevailed, and I have still never sat behind the wheel of a car, but which I have not forgotten either. 'Always remember', he said, 'to behave as though everyone else on the road, whether driver or pedestrian, is either mad or drunk or both.' I have often seen examples of the behaviour on which the principle was presumably based, but today's is the best ever. I go to Zürich to meet Arianna, who could not get away from London before. We hire a car at the airport and drive off. There is a motorway which goes very near Hohenems, and we join it off the airport road. We have been proceeding for about fifteen minutes when we see, but at first are unable to believe that we see, a car coming, very fast, *towards* us, and in the same lane. After we have missed him, and recovered from the shock, we discuss the greatest mystery of the episode, which is not 'What did he think he was doing?' which was amply covered by my friend's principle, but 'How did he manage it?' The road was of full motorway standard, with a substantial central barrier and separate entrance and exit roads for both carriageways; how did he get to where we so nearly met him? After discussion, we conclude that the only way it can be done is by entering the motorway from the appropriate feed road, and immediately making a U-turn against the merging traffic. My friend was right.

Schubert is a great restorer of shaken nerves, and the performance by the Amadeus Quartet of 'Death and the Maiden', followed by dinner in the *Schloss* restaurant, duly restores them. Fräulein Stocker, alas, is not there this year; on the last night of the 1979 Schubertiade we ordered *Gerstensuppe*★ from her, only to be told that there was none left. Not to be entirely outdone, I promptly ordered it for the first night in 1980; she entered into the spirit of the thing, and solemnly wrote it down on her pad: Four *Gerstensuppen* for June 12th next year. ('And two bottles of Gumpoldskirchner, please' – 'And two bottles of Gumpoldskirchner'.)

★ Barley soup; but the bald translation does it less than justice.

MONDAY, JUNE 16TH

We walk up to Bödele, the next village above. Hardly even a village, just a couple of houses, a little shop, and a *Gasthaus* which serves a very acceptable lunch. The air might have been swept clear by a giant broom, for we can see for miles across fields alive with buttercups, and the hills in the distance are practically incised into the sky. Two years ago, I walked up here alone, and in the middle of lunch there was a buzzing as of science fiction giant hornets. Just outside, on a patch of bare land, six huge Austrian army helicopters, one after the other, came in to land in a neat row, looking when they had done so even more like Martian insects. In my best German, I complimented the *patron* on the excellence of his cooking, for which, it seemed, visitors came from across the very mountains. He didn't get the point; possibly my best German is not good enough. I wish I spoke German fluently; I wish I spoke fluently *any* language other than my own. If I am to be damned for the sin of envy (and anyone going about seeking a reason for damning me will have plenty to choose from, starting with gluttony), I shall deny it stoutly – I do not covet my neighbour's ox or his ass, or his maidservant or his manservant – until it comes to my yearning to speak a foreign language at a level deeper than ticket booking and trivial conversation, and to play the piano, even badly. Can I really be damned for such mild covetousness?

TUESDAY, JUNE 17TH

Exciting news for the forthcoming cancelling championship. Herr Nachbauer has lost a good deal more hair, and greets me with the news that Schreier is not coming. On the other hand, Richter is actually here; indeed, he is sitting in the garden, and Herr Nachbauer invites me to go and peer round the door if I do not believe him. But I do; his appearance – with one auspicious and one dropping eye, in equal scale weighing delight and dole – tells the whole story most eloquently. Not quite the whole story: Christa Ludwig, who has hardly had time to pack after substituting for the stricken Gruberova, has agreed to replace Schreier as well, and is to sing '*Die Winterreise*'. I have reservations about women singing men's songs, and vice versa: do they suppose the audience doesn't know what the words mean? But Ludwig immediately melts such doubts in the warmth and beauty of her singing.

WEDNESDAY, JUNE 18TH

A week of Schubert and no sign of flagging. Not every composer would stand it. Beethoven wouldn't, for a start; our soul's ears would become exhausted, for there is something god-like about Beethoven, and ambrosia and nectar are to be taken in small quantities. Nor Haydn; after a time, it would all start to sound the same, which would be unfair to Haydn, but a bar to an all-Haydn Festival. There is Wagner, of course; but nobody could stay throughout the Bayreuth Festival and go to every performance. (I bet some do, though.) There is also Bach, who has Ansbach to himself; but the mysteries of Bach are for me eternally insoluble. No; only Mozart and Schubert can really be listened to exclusively twice a day for a fortnight without tiring their listeners or making them feel the need for a change.

Herr Nachbauer has more news, this time exclusively good. There were dark rumours, last year, of financial difficulties for the Schubertiade, and even darker ones to the effect that some of the older-established festivals had not taken kindly to the appearance of the upstart, and were bringing pressure to bear on the pillars which support it. But all seems to be well; at any rate, plans for 1981 and 1982 – dates and performers – can be officially announced.

Richter – at the top of his steel-fingered form (the great thing about all the leading cancellers is that when they do turn up they play all the better) – joins the Borodin Quartet for a rousing performance of The Trout, a little stronger than usual but no less lyrical, and with all the repeats. (Why do so many players and conductors omit Schubert's repeats, when they must know that the first thought any listener has on hearing any of his works is 'I wish I could hear that again'?) Afterwards, we break the news to Arianna that by joining in halfway through the week, she has missed the best performance of all. The Brandis Quartet, with members of the Berlin Philharmonic, have played the Octet, and in the open-air courtyard downstairs, too. It was a night without a leaf stirring, though the players, taking no chances, clipped the music to their stands with clothes-pegs, and the windows overlooking the *Hof* were alive with candles. The lovely, unhurried performance of this lovely, unhurried work moved towards its close, and as dusk fell the nightingale, most Schubertian of all living creatures in its understanding of suffering and its expression of the ultimate triumph of joy, joined in.

The Enchanted Garden

By all rational tests, Glyndebourne cannot exist. But it does. Consider: John Christie, an eccentric Englishman, formerly a master at Eton, is married to an opera singer, Audrey Mildmay. In 1931, he decides to build a miniature theatre at his Elizabethan house in Sussex, where his guests, friends, tenants, staff and neighbours may be entertained. The building is begun, but in the middle of dinner one evening, his wife turns to him and suggests that if they are going to build an opera house, they might as well build a real one rather than a toy, and put on opera professionally and seriously. The Englishman is much taken with the idea, stops the building work and has the entire plan begun afresh. While the new building is going up, the Englishman announces that a season of opera will be given the following year, and then sets about finding somebody to give it. By a series of chances, his path early in 1933 crosses those of two Germans, Fritz Busch and Carl Ebert, who have left their native land on the Nazi accession to power, and an Austrian, Rudolf Bing, who can see what is coming. Among them, they conceive the idea of founding a music festival where the world's finest performances of opera will be given.

Shortly afterwards, the world's finest performances of opera are indeed being given under these auspices. They are given in the middle of the countryside, in a place no one in the musical world has ever heard of; the performances start in the middle of the afternoon; a special train must be boarded at Victoria, at lunch-time, or a drive of several hours' duration embarked upon; the announcements bear the curt instruction

'Evening dress recommended', though on the opening night neither Lady Diana Cooper nor Princess Bismarck wears it. On the second night, seven people get off the special train, and the entire audience numbers only fifty-four. It is not long, however, before the theatre is full every night, and it has been full most nights ever since. And, on the whole, has deserved to be.

Glyndebourne does exist then, but defies logic to do so; so much the worse for logic. Opera on a full professional scale is the most expensive form of entertainment the modern world knows; in almost all countries with any claim to operatic excellence, the opera, which cannot anywhere pay its way from its box-office receipts alone, is supported, in one way or another, from public funds. Glyndebourne receives no such subvention for its Festival, and never has. In the pre-war years, John Christie met the inevitable deficit from his personal fortune; when this became impossible in post-war conditions, Glyndebourne began the process, since adopted by other opera houses including state-supported ones, of appealing to business and commercial patrons for support, and to individual music-lovers and Glyndebourne visitors as well. By this time, the fame of Glyndebourne was so great, and its social cachet so strong, that financial association with it was felt to be advantageous, and substantial funds were forthcoming from these sources. Gradually, the social cachet diminished, as the social areas from which Glyndebourne's audiences were drawn became wider, and indeed as the performances ceased to be operatically unique, when Glyndebourne was no longer able to compete against richer opera houses for the best singers. By then, however, the tradition of private patronage had been well established, and exceptionally good financial management at Glyndebourne had ensured that its box office and ancillary receipts provided a higher proportion of its outgoings (some 70 per cent) than any comparable institution in the world.

Glyndebourne cannot exist, but it does. It cannot survive, but it does that, too. What other objections are there? Well,

that the standard of the performances no longer justifies the
réclame, let alone the bother of getting into evening dress
before lunch in London in order to hear opera at tea-time in
Sussex. This claim is more difficult to meet, but more important; if a man floats in the air without means of support, he
is clearly not subject to the law of gravity, but if he walks on
the ground no claim to that effect can be accepted without
corroboration or demonstration. Yet Glyndebourne, though
it walks upon the ground, *can* float in the air. No longer can it
be assumed that the world's finest performances of Mozart
will be found there; but different operatic achievements, no
less valid and important, have replaced that one. Most notable
has been Glyndebourne's pioneering of the almost entirely
forgotten operas of Monteverdi; apart from a few performances at Oxford under the inspiration and command of Sir
Jack Westrup, no Monteverdi had been heard in Britain, and
precious little anywhere else, for centuries when Glyndebourne began a world-wide revival of interest in this neglected
genius with its production of *L'Incoronazione di Poppea*, followed some years later, after a similar pioneering task had been
undertaken on behalf of Cavalli, with *Il Ritorno d'Ulisse in
Patria*. The broadening of Glyndebourne's repertoire, once
begun, proceeded briskly; *Fidelio*, *Rosenkavalier*, unfamiliar
Rossini, *Pelléas et Mélisande*, still more unfamiliar Janacek –
all these have strengthened and deepened the appeal of
this magnificent anachronism (until the war, only Mozart
and Verdi had been performed there), attracting in doing so
audiences from further afield in more than simply the geographical sense. Bing left; Busch died; Ebert retired; John
Christie grew old, took sick, died during a performance of
Così Fan Tutte (I was there that night, and did not know of his
death until the following morning, as no announcement was
made and the performance, by his express command,
continued). His son George, groomed as long and carefully as
a Prince of Wales, ascended the throne, bringing new ideas,
new approaches, new artists and directors, a more flexible –

come, less obstinate – attitude to the entire enterprise than his father's. Glyndebourne is; survives; flourishes; justly retains the respect of the opera-loving world. But none of that explains its special, separate, appeal. To explain that, or to attempt to, it is necessary to describe the place.

The drive from London goes through some beautiful Surrey and Sussex country; on a fine day, with uncrowded roads and plenty of time allowed, it offers a glimpse of the soft English south-east at its best. At the last fork, where the other road goes to Lewes, the first yellow AA signpost is encouragingly seen: Glyndebourne, it says. A few miles later, the last corner, the one with the post-box, is turned, and the road dips up and down until the driveway opens on the left. Attendants, attired in implausibly rustic uniforms, the Christie family's Swiss Guards, direct the visitor through the brick archway, round to the left, round to the right, into the car park, where more Swiss Guards marshal the cars into neat ordered rows. A stone path leads to the house along the edge of the car park; experienced Glyndebourne visitors look up to the right, across the cars, before turning left, for there on the hillside the sheep will be placidly grazing. I claimed, some years ago, that these were not real sheep at all, but extraordinarily lifelike flat wooden simulacra, drawn back and forth across the contours by an ingenious arrangement of wires, the whole *mise en scène* having been designed by Oliver Messel. There was no denial by Glyndebourne, and I feel free to consider my theory vindicated.

Between high hedges, the path leads, via the tennis court, to the tea-restaurant. Emerging refreshed, the visitor is ready to explore the gardens. The gardens are one of the twin pillars of Glyndebourne's glory, and the pillars are twins indeed; the Head Gardener's name is printed in the programme in the same size type as are those of the Artistic Director and General Manager. First, there is a plain square lawn, marred only by a hideous bust of John Christie. We proceed down the steps to the lower lawn and thence to the sunken garden, alive with colour that in a more propitious climate would be a real Douanier Rousseau jungle. A few more paces and we pass through the opening in a high box-hedge. Inside, the path separates two more lawns, edged with luscious flower-beds; half-way along there is an opening in the hedge on the right. From beyond comes a Glyndebourne sound that is almost as characteristic as that of the orchestra tuning up; the click of croquet balls. It is said that the only class distinction at Glyndebourne – and that a self-imposed one – is marked by the fact that the orchestra play croquet and the singers tennis; *se non è vero* . . . Beyond the croquet lawn to our right we can glimpse green, but for the moment we are to proceed out of the box-hedge by the opening at the far end, where we see a gigantic oak before us, and beyond that, water. This is the Glyndebourne lake; strictly, the first and chief of Glynde-bourne's *three* lakes. A soft green path surrounds it; lily-pads float on it; ducks splash and bob in it. We proceed between lake and a wire fence, beyond which docile cows pause in their munching to eye the weird-looking strangers, and comment on them when they have passed. At the end of the lake is a wooden gate; and on the other side of it lies another, smaller, body of water; beyond that, the trick is repeated, the terrain getting wilder each time; the hardiest explorers of all find themselves eventually at a final gate and the road beyond it; the back door of Glyndebourne.

Today we shall circumperambulate only the first, official, lake. At the end there is a rustic seat set back among the greenery where many a troth has been plighted in many a Glyndebourne interval. Returning on the far side of the lake, by the path overhung with branches and brambles, we go round the mighty oak to inspect the expanse of green only glimpsed on the way down.

Up a few brick steps, and we are on an immense lawn; on the edge of it, there is a row of low buildings; they look like dressing-rooms, and indeed they are, as we realize from the fact that from them, in this hour before curtain-rise, are pouring sounds and sweet airs, that give delight and hurt not. We stroll on to the lawn. There, before us, is the house, its whole façade in view. It is not an ornate building, and it is not high; but it has a handsomeness and a solidity that make it memorable and inviting. We shall enter it in a moment, but first we must turn round. So doing, we gaze on an apparently unbroken vista, stretching from where we stand to the fields beyond, alive with grazing cows. How – assuming that they are not as artificial as the hillside sheep – are the cows kept from wandering on to the lawn and indeed into the house? We walk down the lawn; no sign of a fence appears but, just before we fall into it, we see that most English of devices, a ha-ha, presenting an impenetrable yet invisible barrier to the most determined of cattle.

Turning again to face the house, the whole sweep of the lawn is before us. If we have got the timing right, and the weather has got itself right, it is dotted with men in dinner-jackets and women in long dresses, and the combination of green grass, blue sky, black cloth and every colour of silk, linen and cotton presents a picture of incomparable charm, beauty and harmony. Here we must stop for a moment, and face a problem.

Our world has long had a habit of turning words of praise into terms of abuse, and none has suffered such a sea-change as 'élite'. Once, this signified the best. Now the word suggests to many that most unforgivable of modern crimes: the possession of some quality, position or ability that some other people do not have. The proposition is easily formulated: that which not all people have, no person may have.

Surveying the lawn, the opera-goers and the house, I survey also this argument, and find it wanting. The truth is that it is excellence itself that is the enemy, precisely because excellence stands out from the ordinary. The individual who insists on his individuality is the enemy, the man or woman who asserts the essential difference between every two human beings, a difference rooted in the eternal oneness beneath. Totalitarian

systems, all of them, have as their basis the need to make all
their subjects identical; authoritarian systems that fall short of
totalitarianism feel the same thirst, but are unwilling to go so
far in slaking it; the *dirigiste* systems of modern bureaucratic
democracy, the elective dictatorships of modern democratic
parliaments, are likewise on the same road. Only a political
philosophy which starts from the assumption that no two
human beings see their own needs and desires as exactly alike,
and therefore has as its basis the intention of making all indi-
viduals as free as possible to pursue those separate inclinations,
offers us hope. The hope becomes slighter all the time, and its
frailty is emphasized, even as its importance is celebrated, here
on this lawn.

A cloud has passed across the sun; it is time to go indoors.

There is a handsome wrought-iron gate to the left, with a
staircase beyond it; this leads to the private part of the house,
where George and Mary Christie live. Glyndebourne is not,
and insists that it is not, a public building; it is still a house
where opera is performed in the adjacent theatre. There are no
litter baskets in the gardens, and picnickers are asked to take
their rubbish away with them, and to treat the gardens as those
of a private house. And as far as I know, they do; I do not recall
ever having seen any part of the grounds strewn with the
débris of an *alfresco* supper, even on a particularly fine evening
which has tempted a very substantial proportion of the audience to bring picnics.

Opposite the staircase, there is an ever-open door; this leads
to the Organ Room, dominated by the magnificent instrument (though it lost its innards some years ago) that fills the
opposite end wall. This beautiful drawing room is furnished
richly but not lavishly; a fine piano; some side-tables, on one of
which there has always stood, in a silver frame, a photograph
of Audrey Mildmay, which has now been joined in this place
of honour by that of her widower; paintings; a minstrel's
gallery opposite the organ; comfortable sofas. The comfort of
the sofas is not accidental; it is to this room that latecomers,

whose entry into the auditorium is utterly forbidden, are conducted by angels with fiery swords, and assured that it is the next best thing to Eden. The performance is relayed to the Organ Room's loudspeakers from the stage, and the latecomers are seated after the interval. Here I reveal an item of forbidden knowledge, for which I may well be banished from Eden for ever. Glyndebourne, in all its brochures, programmes and other printed material, emphasizes the rule that latecomers are not admitted. But it offers one drop of sweet water to cool the tongue of Dives; *the opera always starts exactly ten minutes later than the time printed on the tickets.*

But it is about to start now, as the bells signify.

MONDAY, JUNE 30TH

I have been going to Glyndebourne every year for twenty-seven years. I know this for a very particular reason, for one of my visits each year takes a very particular form, and the form itself ensures that I keep track of the years. I first went there in 1954, and in the following year, Stewart and Douglas and I, friends from L.S.E., went *à trois*: each of us went at other times during the season with our ladies, but one visit – none of us can now remember exactly why – was men only, and was inevitably christened the 'Stag'. Next year, in the same circumstances of pleasing the ladies with other operas, other nights, we did it again. By the time of our visit in 1957, we realized it had become a habit; when we celebrated our tenth Glyndebourne Stag, in 1964, it had become a tradition; I do not care to wonder what it should be called as we now approach the thirtieth anniversary. The original administrative director of the enterprise was Stewart, who, very early on, became a member of the Glyndebourne Society, membership of which, for a trifling annual fee, offers an earlier start on the booking of tickets than is available to the rest of the public; But the membership list was closed very early, since if everybody could join the advantage would be nullified, and new members have only been admitted, over the years, as existing ones die or resign – mostly die, for who would resign from such a delightful club?

Stewart had an additional qualification; as a civil servant he was, and is, the only one of us capable of doing the administration. So every year he receives the advance booking form that is sent to Society members, photocopies it and sends the details to Douglas and myself, whereupon all three of us dine together and select the opera most suitable for our visit. This, of course, has long since become only an excuse to meet and talk over a good meal; we could obtain our tickets in a far less elaborate manner now, and for my other visits I do, but the tradition has become fixed, and moreover it has become a treasured means by which three close friends whose lives have run in very different channels, professionally and personally, may renew and strengthen that friendship, which grows stronger, and inevitably more cherished, as the years – more rapidly now – go by.

On the tenth anniversary of our annual festival within a festival, Douglas and I thought it right to mark a decade of Stewart's selfless organizing, so we had a magnificent heraldic coat of arms made for him; three of the quarterings referred, in a manner unintelligible to outsiders, to aspects of our annual outing, and the fourth was a visual pun on his surname, while the motto was '*Benedicite omnia opera*'. We smuggled it down and had it put on his plate for the dinner interval. Ten years later, somewhat to our own surprise, we found ourselves under the pleasant necessity of doing it again; this time we got a silver salver, which we had decorated with an equally punning motto round the rim. And soon it will be thirty years since this custom began, and we shall think of something else.

Meanwhile, there is the rest of the tradition to be observed. On the appointed day, far from getting into a dinner-jacket at lunch-time, I don mine immediately after breakfast. I then make my way to Streatham, where Stewart lives, and where Douglas, who does not live in London, has been staying the night. Stewart is in the act of tying his bow tie (this is a ritual as deeply rooted as the outing itself, and I have accused him of having scouts posted at the end of the road with walkie-talkie radios, to enable him to get the timing right), and as soon as he finishes the task, he opens the champagne. At noon, we set off for lunch en route; in the earlier years, this was taken at a restaurant which has long since closed, and ever since we have gone to Gravetye Manor. This massive house, now a restaurant, hotel and country club, is to be found, though not easily, a few miles from East Grinstead; it has gardens as remarkable as Glyndebourne's own, and makes a most pleasant staging-post, though the food is so rich, and we eat of it so copiously, and the wine list is so extensive and interesting, and we deny ourselves so little of its contents, that a siesta is essential before continuing the journey. On one of these annual journeys, something more than a siesta was required; finishing the meal with one of the elaborate desserts in which Gravetye's chef – who was at that time an Austrian, Karl Loderer – specialized, I deposited a tablespoon of raspberry sorbet on the front of my dress shirt. Instead of driving direct to Glyndebourne after lunch, therefore, we made a detour via a gentlemen's outfitters in East Grinstead, where I strode up to the counter and said to the assistant behind it, 'Good afternoon; I have, as you can see, recently committed a murder, and wish to buy a new dress shirt, so that I may get rid of the traces.' Either homicide is more common in that part of Sussex than I had supposed, or he did not believe me, for all he said was, 'What size collar, sir?'

At Glyndebourne, we naturally propose to follow the ritual of tea and walk before the performance. To our horror and rage, and in my case also indignation, it is raining. This is the first time in more than a quarter of a century's Glyndebourne-going that I have been rained on there, either on the Stag or any other visit. Nor, in my submission, is that an accident; from the first, I have refused to take a picnic, on the ground that to do so in the English summer is to invite condign punishment for hubris, and the implied bargain I struck with

Providence has *always* been most straitly kept by me, and *until now* by Providence also. True, Providence likes its joke; many a time it has been raining on the journey down, and more than once it has stopped only as the car turned through the gate. Occasionally, indeed, it has even resumed during the performance, to stop, of course, as soon as the interval begins, since another stroll round the gardens before Act II is no less firmly a part of the ritual. But never before has there been rain on Glyndebourne's greensward when I have wished to be upon Glyndebourne's greensward myself. Another cup of tea is taken, in some perturbation; but how can perturbation last when Mozart is on the bill?

Mozart, if you stop to think about him, will scare the life out of you. The fecundity of his genius is demonstrated not merely by its quantity or even the speed of its outpouring, but by its literally incredible spontaneity, incredible because it is impossible to believe that a human being can conceive such marvels of art so completely and in so many cases record them without a change of mind. Mozart himself said that a work presented itself to him as a single point, into which the whole score was compressed; all he then had to do – all! – was to hold that point of light in his head while he expanded it and wrote it down. This is an extraordinary enough statement for an age before atomic theory, though it is a good description of the picture of an atom that scientists held until the most recent discoveries in particle physics; it is much more extraordinary when we reflect that Mozart was describing a work of art that might be of forty minutes' duration.

It will not do to think of Mozart as some kind of semi-conscious creature, working by an instinct he could not understand and could only dimly recognize. That will do for a Nijinsky, but not for creative genius. But if Mozart was not a ouija-board, what the devil was he? Clearly, he was a channel through which music poured ceaselessly into the world's lap; clearly, also, he was a conscious instrument, burning to split the atom of inspiration into its particles of notes. But a channel has two ends; what was putting the music in at the far end?

That is the question that is apt to scare those who think about it, for it asks: what is inspiration? 'Inspire', after all, is a transitive verb; Mozart was inspired *by* something or someone *to* write his music. It may be objected that this, if it is true, is no less true of other artists, but it *is* less true of the others, with the exception of Schubert, for the level of spontaneity these two reached is not to be compared with that of other composers, and it is the spontaneity that is so amazing, and that makes the hair stand on end. Look at the torture of Beethoven's sketch-books, recording the progress of a musical idea to the anvil of Beethoven's implacable search for perfection, on which it is hammered interminably with a Titan's strokes into its final form, and then think of Mozart and Schubert creating complete masterpieces faster than they can write them down.

Peter Shaffer, in his play *Amadeus*, does not undertake to solve the mystery, but he does something nearly as valuable; he depicts it, in all its majesty and awe, so that none but fools can miss it (there are, of course, many fools in the world), and he makes Mozart's rival, Salieri, see the point with such terrible clarity and completeness that it turns God into his eternal enemy overnight. And his charge against the God who has betrayed him, conveyed in the mighty speech that ends the first act, marks out the battleground in lines of fire:

Tonight at an inn somewhere in this city stands a giggling child who can put on paper, without actually setting down his billiard cue, casual notes which turn my most considered ones into lifeless scratches. *Grazie Signore!* You gave me the desire to serve you – which most men do not have – then saw to it the service was shameful in the ears of the server. *Grazie!* You gave me the desire to praise you – which most men do not have – then made me mute. *Grazie tanti!* You put into me perception of the Incomparable – which most men never know! – then ensured that I would know myself forever mediocre. Why? . . . What is my fault? . . . Until this day I have pursued virtue with rigour. I have laboured long hours to relieve my fellow men. I have worked and worked the talent you allowed me. You know how hard I've worked! – Solely that in the end, in the practice of the art which alone makes the world comprehensible to me, I might hear Your Voice! And now I do hear it – and it says only one name: MOZART! . . . Spiteful, sniggering, conceited, infantile Mozart! – who has never worked one minute to help another man! – shit-talking Mozart with his botty-smacking wife! – him you have chosen to be your sole conduct! And my only reward – my sublime privilege – is to be the sole man alive in this time who shall clearly recognise your Incarnation! *Grazie e grazie ancora!*

So be it! From this time we are enemies, You and I! I'll not accept it from You – Do you hear? . . . They say God is not mocked. I tell you, Man is not mocked! . . . I am not mocked! . . . They say the spirit bloweth where it listeth: I tell you NO! It must list to virtue or not blow at all! What else is virtue for, but to fit us for Your incarnations? . . . *Dio Ingiusto!* – You are the Enemy! I name Thee now – *Nemico Eterno!* And this I swear. To my last breath I shall *block* you on earth, as far as I am able!*

Salieri, then, is in no doubt as to the truth, though the motives he attributes to God, and the capriciousness he implies, are the fruits of his own disappointment: what would be said, what *should* be said, by someone who does not see Mozart as the good money of genius come to drive out the bad of mere talent, but who nevertheless sees as clearly as Salieri that there must be *some* reason for Mozart and his selection as the conduit along which there is to flow such enduring proof of – of what?

That is the question. There must be an answer.

Die Entführung aus dem Serail is the slightest of the 'Big Five'; the little finger on such a hand, however, can move mountains

* Peter Shaffer, *Amadeus* (André Deutsch, 1979).

unaided, and this enchanting work can prove far more than an entertainment. We three, indeed, have the proof, for we went *à trois* to Glyndebourne for *Die Entführung* twenty years ago, in Carl Ebert's production with Oliver Messel's sets, and we shall never forget the strength as well as the magic of that performance. There is nothing like that tonight, though since we have all gone expecting the worst, as many of the reviews have suggested that Peter Wood, the director, has butchered it to make a producer's holiday, we are correspondingly delighted to find so much to enjoy. But much of the singing is dangerously thin, in places even sour, and the pace of the conductor, Gustav Kuhn (new to Glyndebourne), so measured as to rob the work of much of its innocence and even spontaneity. I say this after the performance to George and Mary Christie, and to Brian and Victoria Dickie; my opinion is greeted with shrieks of horror and scorn, and it is unanimously agreed that I cannot tell the difference between the slow kind of conducting and the loving kind. Kuhn is Glyndebourne's newest treasure, and I have committed misprision of the coffers.

We drive home for the final stage of the ritual. Stewart's lady, Joan, known for reasons which we have all now forgotten as the People's Friend, is waiting for the signal, sent from a telephone box a carefully judged distance from base; on receiving it, she starts to cook a giant supper of bacon and scrambled eggs, sausages and grilled tomatoes. We have eaten a lavish banquet at Gravetye and a substantial dinner in the Glyndebourne interval; yet we scoff Joanie's feast as though we had not seen solid food for a fortnight. The evening is rounded off perfectly, with Figaro, the ginger cat, supervising the mirth. A minicab takes me home, and I am accompanied all the way to bed and sleep by further reflections on friendship.

MONDAY, JULY 7TH

Something is wrong; it is raining already. It will clear up by the time Arianna and I arrive, no doubt.

It has not cleared up by the time we arrive; it is showing no sign of even pausing. We take the tea and omit the walk.

Rosenkavalier is the other new production of the season, and it, too, challenges comparison with a mighty ghost. Carl Ebert took his leave of Glyndebourne with a production of this opera, and his production of it remains in the mind as one of his finest achievements, unfolding act by act to this almost flawless work's tremendous climax. First, the great trio; next the love-duet; and then, because Strauss was in his way a genius, for all the taint of his character and the extent to which that taint got into so much of his music, the magical, unique colophon, the entry of the Marschallin's little black page in search of the lost handkerchief. A blind man could follow the action with ease; the child's hurrying footsteps outside the room, his entrance, his momentary bafflement, his darting search carrying him into every corner of the room, his de-lighted pounce as he spots the treasure, his joy as he runs out brandishing it, leaving the orchestra, in a final *fortissimo* up-swing, to bring the curtain down with a crash.

The end of *Rosenkavalier* is among the finest things opera can do. I know the argument on the other side – that Strauss was a cold-hearted cynic, calculating exactly what would best jerk the tears and the royalties, heartlessly manipulating his characters' love, true love being an experience unknown to him. The argument is a powerful one; but those who condemn *Rosenkavalier* on the strength of it forget that men can become greater than they know, and can succeed even where they are implacably determined to fail. Strauss, in this final scene, rose above his limitations, as he did again at the end of his life, in the final scene of *Capriccio*, and wrote music that goes to the deepest places in the human heart. That is why I have been looking forward to this *Rosenkavalier* so much, and why in-deed I always look forward to the opera so much, knowing that it is capable, if production, singing and playing rise to the occasion, of providing an experience which can seriously be compared to that provided by *Figaro* itself.

It doesn't work. The designs, by Erté, are acceptable in Act I, more than acceptable in Act III, horrible – and horribly inappropriate – in Act II. An ominous distribution of quality, for if the Presentation of the Rose hath lost its scent, wherewith shall it be scented? But the Ochs is dressed like a comic Ruritanian hussar in an operetta, and although it is true that Faninal is a *nouveau riche*, and may be presumed to have himself and his family clothed, and his house decorated, in a somewhat over-elaborate or even vulgar taste, there is no suggestion in the opera that he is colour-blind as well. The singing, too, is well below a level that would be needed to make this a memorable *Rosenkavalier*, and there is something else, to be mentioned only with circumspection, and certainly not to George and Mary over a drink after the performance. I have been going to opera for more than a third of a century, and dramatic verisimilitude in the appearance of the characters, though it is nowadays provided very much more often than it used to be, so that the sixteen-stone Violetta or eighteen-stone Rodolfo is now, thank God, a rarity, is not the very first thing I look for on the stage. All the same, the story of *Rosenkavalier* is of a man torn between two beautiful women, and I have to say, at whatever cost to gallantry, that if Glyndebourne could not find a more attractive pair of women to sing Sophie and the Marschallin they had much better not have done the opera at all. Only Felicity Lott as Octavian (the 'pants part' as American singers call the *travesti* roles) does anything much to cheer the spirits; and they need cheering, for in the interval the rain has turned into a torrent, and after the performance from a torrent into a flood. To be stabbed in the back by Providence at Glyndebourne once may be considered a misfortune; to be stabbed twice in a week suggests persecution. And I did not take a picnic to *Rosenkavalier* either. *Nemico Eterno!*

That, however, is no mood in which to leave Glyndebourne, rain or no rain; on the drive to the station I close my eyes and conjure up the sight of the gardens beneath the sunshine, the sound of croquet between the hedges, the memory of John Christie's brave, mad, impossible dream and the years through which, season after season, it has borne such glorious fruit. Can a dream bear fruit? At Glyndebourne, certainly.

Singing in the Rain

The warmth of Provence; the moment I step outside the airport building I feel it across my shoulders, the balm that smoothes away the knots tied by months of tensing ourselves against the treachery of London's weather. The warmth of Provence; the certainty that I shall not need a topcoat tonight, after the sun has gone down. The warmth of Provence; memories of my very first visit, which was to the Cannes Film Festival, as the guest of Mike Todd, and the carpet-bag which we all got, a replica of the one carried by Phileas Fogg in Todd's film. (A memory within a memory; of travelling with the bag, some years later, returning to London from Amsterdam. As my flight was called, and I rose to go to the gate, a passenger in front of me tossed the paper he had been reading onto his chair, and I read the headline: 'Mike Todd dies in blazing plane'. I ran back into the concourse and bought a black handkerchief, which I tied round the bag's handle. On the plane, I ordered champagne and drank a toast to the last of the real showmen.)

I ring Pippa Irwin, who lives just along the coast. Before I left London, we had arranged to meet; she would come to the opera with me; serve Arianna right for having business in America.

But there is a catch in it, for I must now hire a chauffeur as well as a car. The good M. Dissaux is summoned, with a vast air-conditioned Citroën, to drive me to Aix. I have not been to Aix and its Festival for more than ten years, and I can date my visit very precisely indeed; I was staying with Derek and

Yvonne Monsey, at their house at La Roquette-sur-Siagne, and we all drove over to Aix to see *Così Fan Tutte*. That in itself would not fix the occasion so inextricably in my mind; the pin that holds it in place is the fact that it was the night on which the first men landed on the moon. I can remember how I felt as the moon rose over the open-air theatre, the courtyard of the old Archbishop's Palace, and how strange it seemed to be watching and listening to a perfect summary of the eighteenth century just as the twentieth was coming to this strange fruition. I couldn't stop looking up at the moon, and all around me others had the same compulsion; I don't know what we expected to see – somebody leaning over the edge and waving, perhaps? – but I remember wondering whether, on the moon, it was full earth, and whether the astronauts would remember to turn their money over. Then we all drove back to the Monseys and watched the landing on television. Derek and Yvonne have both died in this past year; she knew she had cancer and not long to live, and faced the knowledge with courage and gaiety, but Derek died first, his heart attack shockingly unexpected. Yvonne, visibly dying, insisted on being at his cremation, carried gently in and out in a firemen's lift by two real firemen. 'I cannot,' wrote Logan Pearsall-Smith, 'get used to the disappearing-trick that my friends have taken to playing.' Nor can I.

SUNDAY, JULY 13TH

Aix's Sunday market; a considerable surprise. The old quarter of the town is full of pedestrian precincts, news of which does not yet seem to have filtered through to the motorists, who bowl gaily along them without slackening speed, let alone to the motor-cyclists, who use the bollards as a slalom course; it is also full of street-names that come from the trades once plied here; Coppersmith's Road, Tanner's Square, Muleteers' Avenue, Musicians' Alley. And Provençal hands have not yet lost their cunning, if the little fair is anything to go by, for although the prices take full cognizance of the tourists, the wares include astonishingly little of the now ubiquitous trash and souvenirs, and astonishingly much of good quality work made by real craftsmen. There is fine woodwork, silverware, jewellery; mirrors with frames in light natural wood, or handsomely carved or delicately painted; good leather, sturdy toys, tapestries; rough soap, and lovely candles with leaves and flowers pressed into the wax; huge skeins of wool, flung down on a stall in a profusion of fifty colours, like tropical fruit or a painter's palette. The passer-by can have a name poker-worked, while he waits, on wooden egg-cups, bowls, goblets, or engraved in the glass of tumblers, plates, dishes; he can buy fresh food, fruit that does not look as though it is made of plastic, biscuits that smell of ovens, not laboratories, tomatoes of irregular shape. All this will disappear in time, of course, as it has disappeared already from most of Europe, driven out by greed, forgetfulness and indolence. But for a moment I am reminded of man's oldest known function, as a maker of things with his hands, and suddenly I come upon the perfect symbol of man in that capacity; half-way down the street there sits at a little stall a maker of sundials, those magic clocks that, alone among timepieces, tell only the happy hours. A straw hat on his head, a dark cheroot clamped between his teeth, he bends over the beautiful face of the one he is working on. It is shaped and polished, and the blade that casts the shadow is already in place; now he is cutting the numerals into the stone. The lines are marked, measured exactly into the graded spacing that a sundial must have; spread out on his table are a series of tiny hammers, chisels, wedges, the wooden hafts comfortably worn, the metal handles polished bright by human hand. He selects a chisel and a hammer, and begins to tap along his marks, pausing after each few taps to blow the dust gently away. I watch, fascinated, as the numbers take shape; when he looks up for a moment I raise my camera and ask '*Vous permettez?*' He nods, and returns to his work, then – since this is clearly the first time for many years that anyone has asked his permission to photograph him – he decides that something more is called for in reciprocal *politesse*, raises his head again and bows: '*Merci*.'

Pippa arrives in the afternoon; Pippa is one of those of whom nobody has a bad word to say; there are some of whom this is true in a negative sense only, in that nobody has anything at all to say of them, good or bad. But Pippa is one of those rare spirits of whom all speak well, and any conversation about her glows with her absent presence. A concert in the evening, in the Cathedral; but first, the Cours Mirabeau.

The Cours Mirabeau runs east-west through the heart of the city. A double row of handsome plane trees lines each side. O shame! I have to ask Pippa what they are; she is a gardener of exceptional talent, and when she and Peter were living at La Garde Freinet she made things grow, in the beautiful garden she created from nothing, that would not grow at that height for anyone else. But what is remarkable here is not that she recognizes a plane tree when she sees it; it is my own ignorance of nature and its language. There is hardly a bird, a tree, a wild flower, that I can recognize and name. Once, walking in Wales, I came back and announced that there seemed to be an awful lot of injured birds in the area, taking off lop-sided; I did not notice the silence deepening until I added, 'Black and white ones.' Then I noticed stares. 'Magpies,' said somebody, crumbling bread; 'they fly like that. Like a frying-pan, the saying is.' Another time, going up-river at Wexford, someone pointed out a heron. 'Where?' 'There – look, by that log.' I couldn't see it, though I was staring at it and it was staring back at me; I had always believed that a heron was the same as a stork, and I was looking for a tall, thin bird standing on one leg with a half-eaten fish sticking out of its mouth. I have come to make a virtue of the necessity of my ignorance, insisting that I am never happy except with the ring of pavement beneath my heels, and deep carcinogenic draughts of street-fumes going into my lungs; a poor alternative to using my eyes, no doubt, but the best I can do now.

Anyway, here we are at the Deux Garçons, looking up and down the Cours Mirabeau. The vista is closed at one end by a handsome *rotonde* with an elaborate fountain, at the other by a statue of Good King René. He seems to have been an entire fifteenth-century Medici family in himself, skilled in languages, science, music and poetry. Also viniculture; he introduced the muscatel grape into this region – indeed, his statue shows him holding out a bunch of them. (It makes no very grand wine, but it does make Beaumes-de-Venise, which I sometimes think is the finest of all dessert wines, and will even go with cheese, which is more than you can say for Sauternes.) In the middle is another, smaller, fountain, moss-grown, said to be Roman. Perhaps; and perhaps they stick the moss on at night, or in the winter when the visitors have gone.

The Cours Mirabeau is one of those urban landmarks that define not merely a city but a civilization. The Champs Elysées; the Piazza San Marco; the Plaza Mayor in Salamanca; Fifth Avenue; even the Kurfürstendamm defines a very strange and new civilization, but defines it none the less. Where do we *saunter* in London? Carnaby Street, the King's Road (the first fully biodegradable throwaway thorough-fares), the horrible Beauchamp Place.

I presume the French invented the pavement café; if not, they have perfected the art, and the life that has grown from it. The Cours Mirabeau is inaptly named; it is gentle, not stirring, and its great patron, so memorably portrayed by Carlyle, a combination of Wilkes and Fox, would have found it not nearly rakehelly enough for his taste. He would have cut a great swath through the girls though, not that many of them look particularly unwilling to have a swath cut through them.

A concert of Requiems, Fauré and Mozart. Once more, the problem of music in church, this time complicated by the fact that the music is liturgical. The French, however, have no inhibitions about applauding, and do not even look to see what their neighbours are doing before they clap, indeed before they cheer. Perhaps the British hesitancy and the French readiness are reflections not of national temperament, but of religion, the difference between the spontaneity of Catholicism and the calculation of the Protestant offspring that had to make its way in the world. Or: the warm south and the cold north. But there is another problem about music in church; it always makes me dissatisfied with hearing church music anywhere else. The unique resonance which comes from the interaction of sound and stone turns the music into a different experience altogether; Valerie Masterson's voice, which is not a big one, demonstrates this very clearly, as she sends pure, silvery notes. one after another, up into the vaulted roof, there to hover like doves before slowly disappearing. One day, somebody ought to stage *Parsifal* in a cathedral, or at least the Grail scenes.

MONDAY, JULY 14TH

Another difference between here and there; the French celebrate their national day, the British mostly have no idea when, or what, it is, and those few who go about on April 23rd with roses in their buttonholes, longing for somebody to ask them why, seem grotesquely out of place. The French, I dare say, are little more conversant with the details of the Fall of the Bastille than are the British with the history of St George, but the truth is that we never cared much for his sainthood in the first place. The French, though, make real whoopee on *le Quatorze*; every town in France has its fireworks, and Aix is no exception.

But before the evening there is the day, and we go to lunch at the Baumanière, less than an hour's drive away. I had telephoned the day before to ask if they were open on the Quatorze; I had forgotten that though the banks may close on Bastille Day, the French spirit of commercial enterprise does not. Once, many years ago, I spent Christmas in Paris, and was ordering something from a shop. The *patronne* said it would be ready on Tuesday, and I pointed out that Tuesday was Christmas Day. None the less, that was when I could collect my purchase. *'Mais vous êtes ouvert même le jour de Noël?'* She looked at me in genuine surprise. *'C'est notre métier.'*

Pippa   Myself

Filets de Sole au Gingembre   *Soufflé de Homard*
Pigeon farci   *Pintadeau aux morilles*

Les fromages
Tarte Tatin
Les Friandises
Café

———

Bollinger 1979
Gewürtztraminer (Hugel) 1976

In the evening, neither of us feels like much dinner, but we go and sit in the Cours Mirabeau, closed to traffic. At the Deux Garçons end, there is an amplified pop group draped over King René; we decamp to the other end, just in time to get a grandstand position for the firework display. None of the great set-pieces, but some lovely star-bursts in a dozen colours, and a final whoosh of red, white and blue rockets. Back slowly up the Cours Mirabeau; no pushing, no hurrying, just a happy French crowd on a happy French day. The pop group has packed its electricity and gone, and King René, spotlit on his pedestal and still holding out his bunch of grapes in a most inviting manner, smiles upon us all. None is so poor of spirit as not to smile back.

TUESDAY, JULY 15TH

Arianna's birthday. After breakfast, it is five past midnight in California. I am staying in a small hotel on the edge of Aix, but I can dial direct to anywhere in the world. So I could from the Rickatschwende above Dornbirn, so I can from the hotel in the little village half an hour from Bayreuth where I shall be staying shortly. I strike a bet with myself that when I get to Edinburgh, where I shall be staying in the most expensive hotel in the city, I shall still have to go through the switchboard to get a call within Edinburgh, never mind overseas. She is asleep, but nobody can object to being woken up five minutes into a birthday, and she doesn't. I detest the telephone, and never cease to bewail the civilization that has made us all so dependent on it. And the trap is circular; if the telephone did not exist, we would organize our lives differently and more pleasantly, but since it does exist we are bound to organize our lives unpleasantly around it. And the uselessness of the instrument for any purpose more elevated or intimate than ordering a couple of pork chops or finding out the time of the next train to Leicester is undeniable. But she sounds well, and after whetting her musical appetite and sending Pippa's love, I let her go back to sleep.

Pippa has a lunch engagement along the coast; I sip in the Cours Mirabeau. In the evening the big event of the Festival. Aix's Director, Bernard Lefort, cannot compete in the open market against the bigger festivals, so he has devised an alternative strategy; modest but interesting events, with one huge, budget-breaking spectacular set in the middle. It is a revival of Rossini's *Semiramide*, sung in Italian, but Gallicly titled *Semiramis*. (Well, the French call *Figaro*, even when they are singing it in the original, *Les Noces de Figaro*, and for that matter can be heard referring to Louis de Beethov'n; it's a mercy that they haven't called the other repertoire opera of the Festival *C'est comme ça qu'elles font toutes*.) Though I am an assiduous collector of out-of-the-way operas, or familiar ones in out-of-the-way places (*Carmen* in Leningrad, *Il Trovatore* in Tel Aviv, *Tannhäuser* in Slough, the *Barber* in Tokyo and in Japanese), I have never seen *Semiramide*, indeed know not a note of it other than the overture and *Bel raggio*. But no opera that has held the stage as long and successfully can be without merit, as Covent Garden demonstrated when they at last dared Meyerbeer with *L'Africaine*. What has kept *Semiramide* off the bills is its basic requirement: the greatest *bel canto* soprano in the world and the greatest coloratura mezzo to go with her. On the whole, such rare beasts prefer not to inhabit the same cage, be it never so gilded; M. Lefort must have a rare talent for blarney, for he has captured Montserrat Caballé for the title role and Marilyn Horne for that of Arsace, the 'pants part'. The plot (Babylonian queen murders her husband, falls in love with handsome general of her army, throwing over fellow-conspirator in the process, discovers that general is her own son, all meet by moonlight, ghost of murdered husband appears, general aims fatal sword-thrust at co-villain, gets mother instead, is proclaimed king) is sufficiently absurd to satisfy the stoutest appetite for absurdity, but if operas fell out of the repertoire because their plots were absurd the repertoire of most opera houses would be thin indeed. Besides, we can be sure of Rossini; the passions involved may be lurid and the characters too villainous or noble to be trifled with, but cheerfulness will keep breaking in, as it did in the Petite Messe Solenelle, anything but *solenelle*, that I heard in Adelaide in the spring.

Pippa is wearing a beautiful silk trouser-suit, I my new white dinner-jacket; this sartorial information is shortly to become relevant to the proceedings in a dramatic manner, as is the fact, remembered from my last visit and *Così* while the moon-men landed, that the courtyard auditorium is open to the sky, though the stage and orchestra pit are not.

The staging is sufficiently ridiculous to satisfy even those left wanting more absurdity than the plot can provide. The set is entirely white, so are the costumes, so is the cast – faces, hands, even hair; most of them, in addition, are encased in bizarre white sandwich-boards with plaster mouldings, looking partly like Edwardian mantelpieces and partly like blanched playing-cards. Caballé, who, the programme reveals, has recently been made a member of the Order of the Golden Grasshopper, has a touch of gold on her costume, and Horne a scarlet cloak, but everything and everyone else is spectral.

There is a good deal of lurching, but little else in the way of production. We are not here, however, for the production; we are here for the two great voices and for what Rossini has given them to show off with.

He has given them enough and to spare; this is what grand opera ought to be: to wit, grand. There has been talk of rivalry and dissension between these two *grandes dames* at rehearsal; there always is such talk. There is no sign of it on the stage, and Rossini has seen to it that there would be ample opportunity for the display of enmity if it were there. He has written two enormous, and characteristically Rossinian, roles; but they go hand in hand almost throughout, and the ladies throw themselves into the work like loving sisters. Thrilling runs and trills and octave leaps, soaring high notes from Caballé and dark chest-notes from Horne, magnificent cat's-cradle harmonies, ringing climaxes, dazzling ornamentation, sensational effects as the two voices intertwine, separate, pursue, flee from and catch one another – indeed it is easy to see why this brainless but glorious stuff so enthralled audiences when the young Shaw was crying out for Wagner, and easier still to agree that the revival is abundantly justified.

Not only justified, however, but wet, for as the second act begins, so does the rain. At first, it is only a light patter, and all eyes are cocked at the cloudy heavens as intently as they were a decade ago at the serene, moon-filled sky. Will the rain hold off? A few minutes' doubt, then the definite answer: no, it will not, and down it comes in fierce, driving sheets. At the first splash, I have draped my faultlessly ironed dinner-jacket round Pippa's thinly clad shoulders; Gallant Jack Levin could do no less. But now nothing short of a golfing umbrella or a pair of all-enveloping mackintoshes, complete with hoods, belts and buttons up to the chin, will save us. There is one consolation; if the rain shows no sign of stopping, the performance will be abandoned. The rain shows no sign of stopping, in fact grows heavier, but the performance is *not* abandoned. I begin to regret jeering at the Austrians for their fear of getting wet, and to wish the French had had enough *Schlamperei* to install a Hohenems sliding roof.

Well, at least the French will flee; self-indulgent hypochrondriacs to a man and a woman, this nation will not suffer for its pleasures, and amid the general *sauve qui peut* Pippa and I can scuttle out without letting down the old country: dammit, *we* won the Battle of Waterloo, not they, and we can hardly run up the white flag in the presence of the insolent foe. To our amazement and horror, the French sit fast like the Imperial Guard announcing that it will die but not surrender, and no amount of convincing ourselves that they are only doing so because they have paid thirty pounds a ticket will shut out the growing conviction that we are shortly going to die of exposure.

The Duke of Wellington, conqueror, after all, of Napoleon, had saved the situation in peacetime, too, once before ('Try Sparrow-hawks, ma'am'), and however unlikely a saint he makes, I offer up to him a prayer for inspiration. He does not fail me; dragging the startled Pippa by the arm, I push past the people sitting between us and the aisle, heedless of the groans and protests of those who, already damp, are now being trampled on as well. Once clear of the row, I turn *up* the steps, not down, still clutching Pippa; in a few strides we are safe beneath the lee of the balcony, sitting in the aisle warm, dry, and with a perfect view both of the stage and of the French floating in their seats. And that is scarcely an exaggeration; when, at the end, the lights come up and the audience rises to leave, the water literally cascades from them, and an array of bedraggled dresses, transparent jackets and ruined coiffures splash and squelch to the exits. Albion Perfide, with not a hair out of place, notes that the rain has ended at the same moment that the opera did, and we go to dinner, starting with a self-congratulatory bottle of champagne. It is already well after one o'clock in the morning, for Act II didn't start until 11.30, but what does that matter?

I lie long awake, the glitter and sparkle of the music filling my head, marvelling at the genius of Rossini, and at those who are unable to hear it. To be sure, he had no under-standing of character, no interest in it, really, and his idea of drama is crude beside that of Puccini, let alone Verdi. But as a writer of music to thrill and delight, he has few equals. When will Covent Garden revive *William Tell, The Thieving Magpie, Cenerentola*, indeed anything but the eternal *Barber*? Come to think of it, when will Covent Garden revive the eternal *Barber* itself?

WEDNESDAY, JULY 16TH

Pippa has to end her visit; business is taking her back, and I see her off; she is positively purring with the merriment we have shared, and so am I. Back to the Cours Mirabeau, where the musicians have congregated for elevenses. I raise with Valerie Masterson the point about church music in church. She agrees, and goes further; she sang the soprano part in both Requiems on Sunday, and she insists that a performer in such works in such surroundings cannot help feeling involved in something greater than just the words and the music. And if the per-former, why not – indeed how not – the audience?

A walk: posters have appeared overnight on the trees, like leaves in spring, advertising *Une soirée topless, avec Brigitte et Ingrid*. It is nice to know that the French have to borrow our word; possibly they have borrowed Brigitte *et* Ingrid, too. I go as far as the view of the Montagne Ste Victoire, familiar in so many guises, so many weathers, so many lights, from Cézanne's obsession with the unending, unendable struggle to get it down exactly, and for ever. The big exhibition in Paris in 1978 had a score or so of his studies of his artistic Shangri-La, in pencil, water-colour and oil, a whole wallful at one point, giving as deep an insight into the way genius struggles as perhaps it is possible to have.

In the evening, I enjoy a perfect vignette of French life. I have been having a bite and a sup at a café in the *rotonde* in which the Cours Mirabeau ends, where the fireworks were held. I have always wondered how many customers at French pavement cafés try to bilk the establishment by leaving without paying when there is no waiter in sight; the practice of leaving a ticket under the ashtray, putting the customer on his honour either to leave the right sum behind when he goes, or to summon the waiter and pay him, seems to invite losses on a considerable scale. For the first time, I am witness to just such a depredation. Two young men rise from a table on the other side of the café, and stroll quietly away. Nothing unusual about that, if they have left behind the sum required. But I learn from the ensuing mime, exactly like a silent film, that they have not. The waiter comes to the table, looks for money, finds none; this is where the cinema pianist would break into excited arpeggios. A fellow-waiter approaches; a brief discussion ensues; the colleague points, saying, 'They went that way', more clearly than the words I cannot hear. Unhurriedly, the waiter who has lost customer and cash sets off, bearing the plate on which there no less clearly rests the unpaid bill. He vanishes from my sight round the edge of the café; I watch, hypnotized, for him to reappear. Very soon, he does, and his colleague turns to him with a mien of enquiry; the inaudible answer is once again accompanied by most eloquent gestures, which say that the sinners have repented of their crime and made restitution. A final inclination of the head, a spreading of the hands, a shrug; it means, 'And I didn't have to threaten them, or even raise my voice.'

THURSDAY, JULY 17TH

There is an exhibition of the work of Bernard Buffet, who is, as they say, very big in Aix; he has designed the official Festival posters, and the programme-book. There are about thirty of his dreadful pictures, all in the same flat style, with the same trademarks, spiky lines and cross-hatching and dreary colours, and the old cliché comes starkly to life in this room;

when you have seen one, you have certainly seen them all. I go round with the disappointment felt by a child who breaks open his drum to see what is making the noise, then I go round again, searching the canvases for any sign, any flicker, of artistic life, of feeling, of vision. In vain; is it possible that Buffet is the most boring painter now living? It is quite possible; perhaps he is even the most boring painter who has ever lived. Well; it is something, as A. P. Herbert's Lord Justice Arrowroot says, to dot an i in perpetuity.

In the evening, back to the Cathedral for an *a capella* concert by the Uppsala University Chamber Choir. First surprise: I have always believed that Uppsala is in Finland, but I learn from the programme that it is in Sweden. Second surprise: the programme is extraordinarily varied, including Mozart, Pizzetti, Poulenc, Frank Martin, Schoenberg and folk songs. Third surprise: well over half of the girls wear glasses. Do the men of Uppsala never make passes at all? Fourth surprise, and best: they are very good indeed. The conductor has a tuning-fork and gives them a note each time, the perfect-pitchers looking smug; then off they go, with a beautiful, full tone and a great sweetness in the phrasing, and negotiating the most complex harmonies with apparently effortless ease. There is a soloist in national costume for some of the folk songs; all in all, I never thought I could enjoy an unaccompanied choir so much.

Or an opera so little. For after a pause in the Cours Mirabeau I am bound for the chief novelty of the Festival, a work by Claude Prey based on *Les Liaisons Dangereuses*. I am surprised that nobody has thought to make an opera out of it before. (Perhaps somebody has – if so, Harold Rosenthal will certainly be sending me one of his postcards when he reads this. I forget which play it was of which I once rashly wrote that nobody had ever turned it into an opera, and Harold promptly listed five versions for me, three of which he had actually seen. He is at present engaged on bringing up to date Loewenstein's monumental *Annals of Opera*, which is said to list every one that has ever been performed; I wouldn't be surprised if Harold were to add all those which have been written but *not* performed.) Choderlos de Laclos's bitter attack on the manners and morals of the upper classes, which has as good a claim to have helped precipitate the Revolution as is made for Beaumarchais and *Le Mariage de Figaro*, needs an eighteenth-century composer – Mozart with his heart removed would be perfect for it – though Berlioz could have done it, too. So, of course, could Stravinsky. But M. Prey cannot; he has set it in an arid *parlando* idiom, as far removed from the eighteenth century, either before or after *le déluge*, as it is possible to get. I tiptoe away at half-time.

FRIDAY, JULY 18TH

M. Dissaux, punctual to the minute, picks me up to drive me to Marseille. I have never been to Marseille, though I have a very detailed picture of it from the Marcel Pagnol film trilogy, *Marius*, *Fanny* and *César*. Is it going to look as it should? Of course it doesn't; choked, choking rows of cars now surround the Vieux Port, where the friends gathered under the patronage of Raimu. Oddly enough, however, a modern equivalent of the atmosphere does seem to exist. Certainly, though the new harbours and docks have relegated the Raimu area to secondary status, it does not seem at all dead or museum-like; on the contrary, it teems with life, and the first bar I drop into for a glass of wine and a coffee has a little old mini-Raimu in charge of it, complaining that the cars are driving his custom away. Sitting later at a café overlooking the water I am startled by the most extraordinary din; at first I think that the gang warfare for which Marseille is notorious has broken into open conflict under my nose, but the truth, though less alarming, is even more picturesque. It is a bridal motorcade, which differs from other bridal processions, and indeed other motorcades, in several respects. First, it travels at about seventy miles an hour; second, it does not appear to be going anywhere, since the cars, about a dozen of them, simply go round and round the harbour; third, the cars have all been fitted with those Klaxons that play a tune, in this particular case the minor-key version of the opening bars of 'Colonel Bogey'. The onlookers respond with cheers, waves and even a few rude gestures; from my ringside seat I can see the bride and groom come round again and again, laughing every time.

All around me, I hear the strange accent of Marseille; later I perfect my own version of it, which anyone can do. Close your back teeth firmly; hold your nose no less firmly between finger and thumb; speak French in your own fashion. You will find that you are doing so with a passable imitation of a Marseille accent.

SATURDAY, JULY 19TH

To the studios of Radio France, whence I am to transmit my B.B.C. broadcast on the Aix Festival. A scene ensues that Raimu could have used; London can hear me perfectly, but no amount of twiddling knobs and changing circuits can make London audible here. The studio manager gets Broadcasting House on the ordinary telephone; eventually, I find myself speaking to Alan. Unfortunately, the telephone is outside the cubicle, and for technical reasons I do not understand (it would be a laughably simple technical reason that I *could* understand), the call cannot be put through to the phone on the table in front of me. My headphones being useless, I abandon them, and after a good deal of dashing in and out of the cubicle, Alan and I agree that I should go ahead and speak the whole script in one 'take', the only drawback of the method being that if London ceases to be able to hear me after I have been speaking for, say, thirty seconds, they will not be able to let me know until, twenty minutes later, I return to the telephone and ask 'How was that?' Fortunately, the line is clear throughout. Alan and I assure each other that things will go more smoothly in Munich. Walking back to my hotel in the sunshine, I see a poster advertising a *"Festival National de Majorettes, avec le gracieux concours de Pascal Dumas, Champion d'Europe 1980 de Twirling-Baton'*. Another i dotted in perpetuity; to be European Champion at Twirling-Baton is not the same as being the composer of the Jupiter Symphony, but it is not quite nothing. Anyway, I am sure that the Festival of Majorettes will be an improvement on the Aixoise *Soirée Topless*, and Pascal Dumas a cut above Brigitte *et* Ingrid.

FRIDAY, JULY 25TH

Five days pass, spent at Bandol working on this book. M. Dissaux is as punctual as ever, this time to take me back to Marseille airport. He is full of reminiscence, for he was born in these parts, before the South became, from the Spanish border to the Italian, one continuous resort. He gestures at a garage; his parents owned it, he tells me, in the days when the thousands of holiday cars had not yet started to pour along this road, and soon after the war they sold it *'pour une bouchée de pain'*. Another gesture; *'et maintenant . . .'*

A couple of hours later, I am in Madrid for the first time, face to face with my Goya problem and my El Greco problem. Everyone to whom I have confided the problems has, at the discovery that I have never been to Madrid, insisted that the solution is to be found in the Prado. On

SATURDAY, JULY 26TH

therefore, I make for the Prado.

The problem is simply stated: before Goya, before El Greco, I stand entirely unmoved. But a significant, and alarming, difference becomes apparent when I compare my Goya/El Greco problem with my Bach problem. I have no difficulty in hearing the greatness of Bach in the B Minor Mass, the St Matthew Passion, the Double Violin Concerto; I understand entirely why he is a composer who moves his hearers as profoundly as any man who ever wrote music, including Mozart. My problem is not that I am unable to hear his greatness, but that I am unable to respond to it. With the two painters it is worse, much worse; I cannot even see what other people are responding to. I have looked at the 'Disasters of War', and now in the Prado I look at them again; I have never looked at the 'black paintings', but now in the Prado I look at them for the first time; I have looked at countless reproductions of the Maja, clothed and unclothed, and now I look upon the originals. And nowhere in any of this and all the other Goyas in this collection can I see anything but a minimal talent as a draughtsman and a slightly greater one as a colourist. What is wrong with my eyes and my mind, to say nothing of my feelings, that I cannot see what everyone else can? For this is not a matter of the Emperor's clothes; I am prepared to argue that Franz Hals is an absurdly overrated artist, and to explain why I think so, but in the case of Goya I make no such claim to be right where received opinion is wrong.

It is worse still with El Greco. I have never seen more than a few El Grecos together before, and here there are dozens of them. And the only feeling I have is a feeling that they are all hideous, made of implausible shapes in vile colours. Yet I am plainly as wrong about El Greco as I am about Goya. Later, talking to the former Director of the Prado, Xavier de Salas, I put the problem to him. He is neither outraged nor surprised, and gently analyses my problem in terms of the culture in which I have been brought up and the kind of art to which I do respond. He is very interesting on the subject, but it won't do, for others with a cultural background, and tastes, similar to mine can see in the two Spaniards things to which I am entirely blind.

SUNDAY, JULY 27TH

I return to the Prado, but avoid El Greco and Goya. Instead, I concentrate on Velazquez, and am rewarded. I have never seen more than a handful of his paintings together before, either, and my joy in these, and in their sumptuous understanding, is enriched by the relief of remembering that at least I do not have a Velazquez problem as well.

MONDAY, JULY 28TH

Arianna is arriving at Madrid from America. We greet each other soundlessly through the glass wall that separates the customs hall from the concourse, and we continue to do so during the hour and a half it takes her to get her baggage. She looks impossibly well in white jacket, red blouse and Californian tan. Our driver, Pedro, a Spanish M. Dissaux for punctuality, has clearly collected passengers from Madrid airport before, for he displays neither surprise nor impatience, but sets off calmly as soon as the luggage is stowed. We are awaited 150 miles to the south-west, by Tom and Fleur Cowles Meyer. We arrive when it is still light; the beauty of Las Torres de los Bejaranos, and of the garden that Fleur has created for it, are as we remembered them, and the loving warmth of the hospitality overwhelms us at once. Fleur and Tom have thought of their guests' every possible wish in advance, and supplied it. And there is never any pressure on anybody to do anything in particular; read, sleep, sunbathe, work, walk, shop, talk, be silent – all possible variations of behaviour are catered for. I spend the nine days writing, an old carpenter's work-bench providing a perfect table in the open air but in the shade. Peace and happiness; Fleur and Tom provide both in this house (castle? palace?) built from total ruin to its present grace. We are sorry to go, though a chill has fallen on the warmth with the news from London of Ken Tynan's death. I crossed swords with him many times, but salute him as one who put more into the common pool than he took out. His death follows hard upon that of Peter Sellers, who once appointed me King of Flunubria, in recognition of my services to The Goons. 'I know', he wrote, 'that there is no such place as Flunubria, but if there ever should be you will be all ready to take over.' Peter was another one with a credit balance.

THURSDAY, AUGUST 7TH

Pedro is on time; the plane to Munich likewise. To Oberammergau, with a detour first to the Wieskirche. I fell in love with this masterpiece of the Baroque many years ago, and from anywhere within a hundred miles will go about to see it again; it never fails. The moment we step inside, we are assailed by an explosion of light and joy and love; beside this expression of worship the mightiest and noblest of the Gothic cathedrals would seem cold, forbidding, dedicated to a God of justice, not of mercy. A year or two ago, a friend travelling in the vicinity went there for the first time, on my urging. His wife, who felt the same about it, reported to me later the instinctive cry with which he had greeted the interior: 'But this is what religion is about!' I suppose it is; I hope so, anyway.

FRIDAY, AUGUST 8TH

It is also, I suppose, about Oberammergau, or at any rate the Passion Play. I saw the 1960 performance; Arianna has never seen it. We are staying – it feels odd – at the hotel run by a former Christ. The play is still, in its simplicity and beauty, a deep, shaking experience. It has been shortened; it was two sessions of four hours in 1960, with a two-hour break, but now they are two and a half hours each, and the break is three. A few references have been inserted too, in response to the foolish and intolerant campaign charging the text with anti-semitism, or at least with doing nothing to deny the ancient charge of Jewish deicide. The charge always was nonsense, made largely by people who had not seen the play, but the changes have not harmed it, and the great story unfolds in all its majesty, its voice and meaning as clear now as when the events portrayed were unfolding themselves.

Oberammergau itself is much as I remember it, too. Indeed, it is worse; the commercialization of the entire town has gone even further, and we cannot go a yard without seeing a display of mostly hideous wood-carvings, of scenes from the Passion, on sale. Nor is that all, or the worst. I do not recollect, and I am sure I would have recollected if it had happened on my earlier visit, the behaviour of the sellers of the text (five marks, in German, French or English), which also contains the cast and the names of all those participating. The huge theatre, like an aircraft hangar, is open at the stage end, though the auditorium proper is covered (the cast gets soaked several times in the course of the play, carrying on through the showers without pause, dismay or faltering); this means that it is light enough to read the text, and many, understandably, want to follow the lines. But the programme sellers patrol the aisles, including those running across the theatre, *throughout the performance*, holding the books high above their heads, darting towards any potential customer who has indicated an interest in their wares, taking the banknotes, counting out the change. It is hardly possible to believe it, but they do not even pause in their huckstering during the scene in which Christ drives the money-changers from the Temple. Truly, the glorious affirmation to which the play bears witness must be powerful indeed, to overcome such baseness in its surroundings.

But it does. Indeed, it does something more; it drags the Christian witness out from beneath the mountains of best-selling popular theology under which it has been buried for so long. Nobody today would be so foolish as to dispute that the age of faith has gone, never to return, but the best-selling mountains avoid either defying that truth or drawing conclusions from it; instead, they are devoted to a new kind of apologetics, the purpose of which is not to defend Christianity but to remove from it anything which might make it difficult for those of little faith, or indeed for a cannibal voodoo-man, to accept it. The strength of the Oberammergau Passion Play is derived from the fact that it is rooted in a much earlier tradition, in which it is unnecessary to *explain* the Passion at all; all that is needed is to depict it. All that is needed for what? Not for inducing instant conversion among the godless, who must make up the greater part of the audiences, but for making even the most unimaginative spectator realize how and why Christianity has exerted, and continues to exert, so gigantic an influence on the world. (An obvious example, not the most important: where would pictorial art or choral music be without Christianity?)

The play's technique is simple. Old Testament tableaux including, but not confined to, the Messianic allusions or analogues, and accompanied by oratorio, separate the successive scenes in which the last week of Christ's life on earth is portrayed; the play thus begins with Adam and Eve being driven from Eden, and ends with a huge chorus of rejoicing at the news that the tomb is empty.

Anyone going to Oberammergau in search of language comparable to the Authorized Version will be disappointed, but anyone doing that will deserve to be. Alois Daisenberger's 1860 version, based on Othmar Weis's 1810 one, tells the story in clear, unadorned prose; even a spectator with no German and only a slight acquaintance with the events depicted has no trouble in following the play without a crib. And its power is astonishing; to *see*, alive and spoken, the entry into Jerusalem, Judas bargaining with Caiaphas, the Last Supper, the Crucifixion (the words of the two thieves provide one of the most moving passages in the play), is to be able to feel something of the force that, starting from the point at which the play ends, went on to sweep the world.

And there is something else, perhaps even more important. Suppose a spectator who knew nothing at all of the subsequent history of Christianity. He could not, I think, fail to guess its triumph, for it is only necessary to show Christ's Passion to make it plain that a story of defeat, degradation and death is in fact one of victory, glory and eternal life. This, the greatest paradox of all, is the spirit that seems to have seized all the

performers – actors, singers, participants in the tableaux –
and the inevitable result is that we emerge, all 4,400 of us, in a
state of exhilaration.

There are no curtain-calls, of course; but it is interesting that
a not particularly reverent audience (the flash of cameras went
on throughout the play) instinctively refrained from applause.

We have already packed, and have nothing to do but reflect
and leave. And to get stuck in a mighty traffic-jam on the
autobahn, en route to Salzburg.

The Magic Flautist

On the doorstep of the Bristol Hotel, in the handsome Makartplatz, dominated by Fischer von Erlach's Trinity Church, there suddenly materializes Rixi Markus. Once more, I salute an individual who can do something better than anyone else in the world; Rixi is the best woman bridge-player. We arrange to meet; she is bound to have the latest Salzburg gossip (she is entitled to – she is Salzburg-born, and spends the entire month of the Festival here). She is staying at the Österreichischer Hof, and since she is more or less the unofficial Mayor of the city, it occurs to me that she could – and willingly would – have got us a room there. I think that the view across the river from a bedroom at the Öster-reichischer Hof, over a window-sill full of geraniums, to the Old Town dominated by the Cathedral, is perhaps my favour-ite urban sight; even Venice hath not anything to show more fair. But we are nicely settled in at the Bristol now.

Arianna has been to Salzburg once before; but not *my* Salz-burg. The first ritual, therefore, is to introduce her to Salzburg Poohsticks.

I discovered many years ago that Salzburg is the best place in the world for the game. But first, I explain the rules to her. Poohsticks, invented by Christopher Robin and his friend Winnie-the-Pooh, 'a bear of very little brain', is played on a bridge over a suitable river or stream. The players, on a count of three, simultaneously drop twigs – the originators used pine-cones, but these are not always readily available – into the water, off the upstream side. They then rush across to the other side to see whose Poohstick emerges first, carried by the flowing waters, from beneath the bridge. The winner scores a point, and the exercise is repeated until it is time for lunch. The game works so well in Salzburg because its river, the Salzach, is one of the fastest I know anywhere in the world. It rushes along, on its journey first to the Inn and then, thus merged, to the Danube, at an immense speed, particularly when it is in spate after rain, which at this time of the year it mostly is; Salzburg has the most treacherous festival weather I know, capable of changing even more abruptly than that of Hohenems or Oberammergau from cloudless sky to tropical rain. And Salzburg's pedestrians-only bridges make Pooh-sticks not only exciting, but safe; many's the time, elsewhere, that I have narrowly escaped death from the traffic when dashing across to see who has won the round.

But even without the game, it is good to stand on the Mozartsteig and look up and down the rushing Salzach, its water the colour, and wrinkled texture, of an elephant's hide; in the postcards they sell here it is a beautiful blue, but then so is the mud-coloured Danube in the postcards they sell in Vienna.

Good, yes, but not without more complicated feelings. I first came to Salzburg, as I first came to Edinburgh, when I was a student; as I have said, I was just beginning my journey into music. I have paid many visits since, though not so many as I have to Edinburgh, and the consciousness of passing years is strong when I stand on this bridge. Traditionally, Venice is the place for such feelings, but I came to Venice late – I was over thirty when I went there for the first time – and the places that compel a man to listen to his own heartbeat at night are the ones he discovered early in his life.

Behind me there rears up the Kapuzinerberg, backdrop to the New Town as the Mönchsberg is to the Old, now lying before me. Soon I shall see the Cathedral again, its bombed dome successfully restored; the Residenz, with its mighty

Baroque fountain and, inside, its rooms too magnificent, even too large, for this city; the Fischer von Erlach churches in which Salzburg is so rich; the Mirabell Garden, all shining green and blazing red. But first, we have a humbler call to pay.

The Getreidegasse, which wanders east-west, from the river to the opera house (or houses, for there are three of them in one building) through the heart of the Old Town, has gone up in the world. It is now a pedestrian precinct, and the tourists, their buses leaving them at one end and going round to park at the other, fill it from wall to wall most of the day, and photograph it almost as much as they do the Bridge of Sighs. And it caters for them; it contains the most expensive hotel in Salzburg, the Goldener Hirsch, and most of the more fashionable shops. Not all of the Old Town is as smart, and it is still possible to conjure up the human history of Salzburg in the little squares and alleys with which it is hugger-mugger crowded, loud most of the day and much of the night with the clatter of knives and forks and wine glasses from the scores of restaurants. But the Venice-narrow breadth of the Getreidegasse, and indeed the '*gasse*' in its name, betrays its origins as a street for the not-quite-poor. And certainly the family we are to visit today were never particularly rich, and got steadily poorer.

At the eastern end of the Getreidegasse, where it widens into the Hagenauerplatz, stands No. 9, an ordinary-looking building, with four storeys above the ground floor shops and a row of attic windows atop. It is painted egg-yolk yellow, and a banner in the Austrian colours, red-white-red, flaps outside. We pay our twenty Austrian schillings and enter. We pass a modest kitchen, and go on climbing. We come to an interesting collection of theatrical memorabilia: scores, playbills, set-maquettes, costume sketches, programmes; also posters, many of them chosen because they announce the very early work of unknown musicians who later achieved world-wide fame. One of these advertises a concert half a century ago, conducted by 'Herbert Karajan', who has also, it seems, gone up in the world since, by the length of a *von*.

Another climb; now we are on the third floor. There are portraits and musical instruments; the tiled stove that warmed the lodgers. We enter the central room; it contains a piano and a harpsichord, a showcase with a violin and a viola. One corner of the room is roped off; a plaque tells us why. '*Hier stand Mozarts Wiege*': here stood Mozart's cradle. We are a few inches from where, on January 27th, 1756, Mozart was born, Mozart who burrowed more deeply into the divine than any other artist who ever lived, even Bach, even Titian, even Shakespeare, Mozart who lived to be only thirty-six and died in penury, Mozart whose grave is for ever lost, Mozart who is the mainspring and mainstay of the Salzburg Festival, Mozart who could have lived comfortably for a year on today's price for a single seat in the best part of the house for any performance of any opera – *any* opera, not just his, not just the new productions, not just the first nights, not just the performances with the most glamorous stars.

Mozart, decidedly, mistook his vocation; he should have run a ticket agency at Salzburg during the Festival. A single best stall for the opera costs £70; for a concert, £35. Before we dismiss this as grotesque, even disgusting, let us consider a little. First, seats at Salzburg provide an example of that rarest of economists' categories: reverse elasticity, that is, a commodity for which demand *increases* every time the price goes up. At £70 a time, those seats could be sold three times over, and the black market, in which the hotel porters are to the fore, ensures that they *are* sold for three times their face value. Well, there are no doubt enough people today with enough money to afford such prices and enough willingness to pay them; we have no right to criticize others for the way they spend their money, at least if we want to spend our own without criticism. Nor, as it grimly happens, have we the right to criticize the Salzburg authorities for the price they charge for their tickets; the Salzburg Festival receives and, if it is to continue, needs, a massive national and local subsidy, without which those seats would cost not £70 but £150. To put on the performances, and performers, that Salzburg offers does cost a very great deal, and examined in strictly relative terms, £70 a seat is cheap.

Not, however, in absolute terms; and there is worse lurking at the other end of the brochure. Seats at £70, let them buy that will and can; but the *cheapest* seat for the opera costs some £14, and that is what, in the end, will weave old Salzburg's winding-sheet, and reduce it to the condition of a beautiful but lifeless museum. The Philistines of the left will have it that no wealthy man can love art, only buy it. It is untrue, of course, but it is not the opposite of the truth, which is not that only the poor truly love art, but that the incidence of music-loving is distributed at random among rich and poor. Obviously, there are many who go to Salzburg *only* because they can afford it, to meet their friends and be seen. That matters little; but there are many more who would go to Salzburg for less silly reasons, and who cannot afford to do so. That matters little, too, except for one vital qualification; if the young do not get the festival-going habit when they *are* young, though they have to hitch-hike across Europe and sleep in haystacks on the way, they may never do so at all. The highest price for a seat at Bayreuth is £40, which also deters the unmoneyed young; but at Bayreuth they pile the subsidy on to the other end of the seesaw, and the consequence is that the unmoneyed young, or the unmoneyed middle-aged and old for that matter, can get an ordinary seat for £3·50, and one with a restricted view for £2·50, and even some with no view at all (*Hörplätze*, or 'hearing-seats') for £1·25. The Salzburg tills play merrier music; but Bayreuth eyes see further.

Meanwhile, this is Salzburg's Jubilee Year; the Salzburg Festival was founded, by Max Reinhardt, Richard Strauss and Hugo von Hofmannsthal, in 1920, which makes it one of the oldest of extant European festivals, junior only to the Three Choirs and Bayreuth. Nineteen-twenty must have seemed a strange time to be founding a festival, in the ashes of the Austro-Hungarian Empire; but then, the mid-1940s, amid the ruins of Europe, must have seemed even less propitious. In 1920, the Festival consisted of nothing but Hugo von Hofmannsthal's *Jedermann*, and Salzburg possessed not even one Festspielhaus, let alone three; but the idea caught on, and Salzburg is now without doubt, and has long been, the unchallenged Queen of Festival Cities. What is now the Kleines Festspielhaus became a theatre in 1924, adapted from a riding-school; it was rebuilt two years later, and apart from changes made under the Nazi regime, when the 1926 decorations were pronounced 'degenerate', remained the same – I remember vividly the white and gold of the old auditorium from my 1948 visit – until it was rebuilt, in a plainer style, in 1963, matching the Grosses Festspielhaus, which holds nearly twice as many and was completed in 1960. The third auditorium in the Festival complex, the Felsenreitschule, was also a riding-school; it was converted in a fairly rudimentary fashion – the makeshift roof kept the audience dry most of the time, but I remember the sound of the rain drumming on it, which was often louder than the performance – and eventually the place was condemned, in the 1960s, as a danger to the public, and thoroughly renovated, being opened in its present form in 1970.

The Queen of Festival Cities deserves her throne. For one thing, she has long being mindful of her duty to make up to Mozart posthumously for her treatment of her greatest son while he was alive. True, the city of his birth treated him better than did Vienna, which contrives today to forget that she let him die:

> Seven great cities contend for Homer dead,
> Through which the living Homer begged his bread.

And whatever Mozart's troubles with the Archbishop, much exaggerated in the recounting, as Ernest Newman pointed out, 'by people who couldn't tell a Colloredo archbishop from a Colorado archbeetle', Salzburg makes handsome enough amends today. Every year, at least two of his operas are staged, dozens of his orchestral and instrumental works performed. It can be said with more than metaphorical truth that his name is in everybody's mouth, for Salzburg's celebrated chocolates, the *Mozartkugeln*, are sold at Festival-time by the ton, and for the rest of the year by the hundred-weight at least. The very carillons play Mozart; his portrait is in every shop window, not much smaller than that of von Karajan; the staircase at No. 9 Getreidegasse, which we have just climbed, resounds all day to the tramp of visitors' feet; in addition to the Mozart Bridge there is a Mozart Street and a Mozart Square, as well as a Papagenoplatz, and for that matter a Schikaneder Street, though to Salzburg's shame there is nothing named after da Ponte. But Salzburg has long had the pleasant habit of naming streets after the Festival's leading participants; that there should be a Hugo von Hofmannsthal Street, a Richard Strauss Street and a Max Reinhardt Square is no more than simple justice, but there is also a Toscanini Court, an Alexander Moissi Street, a Bernhard Paumgartner Promenade, a Bruno Walter Street, a Maria Cebotari Street, a Clemens Krauss Street, a Ferenc Fricsay Street, a Franz Schalk Street, a Wilhelm Furtwängler Garden, a Lotte Lehmann Promenade, a Richard Mayr Alley, a Vienna Philharmonic Street, a Stefan Zweig Way and a Wilhelm Backhaus Road. There are also streets named after Beethoven, Wagner, Bruck-ner, Pfitzner, Hummel, Hugo Wolf and Hans Sachs.

I remember the Mozarteum well; it looks rather like a grander version of the Freemason's Hall in Edinburgh, with a lovely white and gold organ, and this morning its own or-chestra is playing. When I first came, its conductor was Bernhard Paumgartner, the long-serving President of the Festival; now it is Theodor Guschlbauer, a giglamped young man who gives a spirited performance of an early symphony, which is followed by an equally sparkling rendering of the C major Piano Concerto by Paul Badura-Skoda, dinner-jacketed at 11 o'clock in the morning. The Mozarteum's acoustics are as

I recall them, too, and are obviously incurable; everything sounds as though it is being played inside a petrol-tin, and a simple *mf* from the tympani suggests that the Third World War has broken out.

Well, if it has, there are worse places to be than Salzburg. I spend the day wandering the streets, taking a cup of chocolate at Tomaselli's, an entire Cours Mirabeau in itself, hoping that the weather stays fine until tomorrow evening, for we are to see *Jedermann* in the afternoon, and if the weather report says that a peasant in northern Finland has felt a splash on the back of his neck within the previous fortnight the open-air performance will be abandoned, and the Festspielhaus used instead. *Jedermann* in the Festspielhaus is certainly impressive; but in the Cathedral Square, with the Cathedral's mighty organ pealing out, at the end, the glad tidings of great joy, that Jedermann will yet be saved, it becomes an altogether different experience, comparable to that of the Passion Play at Oberammergau.

In the evening, the opera, in the Grosses Festspielhaus; *The Tales of Hoffmann*, the only new production this year. The Bristol provides a bus for its guests; it is much quicker to walk to the Festspielhaus, and would still be quicker even if the bus never got stuck in a traffic-jam, but the Salzburgertum, native and visiting, has an even greater horror of walking than of getting rained on, indeed almost as great as its terror of being in a railway carriage with an open window. When in Rome . . . we take the bus.

The Grosses Festspielhaus was designed and built in an era of luxury, and shows it. The foyers are vast; the cloakrooms are vaster, and have a separate peg for every seat in the house (and it holds nearly 2,500); the refreshment rooms are vaster than foyers and cloakrooms combined, and everybody gets served with ease and speed. Nowhere have I seen so high a proportion of evening dress among an audience; there cannot be fifty men in the house without dinner-jackets, and even Glyndebourne, these days, cannot match such standards.

True, at up to £70 a seat a *sens d'occasion* is hardly surprising, but old man Christie's rule seems to be operating here, and it is the answer to the charges of snobbery and society that have so often been levelled in Sussex as well as Salzburg. John Christie said that all those involved in the production, from the conductor to the scene-shifters, were taking every possible care to ensure that the performance was as near to perfection as human beings can attain; in return, he asked those in the audience to respond similarly, in the only way open to them, namely by taking trouble over what they wore. Nobody was ever turned away from Glyndebourne for being 'incorrectly' dressed, but Christie's principle was justified, and 'Evening dress is strongly recommended' remains in the Glyndebourne programme, though now qualified, inevitably, by the words 'formal or informal'.

There is little that men can do, in the way of evening dress, that is out of the ordinary though I am myself, even if I do not yet know it, about to do something spectacularly different; if you are looking for fashionable clothes here, it is the women who must be judged. There is no doubt, then, that this is a fashionable audience. Red is the dominant colour (for the dresses, that is – for the shoulders it is a luxurious tan, no doubt acquired on the Côte d'Azur in July to be exhibited here in August), though there is much gold and quite a lot of pale blue, mostly on the older women. Arianna is wearing her black and red trouser suit, and I am vain enough, not that a man needs to be *very* vain in these circumstances, to be pleased at the turning heads. At the final bell, we part; for some reason our tickets are in different areas, one in the stalls, one in the balcony.

The seats at Salzburg look uncomfortable but aren't, unlike those at Bayreuth, which look uncomfortable and are, and also unlike those at Aldeburgh, which are very comfortable and look it. Sight-lines are perfect; the acoustics are huge, full, rich; the stage is immense. At least it is tonight, but it is adjustable, and for unspectacular operas, it shrinks. Tonight, however,

Jean-Pierre Ponnelle has been given his head, together with what must have been a very large sum of money indeed, and has seized a huge opportunity in a fitting manner.

The curtain is up when we enter, and the scene is a vast square. It has evidently been raining, because the whole floor, black and gleaming, has become a vast mirror, reflecting everything and making the enormous stage area seem even larger; later, Ponnelle is to go further still, and slide mirror-walls down both wings, thus trebling the apparent space in an instant.

Meanwhile, he has divined that the spirit of *The Tales of Hoffmann* is one of magic – not black magic, though of course the story is full of it – but the magic of the pantomime, the magic of a child's delight in a conjuring-trick, the magic, in short, of the theatre. As Ponnelle detonates one sensation after another, turning us all into children eager to see what happens next, I realize that this is what has vanished almost entirely from today's theatre, wedded as it is to various forms of realism, most of them less realistic than the pantomime itself. When will our theatres learn – or rather, when will they re-member – that the more they try to make the theatre resemble life, the less it does? One of these days I am going to paint outside every theatre in London, in letters of fire two yards high, the words: 'Real rooms have four walls'. Ponnelle will be dismissed, for this production, as a romantic trifler, though some of his critics will admit that, since a romantic trifle is what *The Tales of Hoffmann* is, that is not altogether inap-propriate. But he has done much more; he has demonstrated that the theatre's task is to be not accurate but *convincing*, and when the entire chorus in Act I disappears abruptly through the floor, when the gondolas in the Venice scene are huge cloaks, dragged slowly and steadily across the stage, when a waiters' ballet distributes three score mugs of beer, two feet tall, in a few seconds, when these and a dozen more such effects have the audience gasping with delight as well as astonishment, he has proved his point.

As for Placido Domingo, he proves *my* point that he is the greatest lyric tenor now living. We are not, it is true, living in a time plentifully supplied with great lyric tenors; besides Domingo there is really only Pavarotti. But Domingo would have stood out in the Golden Age itself, bringing an extraordinary intensity of feeling and drama to match the caressing beauty of the voice itself. I hesitate to call a tenor intelligent, for the idea is so improbable; but Quiet Sunday not only *is* intelligent, he sings as though he is.

We meet in the interval, equally thrilled. Arianna has found, of all people, Marese Murphy, and brings her to the rendezvous by the coffee counter. Marese is one of the pillars of the Wexford community; indeed, it was she who presented me, on behalf of the Plain People of Ireland, with my collapsible opera-hat.

I don't know why we always find it surprising to meet friends abroad – unless, to be sure, in remote jungles or deserts. Yet I find myself greeting Marese not just as a dear friend, but as a dear friend thought lost for ever, and when I see Peter Diamand in the distance, looking as wise, benign and wrinkled as ever, I register a similar surprise, though as a matter of fact it would be slightly surprising if the former Director of both the Holland and Edinburgh Festivals were *not* at Salzburg.

SUNDAY, AUGUST 10TH

The day dawns fine, though in Salzburg that is no guarantee of respectability; *Jedermann* is by no means assured yet, and the clouds come and go throughout the day. By tea-time, however, they have not been seen for an hour or more, and the performance begins, on time, at 5 o'clock. On the way in to the Cathedral Square, which I have never seen without the wooden seating, for I have never been to Salzburg except during the Festival or within a week or two either side of it, and photographs of it dominated not by the grandstand but by the massive statue of the Virgin always look strange, I buy the English translation. The old one, which I remember all too well from my early visits, was a disgrace, clearly done by someone who did not know English and did it from a dictionary. To my amazement, I discover that the same translation is still in use. It was done, I see from the imprint, in 1911, presumably just after *Jedermann* was written and long before the Festival began; the translator's name is M. E. Tafler. A few examples of his grotesque idea of English:

> To what to-day we represent
> A full attentive ear be lent!
> A moral play and never blamed,
> Everyman's summoning 't is named.

But how when at the trombones' ringing sound of all your riches you shall have to give a clear reckoning either for everlasting death or for eternal bliss?

Won't be an easy thing, my folly, for your cook is to good a one and the wine heating the blood nicely, there, I am glad to stay where I am.

Ye dear fellow, but advise me then, who is calling thus dreadfully 'Everyman'?

Years ago, I asked Raimund von Hofmannsthal, the author's son (the possessor of the most enchantingly dreadful handwriting I have ever seen in my life, a series of indistinguishable vertical jabs, like a kind of debased cuneiform, bearing no visible relationship to any letter of the English language), why he permitted this trash to be sold as a translation of his father's work. He was astonished when I showed him the Tafler version; he didn't know it, and said he would look into the matter. So he did, only to discover that for complicated reasons of copyright, he had no control over it. Raimund died some years ago, much mourned; John Julius Norwich put together a little book for his friends, under the simple, and appropriate, title *A Rosenkavalier*. Elizabeth, Raimund's wife, one of the great beauties of our time, followed him last year. I *cannot* get used to the disappearing trick my friends have taken to playing.

Jedermann does indeed still work; it is particularly fascinating to see it so soon after Oberammergau. Salzburg has periods when they engage well-known players for the performances, and others when they cast it without stars; at present we are in the upswing, and Everyman is played by Maximilian Schell, no great shakes as a director, to judge by his feeble National Theatre production of Odon von Horvath's *Tales from the Vienna Woods*, but an actor of considerable skill and effect. As always, it is the setting which transforms the play into an experience beyond the merely theatrical; the imposing Italian-ate front of the Cathedral dwarfs the players, reducing them, however, not to puppets but to human beings enmeshed in a giant universe. And the great *coup de théâtre*, when Everyman is summoned by cries from the belfries, the final '*Jedermann!*' floating across half the city ('Ye dear fellow, but advise me then, who is calling thus dreadfully "Everyman"?'), ceases to be theatrical and strikes to the heart of a spectator as it does to Jedermann's own.

Dinner with Rixi. Her new book, *Play Better Bridge*, is doing well; the jacket bears a picture of a hand holding S AKQJ, H AKQ, D AKQJ10, C A, and I remind her that when she sent me a copy I replied that with a hand like that even I could play better bridge.

MONDAY, AUGUST 11TH

Figaro, also directed by Ponnelle, but much less successfully; the direction is fussy and distracting, in places even coarse. We see Peter Diamand again, this time to talk to, and arrange to meet for lunch.

TUESDAY, AUGUST 12TH

I have seen a beautiful wine-red dinner-jacket at Resmann's in the Getreidegasse, and am much minded to buy it. Arianna comes with me; while I am being fitted, and the necessary alterations being noted, she prowls round the shop. Just as all is ready, and they are promising to deliver it by tomorrow evening, in time for the opera, she irrupts into the dressing-room, eyes a-gleam with wickedness. 'Come and see what I have found.' What she has found is a black velvet evening suit, waistcoat and all. It is useless for me to protest that velvet wears badly, that I shall have to throw it away within a year, that it costs a monstrous sum, that I shall have to buy silk shirts to wear with it, at even more monstrous cost. The trouble is that she knows me too well, and knows that as soon as I have seen it, I know I must have it. The patient tailor starts again, and the pinning and marking, now considerably more elaborate, is done for the velvet. Yes, they will still have it ready for tomorrow evening; but does this mean that I shall not be wanting the red jacket after all? It does; *something* is saved from the ruin of my finances.

In the evening, *Die Zauberflöte*, also directed by Ponnelle, this time in the Felsenreitschule. He makes up for the disappointment of *Figaro*, and a good deal over. There are three ledges cut into the sheer rock wall which provides the stage backdrop in this house, each having arched embrasures all the way along. These natural galleries Ponnelle uses to striking effect, rising to a climax, as indeed is only right, since it is the focus of the work, in the ordeals by fire and water.

There had been an example earlier of Ponnelle's imagination at work with the same intensity that he had brought to *Hoffmann*, at the Queen of the Night's first entrance; she appeared out of the darkness, and as she did so, the whole of the rock wall suddenly came alive with a huge galaxy of stars, with the Queen in the middle like a spider by Velazquez. And for the great twin tests, he rises to the challenge, and since what is challenged is nothing less than a director's ability to portray the apotheosis of ultimate enlightenment, the absorption of the human into the divine, a director who successfully negotiates it shows that he has fully understood what this mighty work is about.

Tamino and Pamina make their way from right to left through the fire, on the lowest gallery; their progress is measured, stately, unafraid, Tamino holding up the flute, symbol of transformation, like a sword. They vanish, and reappear at once on the second level, going the other way, left to right, while the heat fades from the vanquished enemy and the chill shines eerily around them from the new test. This time, it is more difficult, and they hurry, shielding their faces; water is a more profound element than fire, and the negotiation of its chthonic danger and temptation correspondingly more painful. They vanish again, and, as the silver sheen of the water disappears, and the music breaks into triumph and rejoicing, they appear again, this time in the centre of the topmost gallery, which now glows from end to end like a rising sun. At that moment, Sarastro, played by Martti Talvela with all the nobility and majesty that his immense frame (six feet eight inches of it) and immense voice (rich, sonorous, steady) radiate, turns, and with unhurried stride walks off the stage. The symbolism is complete; the newly enlightened pair no longer need his protection.

I have rarely seen a production of *Die Zauberflöte* get so close to the meaning and mystery; though there remains the mystery of why Ponnelle chose to use Schikaneder's feeble spoken libretto uncut.

WEDNESDAY, AUGUST 13TH

We have lunch with Peter Diamand, for which we go out to Schloss Fuschl, a great haunt of the Nazi leaders when they visited the Festival. Peter, who is a very funny raconteur, is as always full of stories, one of them set in this very hotel. He was eating here during the Festival not long after the war, and was amazed to see that one of his fellow-diners was Hjalmar Schacht, not long acquitted – by the skin of his teeth – at Nuremberg. 'I see', Peter had said to the manager, with, no doubt, a good deal of edge to his voice, 'that Herr Schacht is staying with you.' 'Yes,' said the man eagerly and proudly, 'and we have Herr von Papen here as well.'

In the evening, *Aida*, conducted by Karajan with all the sumptuousness that he can command, which is a great deal. There is no point in doing *Aida* except sumptuously, and Karajan, though as a producer he is without imagination, makes it thrilling, beautiful and touching at once. I have always preferred to hear Karajan conducting music I enjoy but do not take altogether seriously; Verdi, Richard Strauss, even Brahms. I am glad that it was James Levine who conducted the *Magic Flute* and Gustav Kuhn the *Figaro*, but in all four operas (Levine also conducted *Hoffmann*) I marvelled again at that extraordinary musical instrument, the Vienna Philharmonic Orchestra. I suppose the three greatest orchestras in the world today are the Berlin, the Chicago, and this one, and in each a different department seems to predominate. When we think of the Berlin Philharmonic it is the firm beauty of its woodwind that comes first to the mind's ear; when we want to conjure up the Chicago Symphony, we hear the blaze of its brass. And the Vienna's glory is still, as it always has been, the strings; the Vienna's strings seem either to be using instruments that no other orchestra possesses, or a technique that all other orchestras have lost or never discovered. And they sound the same whoever is conducting, thus lending some colour to the ancient jibe that the Vienna Philharmonic never knows who is conducting it because it has not looked at the conductor, nor needed to, for a century.

Dinner at the Weinhaus Moser; reservation essential. Another *memento mori*; when I first came here, more than thirty years ago, the Weinhaus Moser, though it made the best *Wienerschnitzel* in town, was only a little *Stube* with no airs, and wouldn't have known what a table reservation was. Now, after the opera, it is full of evening dress, including my beautiful new velvet, and takes American Express cards, and does not serve Gumpoldskirchner by the glass, and if you ask a taxi-driver whether he knows it, he looks at you as though you are mad. Happily, the most important thing has not changed; it still makes the best *Wienerschnitzel* in town.

A nightcap on the way back, at the Café Bazar. Time was when Stefan Zweig and Thomas Mann and Richard Strauss and Bruno Walter used to meet here for coffee, *Sachertorte* and gossip. But the ghosts of the Thirties are silent, and the world they inhabited gone for ever.

The Haunted House

We arrive in Munich. Arianna immediately goes out shopping. The day before yesterday, in Salzburg, she went out shopping and didn't return for five hours. *Ja, das Studium der Weiber ist schwer*. Dinner at Schwarzwälder, as good as ever, though it has unaccountably lost its Michelin star.

FRIDAY, AUGUST 15TH

We leave Munich for Bayreuth. Or, to be more exact and for that matter more cheerful, for Pegnitz.

I discovered the hotel of the good Herr Pflaum, who in English would be Mr Plum, many years ago, 'since when I have used no other'. Bayreuth used to be a horrible little town; shabby, dull and charmless. In those days, it was still living under the shadow of a decision taken earlier, the decision to live by its Festival alone, and to turn its back on the post-war *Wirtschaftswunder*, the fruits of which would inevitably make it just another German town like all the others. At some point, the citizens must have decided that Bayreuth cannot live by Wagnerian bread alone, and the town began to expand. There is a good deal of industry there now, and the huge office blocks with which it is strewn are visible from the autobahn; clearly, Bayreuth has at last begun to participate in the general German prosperity. But though it is no longer shabby, it is still dull and charmless, and as far as I know there is still no good restaurant anywhere in the place, or a hotel with character.

And so it is Pegnitz and Herr Pflaum for us, as it was when

Robert and I came in 1977, and when Robert, waiting in
dinner-jacket on the terrace for me to descend so that we
would board Herr Pflaum's Festival bus, was mistaken for a
waiter by two passers-by who had stopped for refreshment,
and had ordered coffee, cake and ice-cream before their mistake could be explained to them.

Herr Pflaum, bearded like the pard but younger than ever,
greets us warmly; the atmosphere of his hotel, sensed immediately, is even more delightful than before, and it is clear
that it takes its tone from this truly genial and comprehen-
sively efficient man. He is full of news; his brother Hermann,
the hotel's chef, has just won an international contest for a new
dish, against fierce competition, including much from the
French. Hermann Pflaum's creation was 'Duck *en folie*', and
the diploma of his victory is framed on the wall of the hotel.
Also, but in this case alas, we have missed the hotel's own
operatic entertainment; the posters are still up, but the last
performance was at the weekend. As Herr Pflaum describes it,
it seems to have been a tempting mixture of a Wagnerian parody,
a concert, a dance, a firework display and a banquet, the
audience moving after each of the six courses to a further venue
with another stage and another section of the entertainment.
You would have loved it, he says, and I can well believe him.

SATURDAY, AUGUST 16TH

We are seeing the three non-*Ring* operas the wrong way
round; tonight it is *Parsifal*, which would be more fitting last,
on Monday *The Flying Dutchman*, and on Tuesday *Lohengrin*,
which for my part I would be happy to get out of the way first,
as it is far from being my favourite Wagner opera. As it
happens, fate is being kind rather than untidy, though we are
to discover the truth only gradually.

There is a green hill far away . . . The approach to Wagner's
theatre is unique, like so much else about him and his achievement. The Festspielhaus stands on the brow of a hill, dominat-

ing its side of the town; at the bottom of the hill lies the railway station, and the pilgrim, if he starts there and refuses the services of the taxi-drivers who are willing to drive him half a mile in return for a sum which would have kept Wagner, never mind Mozart, for a month, walks along the side of the station and its goods yard until, in a few minutes, he comes clear of the trees that line the pavement (O for Pippa, to tell me what they are!), and finds himself at the bottom of the Grüner Hügel, looking up at a square, severe, symmetrical, red-brick building a few hundred yards ahead and above, its walls creeper-clad to soften the colour, though it has mellowed with time. Over the portico in front there flutters a flag, white with a red border, and in the centre, also in red, a capital W. The W stands for Wagner.

Many people, I am aware, will not stand for Wagner at any price. And it has to be said that Bayreuth is not the ideal spot in which to seek a cure for the antipathy he arouses. I have come here after long wanderings *in partibus infidelium*, amid the fleshpots of Florence and the lobsterpots of Aldeburgh, my head still ringing with the delights of Schubert and Hohenems and my eyes still full of the Baroque splendours of Salzburg; but it is no use approaching Wagner's music in Wagner's town in anything of the same spirit. Bayreuth is for those already infected with the fever of Wagnerism, which has been running inextricably in my veins for a good deal more than thirty years; but anyone who comes here healthy, in the hope of catching the disease, as wise mothers deliberately expose their infant children to measles and mumps lest they catch them only later, at an age when complications may ensue, will find that the antibodies of Bayreuth are strong in their blood.

Take that green hill, which is, after all, the first Wagnerian sight the newcomer who goes straight to the theatre sees. At the bottom of it, a traffic-policeman directs buses and coaches up one of the two symmetrical side roads; only cars and foot-pilgrims go up the centre, which is a wide and handsome avenue, bordered on both sides by beautiful, and beautifully tended, gardens, with shining lawns, lush flower-beds, orna-mental pools. It is very pleasant to walk up this gentle sloping hill in company with hundreds of others on their way to the same goal, but it is the first reminder that in this place we are here to listen to Wagner, and for no other purpose at all. All other opera houses known to me are passed by traffic, on wheels and on foot, going to a thousand destinations other than the music; only on Bayreuth's green hill can we be certain that every one of our companions is on the same errand as ourselves. And if some Martian, having familiarized himself with the works of Wagner and the troubled history of Wagner's family, were to arrive in Bayreuth by accident, not knowing at first where he was, he would speedily learn the chief business of the town. Here is Richard Wagner Street, there Cosima Wagner Avenue; round this corner lies Siegfried Wagner Road and round that Wieland Wagner Street; there is a Tristan Street, a Mastersingers Street, a Tannhäuser Street, a Parsifal Street (true, there is a Parsifal Road in Hampstead, but at least there is no Parsifal Chemists there). By the time our Martian has explored this Wagnerian map, he may be pardoned, on finding himself in Albrecht Dürer Street, if he wonders for a moment in which of Wagner's operas the artist appears.

Bayreuth can boast that it has the most knowledgeable audiences in the world, and so it does. But that is because there is nothing to be got out of Wagner but Wagner. Nobody comes to the Wagner Festival to be seen by friends or photo-graphers, to show off a new fur coat or starlet. The Festival imposes single-mindedness on its visitors; but they come single-minded in the first place. The truth is that nobody would sit in the most uncomfortable theatre in the world from tea-time to bedtime without being interested, to the point of addiction, in what was to be heard and seen there.

We are now at the top of the hill. There is a huge terrace in front of the opera house; at the front of the portico, below the flag, is a balcony, and on it there has just appeared a group of musicians, trumpeters and trombonists. Cameras by the score are raised on the terrace below, as the musicians sound a fanfare, consisting of one of the *Leitmotivs* of the opera before us. They sound it once, which means that there is a quarter of an hour to go before the performance begins; time to look at the catering arrangements, and even to sample them.

In the days before Bayreuth decided to move into the present, the restaurant at the Festspielhaus was a wretchedly inadequate affair. It would hardly compete, even now, with the duck *en folie* of Herr Pflaum's brother, but at least it is efficient and extensive. Upstairs, there is a gigantic cafeteria; downstairs, a restaurant of the same size and a vast terrace beyond. In addition, there is a hatch in the wall from which sausages are dispensed in pairs, and beer to accompany them. Even in the Temple's outbuildings, however, jesting is unknown. When Robert and I saw *Parsifal* in 1977, we were having a piece of cake and a cup of coffee before the performance, and he asked the lady behind the serving counter for whipped cream with his gâteau. She was sorry, she said, but there was no whipped cream. 'Ah,' said Robert brightly, 'no whipped cream at *Parsifal*, eh?' 'That', said the good soul in perfect earnest, 'has nothing to do with it.'

We wander round the building, the back dominated by the gigantic scene-dock. It is difficult to believe, but the theatre is still almost exactly as Wagner designed it; there has been no significant structural alteration, and the gradual decay of the fabric has been dealt with by replacing crumbling brickwork or worn wood with matching materials. O Richard Wagner, thou art mighty yet, and would feel immediately at home in your own theatre if you were to return to it.

He might, too. If so, he would note with satisfaction the fire-engine that stands, at all times, beside it. The interior is largely made of bare wood, and the conflagration that would ensue if the building ever caught fire would be a once-for-all *Götterdämmerung* to rival the greatest achievements of the scene-designers and producers.

The musicians have sounded the second fanfare, this time playing it twice; ten minutes to go. The crowd is reluctant to leave the terrace and the sunshine for the interior of the theatre; I have noticed before, in myself and other Wagner-lovers, that we do not look forward eagerly, as we do when an evening of Mozart or favourite Verdi is before us, to what is to come, except when it is *Die Meistersinger*. We fall under the spell only when the music starts, when, if it is the *Ring*, the E flat steals out of the darkness to begin the sixteen-hour journey from the Rhine to the Rhine. Meanwhile, thrice hath the trumpet sounded, and we are moving in with the crowd.

It is not a large crowd; by most opera-house standards, Bayreuth is small, holding not quite 1,200. Our tickets specify the number of the door by which we must enter the auditorium, and the first shock a newcomer to the Festspielhaus receives comes from the discovery that it is the only theatre in the world with no aisles at all, not even at the sides; the entrances open directly on to the seating, and if you go in at the wrong door you have to come out and go in again at the right one, not that there is much chance of taking a mistake past the well-drilled, smiling usherettes. (I am an obsessional reader of programmes – and much good has that ever done me at Bayreuth, where they are mostly filled with pretentious drivel about esoteric meanings the writer has discovered in the operas – and there is a great deal to read in the Bayreuth *Heft*, apart from the drivel, for Bayreuth, mindful from the start that everyone involved in the Festival has a part to play, is meticulous about giving credit, and lists everyone, including the box-office personnel, the carpenters and even the *Türsteherinnen*, or 'doorstanders'. What is more, the listing carries, in parenthesis after the name, the home town of each participant, which gave me the opportunity, some years ago, to demonstrate apparently occult powers. I noticed in the programme that one of the girls – called, let us say, Janet Selder – came from Glasgow. To my delight, the *Türsteherin* who tore my ticket spoke with a Scots accent, and since Scots accents are not exactly common in Bavaria, I made the obvious deduction. 'Good evening,' I said, 'you must be Janet Selder.' Her eyes opened wide in genuine horror; if she had been a Catholic I am sure she would have crossed herself, since she clearly believed that she was in the presence of the Devil. I thought it hardly fair to let her sit through *Rheingold* in such distracting terror, so I explained).

The next shock consists of the extraordinary subfusc in which the auditorium is decorated. The dominant colour is grey – walls, buttresses, curtain; the floor is uncarpeted, the globe-lights undecorated, and only a touch of blue and dull gold in the ceiling relieves the monotony that greets the eye. A worse surprise is the discomfort of the seats. These are of brutally hard wood, entirely uncushioned, and the backs of them are apparently designed to sever the spinal column of anyone daring to tilt even a few degrees out of the vertical. At Martti Talvela's Savonlinna Festival they sell for a trifle cushions of foam sponge, overprinted 'Savonlinna Festival'; I took mine home, with the intention of bringing it to Bayreuth and leaving it ostentatiously on my chair, words upwards, during the intervals. Alas, I forgot it, and although I had little hope of shaming Bayreuth, by its display, into improving the seats, I would at least have sat more comfortably myself. The seating, too, is not only uncomfortable in itself; it is laid out in rows so close to one another that I find myself involuntarily playing hands-knees-and-boomps-a-daisy with strangers, as I make my way along the row to my seat.

The auditorium is fan-shaped; Wagner based it on the proportions of the classical Greek amphitheatre, and every seat has an uninterrupted view of the stage. That is, an uninterrupted view of the entire proscenium opening, but with the wilfulness of modern producers, it is quite possible for large parts of the action to be invisible for large numbers in the audience.

This must be the worst place in the world for claustrophobics. The shape, and the lack of aisles, means that at its widest the auditorium is sixty seats across; imagine having one in the middle and then being overcome by heat, or the recollection of an urgent appointment elsewhere. Some manage to get away from time to time, as an occasional stab of light from a briefly opened exit door testifies; it is not true, however, that the local cemetery is full of patrons of the theatre shot while attempting to escape.

This year it has a new occupant, dead of natural causes. Winifred Wagner, for so long chatelaine of Bayreuth and custodian of the Wagnerian Grail, has gone at last. She outlived her husband Siegfried, the composer's only son, by fifty years, as her mother-in-law outlived Richard by forty-seven; these Wagner women, though their devotion to the cause is unquestioned, do not carry it as far as suttee.

I am glad I never met her; I should think she is in Hell, if there is such a place, and fairly deep, too. I saw her once, in London, at a concert performance of one of Siegfried's operas; she was chatting happily to Friedelind in the interval, both of them all smiles. I wondered whether to send a note across: 'Mr Levin presents his compliments to Frau Wagner, and wonders whether she remembers the occasion when she threatened to have her daughter murdered, as the surest means of dissuading her from saying unkind things about that nice Mr Hitler.'

De mortuis, as H. L. Mencken gloomily observed, *nil nisi bunkum*, and the programme-book contains, amid the drivel aforementioned, something with a considerably gamier taste. The funeral orations for Winifred were delivered from the stage of the Festspielhaus, and two are reprinted here in full. One is by the Mayor of Bayreuth, Hans Wild, the other by the Chairman of the Friends of Bayreuth, Ewald Hilger. From the latter the reader who knows nothing of Winifred would never gather the smallest inkling of the truth, which is that her admiration and affection for Hitler remained undiminished, indeed proudly proclaimed on many occasions, to the end of her life; in 1976, indeed, when the preparations for the festivities surrounding the centenary of the *Ring* were coming to a head, she made a public statement in such extravagantly Hitlerite terms that her son Wolfgang, sole director of the Festspielhaus since the death of his brother Wieland, and conscious of the fact that the eyes of the whole musical world were turned on Bayreuth, barred her from the precincts of the Festspielhaus throughout the Festival. Here is Herr Hilger on the subject:

> It should not, and need not, be passed over in silence that Winifred Wagner's life was not immune to error and misjudgement, but I am convinced that her outstanding achievements as Directress of the Festivals from 1931 to 1944 will soon receive a fairer estimation, seen in their historical perspective, than seems perhaps possible today.

I fear Herr Hilger is all too likely to be right. The Mayor is not quite so bad – he does at least say that the court which condemned her as a major Nazi collaborator gave her a fair trial – but he, like Herr Hilger, praises Winifred for selflessly handing over control of the Festival to her sons after the war, whereas the truth is that she had no option if the Festival were to continue at all, since the court which condemned her for her Nazi activities sentenced her to relinquish such control in perpetuity.

With friends like these, Wagner needs no enemies. But he has many. Once again, I sit in the Stygian darkness that envelops the Bayreuth audience the moment the house-lights go down, for the exit lights are dim and tiny, and there is not a glimmer from the orchestra pit, covered as it is with the *Schaldeckel*, the gently curved lid which runs right across the auditorium and is open only on the stage side; I reflect, before the *Parsifal* prelude begins, on the extraordinary, the unique, hostility this composer, and this composer alone, provokes not only in people who have never listened to his music, but even in many who have.

It is a phenomenon the great oddness of which does not

seem to me to have been sufficiently remarked. There is no composer whose music pleases everybody; but those who find themselves disliking Mozart, Puccini, Bach or Ravel are content simply to stay away from performances of their work. In the case of Wagner, and of him alone, the dislike becomes positive; I have often encountered an antipathy so strong that it seems to take the form of a desire to prohibit Wagner's music altogether.

Of all the ways in which he is unique as a composer – his stupendous originality, his use of the orchestra as the protagonist of the drama, his weaving of a single musical fabric, without joins or breaks – the strangest and most significant is surely the way in which he inspires such detestation along with the devotion. I can see no possible reason for this attitude other than the most obvious one; we hate what we fear, and what Wagner-haters hate is their own fear of what his explorations of the deepest parts of the psyche may reveal. He deals in forbidden subjects, he speaks in his music of blood and passion and will, incest, murder and revenge, love that consumes like a fire and self-sacrifice even unto death. Wagner opens doors that human beings strive to keep closed; no wonder he arouses fury when he points out what lies on the other side of those doors, and that is what I mean when I say that even we who love this music feel a strange reluctance to enter his darkness, and that the exception to this feeling is *Die Meistersinger*, to which we hurry on eager feet because it is the one Wagner opera that is bathed in sunshine throughout, and never goes down into the darkness below.

Meanwhile, there is darkness in the theatre, and the music is about to begin. That darkness provided one of Peter Diamand's best stories at lunch the other day. He told us that in 1976 he was Wolfgang's guest at the centenary *Ring*, directed by Patrice Chéreau; they went on talking so long in Wolfgang's office before *Das Rheingold* that the performance had begun before they realized it, so Wolfgang took him to the door of one of the boxes, opened it and thrust him inside.

Peter's eyes, unaccustomed to the gloom, could see only a diagonal line of very faint lights; he had already heard much about the controversial production and designs, and concluded that this darkness, pierced only by the faint glimmerings he could see, constituted Chéreau's idea of the Rhine and its maidens. Still blind, and afraid to move in case, in the darkness, he stumbled into the lap of one of the other occupants of the box, or even fell down invisible steps, he was wondering what to do when one of his fellow-guests said to him out of the darkness: 'Do you intend to stand for the whole opera?' Peter whispered back the nature of his predicament, and she took him by the arm and led him gently to a seat. In doing so, however, she turned him through ninety degrees, and he thereupon saw the fully-lit stage for the first time; the dim lights he had been staring at so intently were the ones over the exit doors on the other side of the theatre.

The music has now begun, and the effect of the *Schaldeckel* is immediately apparent in the extraordinary, indeed unique, acoustics. Since the sound is thrown first towards the stage instead of the audience, the singers can ride the waves of Wagner's orchestra like the most skilled and intrepid of surfers, instead of, as is the case in most theatres which play Wagner, struggling in the flood, not waving but drowning. In addition, the sound arrives at the audience's ears ready-mixed, a kind of instant musical layer-cake, and no section of the orchestra predominates unless the score calls for it to do so. And on top of this, the amount of wood in the auditorium turns the whole place into one gigantic sounding-board. (The *Schaldeckel* has another use altogether, as I discovered many years ago; I was sitting in the front row for *Götterdämmerung*, and stretched out my legs to rest them on it, whereupon I realized that he who has never heard Siegfried's Funeral March through the soles of his feet cannot really be said to have heard Siegfried's Funeral March at all.)

But something has gone badly wrong at Bayreuth, if this production of Richard Wagner's *Parsifal* by Richard Wagner's grandson is considered acceptable. Unfortunately, of course, the only arbiter of its acceptability is Wolfgang himself, who is hardly likely to reject it as lacking the most elementary fidelity to the work. Yet such a lack is indeed what it suffers from, and it suffers from it, moreover, in a peculiarly sinister form; to ask that a director shall carry out in a full literal sense a composer's stage directions is to misunderstand the function of a director, and indeed the place and value of symbolism in *mise en scène*. But it is not only literal fidelity that is missing here; it is also artistic integrity in accepting the duty to convey the spirit and meaning of the work rather than the ingenuity and perversity of the director.

It begins ominously; the swan is brought in dead a mere dozen bars after the news that Parsifal has shot it, but it has already developed an advance condition of *rigor mortis*. Surely Bayreuth, if it is going to have a naturalistic swan, could have one that brings less uncomfortably to mind those deep-frozen grouse served by expensive restaurants on the Twelfth of August to convince gullible diners that they have just been shot on the moors and flown straight to the table. But this is only the *hors-d'oeuvre*, like the deep-frozen smoked salmon that precedes the grouse. Richard Wagner is not commonly regarded as a composer who didn't know his own mind, needing assistance from directors who could tell him what he was thinking. I have already said that a literal adherence to the detailed stage directions of a composer, or a playwright, for that matter, betrays a misunderstanding of the way an artist works. But there is a far worse misunderstanding at work on this stage.

Item: when, in Act II, Parsifal seizes from Klingsor the sacred spear which pierced the side of Christ, regaining it for the safe keeping of the Knights of the Grail, Wagner calls for him to make the sign of the cross with it, whereupon, at this tremendous symbol of the victory of Christian truth, the evil magician and his palace of denial crumble into dust. Alas for the composer's wishes and the great hinge of the drama; this

Parsifal made no cross, but merely held up the spear like a lecturer pointing to a blackboard.

Item: in Act III, Amfortas, in his delirium of pain and guilt, begs the Knights to plunge their swords into his side and free him from the life that has become unbearable, but they shrink in horror (*'Alle sind scheu von Amfortas gewichen'*) from his wild and unthinkable request. Thus, at any rate, Richard Wagner: but Richard Wagner's fat-headed grandson has the Knights draw their swords and advance upon Amfortas with the evident intention of fulfilling his wishes – indeed, Parsifal, entering at that point, actually has to push them aside to prevent them from doing so.

Item: in the final pages of the opera, the composer requires Parsifal to hold up the Grail, while the music pours out mystery and worship. This is, naturally, the climax of the work; the Knights have a new King, the Blood of Christ and the Spear which shed it are once again united, for ever now, and the sacred vessel, glowing with the holy radiance of the Redeemer, provides in this moment the focus, the reason and the explanation for all that has gone before. But tonight it doesn't; Parsifal simply plonks the Grail down on a table, which anyway looks like an upturned beer barrel, and walks away to a corner of the stage.

Item: in the last moments before these last moments, Kundry 'sinks slowly, lifeless, to the ground'. Her role in the opera would make no sense if she didn't; only in death can she expiate her original sin, and her death is granted her, as a boon, by God, to show that God's mercy is infinite, and that her sacrifice is understood and accepted. But God, like the composer, reckoned without Wolfgang Wagner's rather special notion of his function; in this version Kundry survives, kneeling upright and healthy in the middle of the stage as the curtain falls.

Booing at Bayreuth, once unthinkable, has now acquired a tradition of its own, so that there is always a faction that demands the right of audible dissent, usually the implacably literal traditionalists, who are more numerous, and more tire-some, at Bayreuth than anywhere else on earth. But booing is not always unjustified, and Wagner's grandson richly deserves the catcalls that greet him in Wagner's theatre. (He looks immensely pleased with himself. He has also become fat; the two things may not be altogether unconnected.)

The music saves something from the wreck; Theo Adam's Gurnemanz could hardly be bettered, unless Martti Talvela would bestir himself to sing it again, and Horst Stein, in my experience usually a conductor of anaesthetic dullness, makes the music spring and flow, alive and exciting, from end to end. And the glory of Bayreuth is still the chorus, as the strings are still the glory of the Vienna Philharmonic. Its present chorus-master, Norbert Balatsch, continues the tradition set for so long by Wilhem Pitz, and I know no other choir, in opera house, concert hall or church, to touch it for power, musician-ship or drama. All the same, this is a dispiriting start to a visit to Bayreuth. It is cheered up when we make contact with the Snowmen, who have just arrived; we shall all meet on Mon-day, for *The Flying Dutchman*.

SUNDAY, AUGUST 17TH

The disadvantage of Herr Pflaum's Festival-commuters' bus is that it gives us no opportunity to linger in Bayreuth. In general, I would not wish to linger in Bayreuth, as I have made clear. But there is one shining exception to Bayreuth's dullness; the other opera house, to which I must make a pilgrimage now.

Straight down the hill from the Festspielhaus, past the sta-tion, past the Parsifal Chemists, past the Hotel Weihestephan, where the artists congregate to bitch those not present, there lies one of Germany's greatest secular Baroque masterpieces, the court theatre of Wilhelmine of Prussia (the Prussian arms are entablatured over the stage). Wagner, when he first came to Bayreuth, thought of taking the theatre for his operas; its stage, though tiny by modern standards, was at that time one of the largest in Germany. But it is impossible to envisage Wagner in this lavish auditorium, with its elaborately carved and decorated pillars, its rich painted ceiling, its trumpet-blowing angels and false proscenium painted like a stage curtain, its rows of jewelled and mirrored boxes, its figures of Justice and Freedom, its sconces for candlelight and its tiny enclosure for a miniature orchestra.

After seeing the building, I stroll through the town; everywhere there are ticketless ones stopping strangers and begging for one of the precious pieces of cardboard; up at the Festspielhaus they crowd the pavements; just before the opera they fall like birds of prey on anyone emerging from car or taxi, eager to learn that somebody's wife or husband has broken a leg or developed pneumonia. It occurs to me that while this state of affairs exists, Wolfgang can do what he likes on the stage. It also occurs to me that if he does too much of it, this state of affairs will not exist much longer.

MONDAY, AUGUST 18TH

The Flying Dutchman, in a strange, exciting, production by Harry Kupfer. The whole opera is a vision seen in a dream by Senta, who remains on stage throughout, visibly dreaming it. Kupfer has achieved a real feeling of nightmare, with the Dutchman's ship turning into a tropical jungle, and the Sailor's Dance performed by corpses. Much good singing, and much booing from the outraged traditionalists, who this time have missed the point.

TUESDAY, AUGUST 19TH

Back at the hotel, at one minute past midnight, there is a knock on our door; a smiling Herr Pflaum enters, bearing champagne and a complicated flan (one of his brother's specialities) covered with candles. Arianna produces wrapped presents, heaped up like Alberich's gold in the last scene of *Rheingold*. I blow out the candles, Herr Pflaum proposes my health, we consume the champagne *à trois*, the flan is delicious.

At what age do the years suddenly start to go faster? Traditionally, for men at least, it is forty, but I remember my fortieth birthday well, and felt no dismay, let alone an impulse to write one of those 'Now I'm forty' articles that were pouring off my contemporaries' typewriters. As for fifty, I had no opportunity to feel anything but happy, for that was the day of the monster surprise party Arianna organized in the house we had rented for the summer in France, when thirty of my friends flew from London to be with us, and as many more came from elsewhere in Europe; bathed in love and friendship, I could have discovered that I was a hundred without a qualm. I had had a few qualms on the day that saw out my thirtieth year, when I realized I had been a promising young man far too long, and that it is impossible to go on being promising, or young, for that matter, after the three has been rung up on that board; all in all, though, birthdays have never worried me; New Year's Eve is my time for reckoning up life's accounts and finding a debit balance so large that self-ending seems the only appropriate response. If I ever do make away with myself, it will certainly be on New Year's Eve.

Why do we so object to growing older? Not just because we are approaching death, not even because we are conscious of failing powers. We mourn the passing years, unless we are among the happy few who have really understood their meaning, because with every one that passes we have left more undone and have less time to do it. Worse; we have left more undone and are less able to believe that we ever shall do it. But what is 'it'? The writer has not yet produced a novel better than *War and Peace*; the composer, a symphony better than the Fifth; the childless woman, children; the politician, anything to secure lasting reputation; the aimless a goal, the frightened courage, the unhappy happiness. But these are all only disguises for the truth, substitutes for the only true creation any of us can really achieve. Of what use the statesman's treaty, the painter's masterpiece, the general's victory, even the gardener's living tree? In the end, it is our own wholeness we must seek, and our only possible creation is ourselves; it is the realization that we have not yet achieved it, indeed that we have hardly begun on it, that brings the sound of time's winged chariot hurrying near. In this truth, Beethoven and Tolstoy are one with the barren woman, the failed husband, those who are afraid to die though they have never been alive. Is there a reckoning that awaits us all? I do not know; but there may be a terrible understanding *in articulo mortis* more painful than the torments of the damned. It *is* later than we think.

In the evening we have a birthday dinner with Kenneth and Sallie, during the interval of *Lohengrin*. It does much to dispel such thoughts; Kenneth has drawn me a beautiful pen-and-ink sketch of Hohenems, recollected in tranquillity, and there is a box of liqueur chocolates to accompany it. The *Lohengrin* helps too; who would have thought that Götz Friedrich, the bad boy of the Covent Garden *Ring*, would produce the most straightforward reading of the three operas we have seen? He has no excuse for tucking a third of the action so far into the right-hand side of the stage that it is invisible to a third of the audience (I don't think I ever set eyes on the King), but apart from that he is without blame. Nobody comes in riding a bicycle, nobody sings his lines with his head in a bucket, nobody is made up to look like the Pope or Franz Josef Strauss. Instead, there are square, plain groupings, simple, clear movements, natural and plausible relationships, fidelity to the composer's stated intentions (well, there is no swan, but there is a perfectly acceptable symbolic representation in its place); and there is a tenor with the magnificently Wagnerian name of Siegfried Jerusalem, who – rather more important – has a magnificently Wagnerian voice to go with his name. He sings like a silver trumpet – but we have been through this a dozen times in the search for a new heroic Wagner tenor, and every time the light shining in the east has proved to be a false dawn.

And we – we Wagner-lovers, that is – are now in a worse plight, for not only is there no true *Heldentenor* in the world, there is no satisfactory Brünnhilde, and soon, when Donald McIntyre begins to give up the heavier roles, there will be no Wotan either. Richard Wagner created a new music-drama, a new kind of opera-theatre for it to be performed in, a new orchestral instrument to make sounds he could hear but which no existing instrument could produce, and a new kind of voice, without which all the rest would have gone for nothing. The operas remain, until the end of time; the theatre has changed for ever into what he wanted it to be; the house he built upon a rock still stands, lest the rest of the operatic world should forget what he taught it; but the voices with which he filled his theatre seem to be dying out of the human race. Let us hope that Siegfried Jerusalem will usher in a new era on Wagner's green and pleasant hill.

WEDNESDAY, AUGUST 20TH

As we leave, I am going through my usual Bayreuth crisis. The absurdity and discomfort of the conditions under which we listen to Wagner in Bayreuth is balanced against the uniquely sumptuous fidelity with which the Festspielhaus brings us the music; the sheer cheek of an opera festival that, year in and year out, selects its repertoire from the same ten works is outweighed by the strength Bayreuth gets from its unbroken tradition, symbolized by the way in which every player in the invisible pit (they say the invisibility leads them to play in shirtsleeves and braces, even to keep mugs of beer beside their music-stands) signs his name on his score – and the Bayreuth orchestra still plays from the original edition. The disquiet aroused by Bayreuth's febrile search for new ways of producing the operas shrinks beside the realization that no producer, however perverse, can ruin these mighty works; the fervent wish that Richard Wagner had never been born goes hand in hand with a yearning to hear once more that incomparable silence, the 'Bayreuth hush'; the certainty that I shall never come again made mock of by the knowledge that I shall. Perhaps I shall come for the new *Ring* in 1983; perhaps for the next new *Mastersingers*; perhaps simply whenever the fever next runs high in my blood. My last thought is for the crew of that fire-engine beside the Festspielhaus; may they stay at their posts, and alert.

The Ghost in George Square

Arianna has to spend a couple of days in London before joining me in Edinburgh; the Shuttle will get me there with an hour to spare, long enough to unpack and change before going to the concert, a recital by Emil Gilels; I have just got time to catch it.

No I haven't, though; by the time we have got the baggage back and cleared customs, I have missed the plane by minutes. Still, catching the next one, I shall yet have time to arrive in Edinburgh, drop my cases and get to the concert.

But that will not do; oh indeed, it will not do at all.

Many, many years ago, as soon as I had reached a professional position in which it was possible, I made a vow, to the effect that I would never go out in the evening, in any circumstances at all and whatever the cost, whether to the theatre, the opera, a concert or a dinner public or private, without going home first to bathe and change. Of all the vows I have made in my life, that is the only one that I have never broken, not even once, not even with an excuse which even the sternest judge would accept. I have spent untold sums of money keeping taxis waiting while I have gone through the ritual; I have come close, on countless occasions, to experiencing a coronary from the stress induced by cutting things too fine (for, obviously, the vow has to include being on time for where I am going); I have been tempted, again and again, to break it just this once; but in the end I have never failed to obey that self-imposed ordinance. And now it looks as though I shall have to, for I really shall not have time in Edinburgh to do anything but go from the airport to the Usher Hall, pausing for not longer than it takes to leave my luggage at the Cale-donian Hotel. Either I am going to break a vow unbroken for twenty-five years and more, or I am going to miss the first half of the concert, which counts as breaking the vow anyway; the irresistible force has come up against the immovable object.

Inspiration strikes, in an access of what I suppose is lateral thinking. In the Shuttle waiting-room, I demand my checked luggage back, trying to resemble a man who has just been intolerably insulted by British Airways and intends to shake their dust from his feet; from the look on the face of the girl of whom I make my demand I deduce that I have succeeded only in resembling a lunatic. Very well, I am a lunatic who wants his luggage back, and a taxi to put it in; off I go to one of the nearby airport hotels. 'I am a lunatic,' I announce (in for a penny . . .) 'and wish to take a room for the night *but not sleep in it.*' 'Yes, sir,' says the young man behind the reception desk, 'that's what we call a day-let, and it will cost you £25·40.' Evidently lunacy is common on the Great West Road; does the Home Office know? No time for that now; I am in the room, I am flinging open my case, extracting a suit, a shirt, socks, shoes, underwear, handkerchief, tie, razor, toothbrush. Into the shower; out; dress; repack; taxi; Shuttle gate, trying to look like a man who has decided to forgive British Airways its intolerable insult.

I am in Edinburgh; but now I have a little time in hand. Not much, but enough; I leave my cases at the hotel and am about to leave my room when the telephone rings. It is Sidney Bernstein, with Sandra in the background, singing 'Happy yesterday's birthday'. I have kept my vow; I feel refreshed; I am in time for the concert; I am among friends; and I am in the city which I love above all the cities of the world, more than my native London, more than San Francisco, than Amsterdam, than Salzburg, than Venice herself.

I came to the very first Festival, in 1947, and must have been back upwards of twenty times, though since the early years mostly only for a weekend. On that first visit, I came up on the night train; a sleeping compartment being far beyond my student pocket, I travelled steerage, and slept in the luggage-rack. That in itself opens the sluices to a flood of memory, for to those familiar only with modern carriages, in which the rack is made of unyielding metal, the claim must seem most improbable; in those days, however, luggage-racks were made of stout netting, and I slept as peacefully as a sailor in his hammock.

A la recherche du temps perdu, I continue to search the bottomless well of the past. The first sight I saw at Waverley Station all those years ago was an enamel advertising sign, old and chipped even then, and long gone now, the memory of which inescapably dates me and my generation, for it went back to the days before everyone wrote with ballpoints and fibre-tips, indeed when fountain pens themselves were by no means universally possessed, and writing was done by fitting a nib into a penholder. It was the manufacturer's various nibs – for nibs could be broad or fine, flexible or rigid, square-ended or with a corner cut off – that the sign was advertising:

> They come as a boon and a blessing to men,
> The Pickwick, the Owl and the Waverley pen.

More memories come up. I had read Robert Louis Stevenson on his native city before that first visit, and wondered what he could mean by his description of the weather:

> The delicate die early, and I, as a survivor, among bleak winds and plumping rain, have been sometimes tempted to envy them their fate.

I speedily discovered what he meant, and have never since failed to obey the rule: for Edinburgh in August, dress as for Reykjavik in February. Those who do are rewarded, for there is something exhilarating about walking along George Street in the teeth of a gale so fierce that the walker is obliged to lean into it with his nose almost touching the pavement, to avoid being blown bodily backwards into St Andrew's Square. I also learnt very early that it is inadvisable, in those circumstances, to open an umbrella, even when Stevenson's bleak winds are accompanied by Stevenson's plumping rain; some of us old Edinburgh Festival hands were hang-gliding before the sport was given a name.

In 1947, Edinburgh made the first of her promises to build an opera house; even then the King's Theatre was hopelessly inadequate for opera, which is why the world's leading companies have either refused to come at all, or, having made the mistake of coming once, have refused to return. The promise was renewed annually for nearly thirty years, and broken as often; only in the 1970s did Edinburgh finally admit that she was never going to build an opera house, and that was only after Glasgow – Glasgow, where they assault each other with broken bottles! – had built one of her own, and within fifty yards of Sauchiehall Street, too, where the broken bottle ceremony is carried out on Saturday nights. But it is impossible to shame Edinburgh; after she finally admitted that the opera-house promise was never meant to be taken seriously, the municipality not of the capital itself but of the Lothian Region set to and converted a huge, abandoned cinema (the Playhouse) into a theatre that would be, or could easily be made, perfectly suitable for opera. Unfortunately, Edinburgh by then had already contrived to quarrel with the Lothian authorities – to such an extent, indeed, that the latter's grant to the Festival had been withdrawn – and until a peace treaty is concluded, no Edinburgh Festival performances, whether of opera or anything else, may take place there. We old Edinburgh hands know that when they do, Edinburgh will claim the credit.

It is this wretched provincialism that trims the ardour of even the most fervent lover of Scotland's capital. There is not a single restaurant of international standard in the city, nor a hotel that can compare even with the best in London, let alone in other countries. A shortage of taxis at the airport is mirrored by the way in which the programmes at Festival events are allowed to run out (imagine that happening at Salzburg or Bayreuth!) only because if enough were printed there might be a few left unsold. The meanness and bad faith in the opera-house story is only part of the meanness and bad faith of Edinburgh's attitude to the funding of the Festival in general; from the first, her citizens and their elected representatives have never stopped squealing in dismay at being asked for a contribution to the cost of an enterprise that must by now have brought into the city, from sojourners, purchasers and international publicity, something like £100,000,000, if not a good deal more, and the squeals invariably rise to an appalling intensity if, when the books are finally balanced, a modest deficit, requiring a supplementary grant, is revealed. I long ago called for a new ceremony, akin to the Tattoo, called The Grudging of the Money, and may yet live to see my proposal carried out. And Edinburgh's ambivalent attitude to her own Festival goes further still, for though it is a myth that the Edinburghers do not themselves attend the Festival events (a third of the seats are filled by them), their artistic conservatism is appalling and paralysing; almost the first thing I have learnt on this visit is that, the New York Philharmonic having included in one of its concerts a work by that strange young composer of the atonal avant-garde, Gustav Mahler, there are seats going begging.

The truth is that, with part of herself, Edinburgh hates the Festival and everything about it, particularly the idea that art is something to be enjoyed and celebrated, and wishes she had never started it. What is strange about this attitude, apart from the attitude itself, is that it is combined with an extraordinary warmth and generosity of spirit towards the Festival visitors. Shopkeepers in Edinburgh at Festival-time really do smile at their customers, and the smile is plainly genuine, not adopted simply for commercial purposes. Edinburghers will go out of their way to direct – even accompany – a stranger to his destination. Princes Street, though crowded as a fairground, is full not of surliness, but of gaiety and good heart. No doubt all this is the shining face of the coin of provincialism, balancing the dull metal of narrowness and parsimony on the other side. No doubt, too – and, alas, there *is* no doubt – Edinburgh has declined over the decades, so that the pleasant shock a newcomer to the city gets at finding so warm a welcome is less powerful for those familiar with it, who have memories to compare.

And now I am back plumbing the well again. My first sight of the city, just coming awake in the early light. The stones I know so well: the red ones of the Scott Monument (Edinburgh's answer to the Albert Memorial), the brown ones of the Assembly Hall of the Church of Scotland, with its terrifying statue of John Knox in the courtyard, the yellow ones of the National Gallery, the grey ones of St Giles, the Castle, the Register House, The streets I have walked so often: George Street, with its handsome proportions, its elegant shops and the Assembly Rooms, used in Festival-time as the visitor's club, where Scott finally admitted, to nobody's surprise, that he was the author of the Waverley Novels; Queen Street, with its unbroken calm, lying only a few yards from the tourists and the bustle; the Royal Mile (Canongate, High Street and Lawnmarket) cutting through the heart of Old Edinburgh from the Castle to the Palace; the lovely green valley of Princes Street Gardens, which contains Edinburgh's best conjuring-trick, for the main railway line runs, untunnelled, straight down the middle, but so cunningly concealed that its very existence is unsuspected by the visitors walking only a few feet away; and George Square. In George Square, the well of memory sends up tears, but tomorrow I must visit it, whatever the cost in vain regrets. Tonight, however, there is Gilels playing the E flat major Variations and Fugue of Beethoven, the set based on a theme that clearly obsessed him, for he used it three times; first in the music he wrote for a ballet, *The Creatures of Prometheus* (does any ballet company perform it? I think I would go to the ballet myself if it were in the bill), second in this set of variations, and yet again, in its most familiar form, in the last movement of the Eroica, which is also, come to think of it, a set of variations. Well, if there is a mythological figure to whom Beethoven can legitimately be compared, it is surely Prometheus who stole fire from heaven and was dreadfully punished for his deed, and Gilels plays the *Prometheus* variations with fire of his own. Why should it seem strange, incidentally, to see a musician with red hair? While I am on the subject of strange sights on the concert platform, why are there no left-handed violinists? If it comes to that, why are there almost no homosexual conductors?

THURSDAY, AUGUST 21ST

On the walk to George Square, which I could do blindfold or fast asleep – along Princes Street, up the Mound (down which, in the old days, the trams used to clatter, taking the huge double bend at such speed that they always seemed to be about to come off the rails), over the George IV Bridge, round the corner by the Infirmary, into Meadow Walk, through the concealed entrance – I am reliving not just my first visit to Edinburgh, but my life. For that nineteen-year-old boy, straight off the luggage rack, stayed in a student hostel in George Square, and the middle-aged man he became can even remember the name of it: Cowan House. In those days I thought nothing of sitting in the gallery for four Festival events in a day, and talking the night away on cocoa after the last of them, and though I have never lost my dislike of going to bed before the small hours, I no longer cram the Edinburgh days and nights with performances, and I do not drink cocoa; for that matter I sit in the stalls. But these changes only serve to remind me of that youth, who had all the world and time, and that is why Edinburgh, for me, tugs at the heart with the glimpse it gives down that avenue of unreturning years. Housman had a word for it:

> When first my way to fair I took
> Few pence in purse had I,

And long I used to stand and look
At things I could not buy.

Now times are altered: if I care
To buy a thing, I can;
The pence are here and here's the fair,
But where's the lost young man?

 – To think that two and two are four
And neither five nor three
The heart of man has long been sore
And long 'tis like to be.

George Square, in those days, was one of the loveliest squares in a city particularly well supplied with them. Scott lived here, only a few doors from Cowan House, and must have walked on the curious miniature cobblestones that make up the inner pavement, surrounding the beautifully tended garden (locked, of course, another sign of Edinburgh's miserable timidity) that constitutes the middle of the square. No doubt his ghost walks here, and that of Adam Smith too, and for all I know, Mary, Queen of Scots; but the ghost I fear to meet is the ghost of my younger self, who would accuse me of wasting his life, and leave me without a reply that would convince me, let alone him.

The tears, then, are never far away in George Square. But nowadays they are kept at bay by the adrenalin of rage at what has been done, slowly and steadily, to this beautiful oasis of peace and harmony. Three sides of the square have been torn down, their eighteenth-century handsomeness being replaced by huge blocks of such brutal and lifeless architectural nastiness that even London – nay, Birmingham and Newcastle – can scarcely match them. And this crime has been committed not by any greedy or corrupt property speculator, but by Edinburgh University, with the connivance of the City Council. Why are universities such abominable barbarians?

Arianna arrives, and we go, with Sidney and Sandra, to the

opera. There is news awaiting us at the King's Theatre; a mere thirty-four years after the Festival began, the bar there has at last been persuaded to stock champagne. This may not seem the greatest achievement since Newton's discovery of gravity, but it is in its lesser way a distinct mark of human progress. For hitherto, the bar at the King's Theatre has not simply refused to stock champagne; its staff, telling a customer that they do not do so, have announced the news that such filthy foreign stuff is not available with an enormous pride in their voices – so much so, indeed that they might have been John Knox telling the Pope that his brand of Christianity was not obtainable in the city. Now although it is only to be expected that Edinburgh should suspect anyone who wants to drink champagne of being an embezzler, and probably also a child-molester, to take audible pleasure in refusal is very far from being an Edinburgh characteristic, or indeed a Scottish one; that kind of attitude is more commonly found in London. It has therefore been a matter of double regret to me over the years that my request for champagne at the King's Theatre should be met with a horrid display of satisfaction as well as a failure to comply with the customer's wishes, and I am in consequence no less doubly delighted now when my request for champagne is greeted not only with a promptly produced bottle but with smiles and an obvious pleasure in serving it. I make a note to go and thumb my nose at John Knox tomorrow, and we proceed to the opera.

Così Fan Tutte, the Cologne Opera's first offering of the Festival, is directed by Jean-Pierre Ponnelle, which makes four operas realized by him that we have seen on this tour. The performance has not been well spoken of, so I am pleasantly surprised at its quality; a dazzling Fiordiligi from Julia Varady (Mrs Dietrich Fischer-Dieskau), a sweetly tintinnabulating Despina in Georgine Resick, and most interesting conception of Alfonso, much further down the social scale than usual.

FRIDAY, AUGUST 22ND

The style of the new Director, John Drummond, whose second Festival this is, cannot be fully judged yet; but the rustle of new brooms is already audible. For a start, the number of venues in use for official Festival performances has increased, which is why I am in the Queen's Hall for the first time, a delightful building with a pillared gallery, listening to a no less delightful ensemble called Canadian Brass. This consists of two trumpets, a French horn, a trombone and a tuba, though these five virtuosos, I suspect, could turn their hands to pretty well anything in brass, up to and including the giant helicon, the only musical instrument that the performer has to climb into before he can play it. Canadian Brass are all dressed in the same uniform of grey sports jackets, dark blue trousers and sweaters, and just as the casual clothes are belied by the fact that they are all wearing the same, so the relaxed attitude they display on the platform is not carried over into their playing.

On paper, so narrow a range of musical colouring as these instruments imply promises monotony; in practice the concert is lively and varied, from Purcell to Dixieland, and reminds me again of the strength the Festival has always drawn from the mid-morning concerts that have been a feature of it from the beginning. But these players add to their performance something very rarely found in the concert hall, and even frowned upon by many – particularly by the respectable Edinburghers who believe that those who drink champagne in the intervals of the opera are damned, and those who go to concerts on a Sunday are in a fair way to following the champagne drinkers to perdition.

Yet why should not laughter accompany music? Clearly, the Canadian Brass players see no reason why not, and they introduce each item with lively patter, including a running joke about the yearning of the trombone and the tuba, least glamorous of orchestral instruments, to be the stars for once. Is it true, as I have heard, that the conductor, Serge Koussevitzky, who started his career as a player of the double-bass, gave a performance of the Mendelssohn Violin Concerto on it? Well, at least I have now heard Charles Dallenbach play Rimsky-Korsakov's The Flight of the Bumble Bee on a tuba.

Arianna had been to Salzburg, but not my Salzburg; she has been to Edinburgh, but not my Edinburgh, Festival Edinburgh, the Edinburgh in which Princes Street is brave with an army of banners. A walk of exploration and introduction is therefore called for, omitting George Square as too dangerous to the emotions. She is much taken with the story of Deacon Brodie (respectable clergyman by day, highwayman by night) and I promise her, as a final treat, the Outlook Tower; when we get there, unfortunately, the day is too cloudy for it. But it is not too cloudy for my memories of it.

The Outlook Tower contains a craft shop, which is neither here nor there. But it also contains a *camera obscura*, that remarkable invention which, without even a lens, let alone a photographic plate, throws on to a screen a picture of whatever the aperture is being pointed at. In the Edinburgh one the screen is a huge stone table, slightly concave in shape; the customers are ushered into the room and surround the table, some ten at a time. Then the door is closed, plunging the room into Bayreuthian blackness, and the operator, reaching up for the lever which operates the viewfinder, lights up the table with a living view of Edinburgh. It is like standing on the top of the Campanile in Venice, looking down on the Piazza San Marco, and in the old days the custodian had a speech which he had obviously delivered thousands of times, the high point being when he swung the picture on to Princes Street and showed us a bus going up the Mound. 'Look at that bus struggling up the hill,' he would say, 'let's help it', and he would put his fingertips on the table, keeping hand and arm straight, and gently raise his elbow, whereupon the bus would run up his hand and arm. A later visit to this magic-lantern show is promised, and a few yards down the hill a commination is uttered against the authorities who have chosen

Festival-time to shroud the Cathedral's great lantern-spire in scaffolding. Here is the spot from which Jenny Geddes threw the stool at the Bishop; there is Usher's Folly, the unfinished Greek temple on Calton Hill; this is the great, sinister bulk of Holyrood House; that statue is of Greyfriar's Bobby, who pined away on his master's grave, or so they say; and there, just at the corner of the Infirmary (careful, now, or we shall be in George Square), is the spot where, more than thirty years ago, I met a man all battered and bloody, who would not be persuaded to go to the hospital two yards away, lest he should be asked questions, about how he got his injuries, that he would rather not answer.

Billy Bishop Goes to War is a two-man show – written and directed by one of them, John Gray, and performed by the other, Eric Peterson – and it tells the true story of a Canadian ace pilot of the First World War who joined the Royal Flying Corps in 1917 simply to get out of the mud of Flanders, and went on to become one of the most daring, successful and profusely decorated fliers of the entire conflict ('Well, Bishop,' said George V, pinning on his chest three medals, including the V.C., 'you've been a busy bugger'). There is, however, a catch in it; it would have little point otherwise. We see Billy begin as a hero of convenience, and gradually change into a war-god as the relish of killing takes hold of him; in the last few minutes we see him wheeled out as a totem-figure to inspire his successors in the Second World War by spouting the kind of recruiting slogan he despised with such ribaldry in the First. But even that would make only an interesting play; what tucks the evening firmly into the memory is the performance of Eric Peterson. He is clearly a talented actor, but there are plenty of those around; as a mimic, however, he is altogether exceptional, of a quality that I have not seen since Ruth Draper. He plays a dozen parts besides that of the hero – society ladies, society butlers, fellow-officers, drunks – and switches in and out of roles with no more to mark the transition than a hunch of the shoulders, a straightening of the back, an unexaggerated modulation of the voice. More; he does something which I would have sworn was impossible – he imitates aircraft engines, guns and bombs without generating any of the usual embarrassment at seeing a grown man flapping his arms to indicate a plane and making boom-boom-boom-brrrr-brrrr-pow-pow-pow noises to mark the noise of battle. On the contrary; he brings the battle alive for even the most blasé of spectators – the deepening stillness of an audience that is locked in the drama's grip is unmistakable.

> . . . Or may we cram
> Within this wooden O the very casques
> That did affright the air at Agincourt?

Eric Peterson can. And he has achieved something else, all unknowing. It has been a very long time since the theatre side of the Festival produced any of the most memorable of the Festival's evenings; lately, I have often felt that it would be better to drop the theatre altogether from the official programme and leave the drama to the Fringe.

The Fringe is an example – one of the most astonishing known to anthropology – of parents eaten by their cannibal children. Year by year it has grown more and more gargantuan; this year it is offering 390 items, and even more halls, churches, cellars, vestibules, telephone boxes and laundry baskets are being pressed into service for the performers and their performances. Most of what the Fringe does is ephemeral, of course, particularly the five-hour epics on the childhood of Fidel Castro, of which there always seem to be half a dozen, some in verse. But we have to remember that most of everything is ephemeral, and the Fringe does have a remarkable record of turning out a few players and a few plays, almost every year, destined to make their mark later on a literally wider stage.

This year there are ominous signs, though. The Fringe now calls itself 'The Fringe Festival', and the umbrella organization which controls its constituent parts is more official and practical than ever. It cannot be long – it *shouldn't* be long – before there is Fringe to the Fringe, as Off-Broadway acquired an Off-Off-Broadway; only thus can the inevitable ossification of artistic progress be avoided, though where the Fringe's Fringe will be accommodated is another matter.

After the play we go up to the Castle for the Tattoo. The Stevenson weather in which I arrived has cleared up, and the day has been sunny. But when dusk falls in summer Edinburgh, so does the temperature, and even in an enclosed box on the Castle esplanade, the chill is not to be kept out. There is plenty to stir the blood, though; it is impossible not to feel excitement at the massed ranks of bands and marchers, the precision with which they interweave, coalesce, part and re-form, the martial music that accompanies their display. This year – the well of memory has nothing like this – there are high-kicking American drum-majorettes, no doubt rivals to that Pascal Dumas, Champion d'Europe 1980 de Twirling-Baton, whom I encountered in Marseille; there is also a group of cadets from Rutgers University giving an alarming display of precision marching carried out with Lee-Enfield rifles *and fixed bayonets*. Not only are their manoeuvres complex in the extreme, but the lethal rifles are treated like the drum-majorettes' twirling-batons, the circles of glittering fire described by the bayonet-points hypnotic in themselves and in the danger that gives the display its extraordinarily thrilling quality. Thrice during the performance, which is carried out with no orders whatever, weapons are exchanged by being hurled, in mutual pairs of arcs, through the air, like jugglers exchanging quoits on opposite sides of the stage. But quoits can't kill, and the cheers at the end of this act are composed equally of admiration and relief, the relief breaking out again at the end, the cold by then having become unendurable, when 'Scotland the Brave' sends us down the hill to unfreeze our bones with a dram or two. Dinner with Sidney and Sandra, and Alistair and Jane Cooke. They have fled the Tattoo at half-time, *and* had a warming bath.

SATURDAY, AUGUST 23RD

In the morning we go to the Freemason's Hall, best-loved and least-changing of Edinburgh's concert halls (even the Usher Hall has had its seats re-upholstered since 1947). A happy reunion before the concert with Jennifer Simon, a friend from Aberdeen, where she works on the local paper; her eyes, as always, are a-gleam with life, relish and mischief. The Edinburgh Quartet, joined by Roger Woodward, play the Shostakovich Piano Quintet. Two years ago, in this hall, the Beaux Arts Trio played his Piano Trio; I had never heard it before, and thought it a noble and searching work, but the Quintet is superficial and trifling by comparison. The reason is to be found in the date of its composition, 1940; Shostakovich was experiencing the full force of the *Zhdanovchina*, Stalin's policy of the total extirpation of Soviet art and its replacement by 'socialist-realist' rubbish. As Shostakovich's posthumously published memoirs make clear, he was lucky to escape with his life after his opera *Katerina Ismailova* ('Lady Macbeth of Mtsensk') was condemned for 'formalism' (i.e., Stalin couldn't hum the tunes). The book, published in Britain a year or so ago, is the best picture yet of the tragic fate of the artist in a totalitarian society, but the Quintet says it all more briefly, though no less tragically.

In the afternoon Agapi, Arianna's sister, arrives by train. Does Edinburgh, I ask myself nervously, know what it may be in for? When the two of them join forces, Pandora retires, acknowledging her inability to compete.

I have got Agapi a ticket for the ballet; Jennifer is going to the Usher Hall to hear the European Community Youth Orchestra; we are going to the opera, as are Sidney and Sandra; we shall all meet, together with a niece of Sidney's and her husband, at the Cosmo. The Cosmo does not pretend to *haute cuisine*, but it is the most successful of Edinburgh's restaurants (it is twice the size it was when I first knew it) because it cooks within its capacity, and there does very well.

The opera is a rarity, Cimarosa's *Il Matrimonio Segreto*. We arrive to news of disaster; two of the singers have been struck down by illness. This is bad enough news when one of the world's leading opera houses is the victim, but the thankless task of ringing round Europe for replacements is made worse when it is for a briefly visiting company (and a lesser one, too) in the notorious King's. I am reminded again of Rossini's claim that opera-house directors all go bald; John Drummond is still well-thatched, but this *is* his first Festival. His luck is in; he has found situation-savers at Stockholm and Düsseldorf. He is luckier even than that suggests; both have sung the opera recently. It is a charming work, slight but worth reviving; it has suffered from comparisons with Mozart and Rossini, but at its own level it is spirited and melodious, with much to enjoy. And without the slip of paper in the programme, and John Drummond's announcement from the stage, no one would know which the replacements were. Dinner at the Cosmo is eaten in a cloud of happiness; Edinburgh's spirit has entered into everybody, even Agapi, though it is her first visit and she has had no chance to see it yet. She reports with moderate enthusiasm on the Australian Ballet; the opera-party have all enjoyed Cimarosa; Jennifer, impressed by the European Youth Orchestra, has preferred Claudio Abbado's conducting to that of Edward Heath.

SUNDAY, AUGUST 24TH

The New York Philharmonic, with Zubin Mehta conducting the Eroica; surely a crowd-pleasing combination anywhere. Not quite anywhere; the programme also includes the European première of Penderecki's Second Symphony, and there are plenty of empty seats to be seen, together with plenty more that rumour has it are filled with paper. The irony is that the symphony, in a single half-hour movement, is musically most accessible; it even includes, as a kind of *Leitmotiv*, that most popular of Christmas carols, 'Silent Night'.

MONDAY, AUGUST 25TH

A day for catching up with the newspapers I have missed on my travels. Edinburgh Public Library keeps files of *The Times* and the *Sunday Times*, and I indulge my only serious addiction. It *is* an addiction, too; deprived of newspapers, I go through an entire repertoire of withdrawal symptoms – restlessness, bad temper, inability to concentrate, eventually a hopeless lethargy – and I have no doubt that if it went on long enough the lethargy would become coma. Not that there is any very sensational news for me to learn; wherever I haven't been able to get *The Times* there has been the local press, or at the very least the *Daily Telegraph*. But I am always careful to ensure that I have seen at least one British national newspaper for every day I have been abroad, even if it means catching up only when I finally get back to London, and there is a reason for my caution. The first time I ever went abroad was in 1946; I went to Switzerland with my sister. We were in a remote village, and in any case communications within Europe were not what they have since become; the consequence was that I saw no English papers for the best part of a fortnight. Early in that fortnight, H. G. Wells had died, and by the time I returned all the obituaries and tributes had come and gone, and I knew nothing of his death until a year or so later, when the first posthumous biography appeared.

I remember telling this story to Alan Moorehead, and he offered me in return a far stranger one. He and Nevil Shute were close friends, and corresponded regularly; Shute lived in Australia, Alan in Italy. Alan got a letter from Shute in the ordinary way, by airmail, which included a reference to a book he was sending Alan by sea mail, together with a further letter. A few days later, Alan learned that Nevil Shute had died, and he said that he found very strange and disturbing the thought that, moving slowly half-way round the world, a letter from a dead man was on its way to him.

TUESDAY, AUGUST 26TH

Another, and greater, theatrical sensation. The Polish company of Tadeusz Kantor have brought a work called *Wielopole Wielopole*, which is the name of the village where Kantor was born, and also the Polish for 'many fields'. It is an *olla podrida* of speech, song, mime, stylized movement, dummies and wordless sound, the whole adding up to a tour through Kantor's subconscious as he recalls the people, the happenings and the meaning of his childhood; a bleak and terrifying picture, strewn with recurring images of war, cruelty and avarice. The priest, alternately officiating at a crucifixion and being crucified himself, never loses his smile; the soldiers, bloodless corpses all, kill the same victims again and again; the old scavenger-woman sweeps up the débris, inanimate and human; it ends with an agonized version of the Last Supper. Kantor remains on stage throughout, directing the action like an orchestral conductor; he allows no compromise in this nightmare of flashback truth, and the result is a work of explosive force.

WEDNESDAY, AUGUST 27TH

A bonne-bouche to end with; *Don Giovanni*, out at the Leith Theatre, an unfrocked Town Hall, done by an outfit called the Cambridge Opera. Opera on the Fringe is exceptionally rare; who are these, and why Cambridge? The programme gives no clue, and I enquire of one of the young people in what looks like charge. She explains that they are mostly just-graduated from faculties or academies of music, that some are still students, that a few have had their first professional engagements, that they have formed the group solely to come to the Festival, that the producer, David Finch, is a Cambridge man. I am early, and wander about; outside, I see two members of the orchestra, a boy and a girl, laughing together, both so young, so innocent and so fair that the sight nearly stops my heart; Varus, Varus, give me back my legions!

The performance is uncommonly good, not only crackling with the electricity of enthusiasm, but polished and mature in execution, with a Zerlina who could take her performance straight on to the stage of Covent Garden, and shine there with it. Patricia Rozario; I note the name, and strike a bet with myself that I have not heard the last of it, or its owner. There is just time to put a paragraph about the production into my broadcast to be recorded tomorrow morning. Nothing to do now but pack, and try not to dream of George Square and the ghostly footfall of a boy of nineteen that I heard behind me on my visit there. Stands the Floral Clock at ten to three? And are there oatcakes still for tea?

Unfinished Symphony

It is said that everyone in the Western world old enough to have been doing anything on Friday, November 22nd, 1963 remembers what it was; the assassination of President Kennedy has acted on memory like the fixing solution on a photograph. I was sitting at home, and had not turned on radio or television for many hours. Very late in the evening, the telephone rang; it was Ned Sherrin, to discuss a television programme which he was producing and in which I was to take part on the morrow. His message was that in view of the circumstances the format and nature of the programme would obviously have to be changed, and my contribution likewise. He based his remarks, however, on the reasonable assumption that I had heard the news, and the conversation continued for some minutes in growing bewilderment on my part; words which would have made perfect sense to anyone who knew what had happened in Dallas seemed to me to be gibberish, or to be couched in a code to which I lacked the key. Eventually, on the edge of panic, I interrupted Ned to ask what the hell he was talking about; to my horror, the gibberish code became even more impenetrable, for he was still unable to realize that I was not in possession of the tremendous and terrible fact that provided the context for what he was saying, and assumed that what I did not understand was the revised plan he was proposing, and which he then proceeded to relate again, in what he thought was simpler language and a fuller exposition but which to me was powerful evidence that I had gone mad. The difficulty was eventually cleared up; but *my* answer to the question 'What were you doing when President Kennedy was shot?' has, ever since, been: Filling the role – which somebody had to play, after all – of the very last man to know about it.

Landing in Barcelona, then, I remember my only previous visit to this city, and the date of it; Tuesday, September 6th, 1966. I remember the reason for remembering the date, too: huge headlines in the afternoon papers were announcing the fact that something had happened to Dr Verwoerd, who had been Prime Minister of South Africa since September 1958. The size of the headlines suggested that whatever had happened to him it was something fairly dramatic: but what was it? My question was not to be solved merely by buying a paper, for I spoke scarcely a word of Spanish. There was only one way to solve the problem; I bought the newspaper anyway, then went into a bookshop and bought a Spanish-English dictionary. Then I settled down on a bench in the Ramblas, in the mild afternoon sunshine; I had, I recall, great hopes that the news would be that Verwoerd had been discovered in bed with a dark lady of advanced tastes running to whips, chains and a great quantity of brass-studded black leather. A word at a time, I worked out the truth, which was that that wicked man had been assassinated in the very Chamber of the South African Parliament.

I inspect the afternoon papers warily: I still speak no Spanish, and the purchase of a dictionary every fourteen years would begin to prove costly after a time. The first thing I notice about the papers, however, is not their headlines but their number, and if I did speak Spanish I would also note that the freedom of comment they contain is very considerably greater than on my previous visit.

The political transformation of Iberia is one of the most remarkable and heartening stories of the postwar world, and it is heartening for a particularly modern reason. Apologists for the tyrannies of the twentieth century are much given to arguing that whatever the nature of the regime being de-

fended – its oppressions, its cruelties, its arbitrariness, its un-
acceptability to those who live in freedom – it enjoys popular
support at home. The evidence for this claim is its apparent
stability and endurance, which cannot, the apologists claim,
be based only on force. The claim would be obvious nonsense
even if it were not publicly disproved every few years, sometimes with a great deal of violence; the Hungarian Revolution
of 1956, the 'Czech Spring' of 1968 and the Polish strikes of
1980 were all very different phenomena in terms of the course
of events, but in each the same welcome demonstration was at
the heart of the uprising – the demonstration that the regime
against which the uprising was directed enjoyed no popular
support at all.

The same was shown to be true at the time of the bloodless
revolution in Portugal in 1974 and in the more slowly unfolding events that followed the death of Franco in Spain the next
year. In the first, a dictatorial regime which had ruled without
a break and without serious challenge for more than four
decades vanished literally overnight into the oblivion of
history; in the second, there was never the slightest possibility
that Francoism would survive its founder's death, nor did it,
and the transition from a shoddy, aimless and run-down au-
tarchy to a true parliamentary democracy was made with far
less difficulty than could have been guessed at.

Perhaps Franco thought that, like El Cid, he could continue
to lead his country sitting dead but upright in the saddle; if so,
he was mistaken, and in Barcelona I can see nothing to mark
his rule but the name-plates on the Avenida del Generalísimo
Franco, which in any case is invariably known as the Diagonal,
and weatherbeaten posters announcing a mass for the soul of
Adolf Hitler, doubtless organized by a few mouldering ir-
reconcilables among the remnants of Franco's army. Before
the week is out I shall have seen the afternoon papers carry the
results of the Portuguese and West German elections; on that
day, fourteen years ago, news in Spain of the free choice of
their political leaders by the people of another country would

have stirred longings in many a Spanish heart, as indeed, I dare say, did the assassination of Verwoerd itself, which must have been a grim *memento mori* for Franco, and for all the other rulers who govern without the consent of the governed, though not, I continue to be certain, for ever.

Barcelona recalls a phrase, somewhere in a Saki short story, about a country which 'produces more history than it can consume locally'. Catalonia's obstinate refusal to consider itself part of Spain is a good deal more tenaciously rooted than the show, largely for the benefit of the tourists, that Venice makes of still being the Serene Republic. Catalan is to Castilian Spanish what Venetian is to Italian, except that more people speak Catalan, and its relationship to the mother-tongue (or sister-tongue, as both Catalans and Venetians would insist) is more distant. This, incidentally, has the effect of rendering Spanish phrase-books virtually useless in Barcelona, where trying to get about with one is liable to make the visitor suspect that he has gone as mad as Don Quixote, for all that the Knight of the Woeful Countenance called Barcelona 'a refuge for foreigners'. Venetian may suddenly shove an x, a letter unknown to Italian, into an otherwise normally intelligible word, but Catalan is full of words that bear no etymological similarity to Spanish at all.

'*Cerrado* – closed', mutters the Anglophone tourist, trying to commit the Spanish word to memory. Then he tries to enter a shop at siesta-time and finds that the closed door bears the legend '*Tancat*'. A few experiences like that, and I begin to be almost relieved when I see, as I do in neon lights, wherever I go, a word that now seems to be a world-wide Open Sesame, as it will apparently fit without difficulty into any language: Bingo.

It is come to this? Is the heroine-city of the Spanish Civil War, the one centre that fought for the Republic against both Franco and the Communists, to line up with the rest of the world, eyes down, and pay homage to catatonia? It brings to mind Forster on India:

What an apotheosis! Last comer to the drab nineteenth-century sisterhood! Waddling in at this hour of the world to take her seat! She, whose only peer was the Holy Roman Empire, she shall rank with Guatemala and Belgium perhaps!

No, there is none that shall escape the contagion; all the world shall be one, not in love or brotherhood, or even in war and destruction, but in covering numbers on a board with counters, and crying, at intervals, 'Shake the bag!'

Fortunately, there is more than that to be seen. A first attempt to walk right along the Diagonal collapses in ignominious recriminations against maps without a scale; the street is six miles long. But before I retreat I have noted the beauty of this sprawling city, the elegant breadth of its avenues, the harmony of its layout beside which Paris seems lifeless, the extraordinary courtesy of its motorists, waving pedestrians across the road even when the traffic-lights tell the drivers that *they* may proceed.

Barcelona, too, may well be the most literate city in the world; every few yards there is a bookstall, and most of these sell real books as well as pulp novels and magazines. The magazines provide further evidence that the harlot's cry from street to street is the same the world over; the language may be Spanish, but the sprawling thighs and the elephantiacal breasts are identical to those in London, Paris and New York. Spain, however, has one variation that I have not previously encountered; here is a paperback edition of *Dr Zhivago*, sternly labelled – I spell out the legend as laboriously as I did the news of Verwoerd's death all those years ago – as not for sale to anyone under eighteen. What on earth is there, can there be, in Pasternak's masterpiece to warrant such restricted sales? I look more closely: the book is one of a series called 'Porno versions of famous films'. Pasternak's unhappy love has died twice indeed:

One day Lara went out and did not come back. She must have been arrested in the street, as so often happened in those days, and she died or vanished somewhere, forgotten as a nameless number on a list which later was mislaid, in one of the innumerable mixed or women's concentration camps in the north.

The porno version of *Dr Zhivago* was on sale in the Ramblas, where I had once played my game with the newspaper and the dictionary; it is Barcelona's most splendid and most human thoroughfare, falling gently, like some great river through a series of locks, from the Plaza Cataluña to the waterfront, its broad central pavement crowded with flower stalls and pet shops by day and cafés by night, and impassable at the weekends, when the whole town turns out to stroll, arm in arm, down this royal mile.

Royal and dirty, for Barcelona may well be the grimiest city in Europe; at any rate I have seen nothing to touch it in that respect outside India. Barcelona's Gran Teatro del Liceo fronts on to the Ramblas; I walk past it three times – down, up, down – before I find it, unable as I am to believe that this filthy aperture can really be the main entrance of the opera house in Spain's second city. Only inside the San José market does a visitor leave Barcelona's dirt behind, and there it is like walking into a Matisse. There are huge mounds of apples, green and red, peppers likewise, cucumbers and oranges, melons and bananas; great banks of nuts, walls of beef, seas of flowers; one mighty avenue – the Diagonal of the market – devoted to fish, laid out in giant wheels and squares and wavy lines, all of it lying on glittering beds of crushed ice, and in the case of the lobsters, demonstrating with the twitch of a claw that they are as fresh as the vendors claim.

From the Ramblas to the Gothic Quarter, centre of a most ungothic trade in digital watches, pocket calculators and cameras. But there, too, is the Cathedral, Gothic within and without to the most casual glance, its chief glory the carved canopies over the choir-stalls. As I leave, there is a sight that holds me motionless, as did that of the Florentina surreptitiously comparing her palm with the sixteenth-century cheiromantic engraving in the showcase of the astrological exhibition. A girl comes through the swing door of the Cathedral carrying a letter, the envelope open; her casualness is clearly, almost painfully, assumed, and she belies it by looking hurriedly around to see if she is observed. Then she moves swiftly to the font, crosses herself, dips two fingers in the water, runs them round the adhesive on the envelope, seals it firmly, crosses herself again and hurries out. What is in the letter that Heaven's aid is called for to speed it on its way? An application for a job? Acceptance of a proposal of marriage? A plea for forgiveness? An ultimatum to a dallying lover?

At the waterfront, I must call it a day, though I have seen nothing yet of Barcelona's chief glory, which must wait until tomorrow. But the Columbus statue, standing on a mighty pillar, is a good enough spot at which to turn back, for almost beneath his outstretched arm as he points is the reconstruction, to its exact size, of the *Santa Maria*. It is impossible not to be moved by the thought of this tiny cockle-shell and the madman on its bridge who did not understand, and would not listen to those who tried to explain the point to him, that if you sailed to the edge of the world, traversing an unknown sea to find an unknown land, you would fall off.

It is as difficult for modern man to think himself back to a world in which a different cosmology ruled as it is for a literate adult to remember a time before he could read or write. And the courage of Columbus is greater than that of Galileo a century later, for recantation would save the scientist, and in the event did, whereas if the mariner was wrong and his mutinous crew right, nothing would save any of them. But he was not wrong.

It is beginning to get dark, and the lights of Montjuich are beginning to sparkle high above the city. Back to the hotel, distinctly less ritzy than its name; the bedroom carpet in my room is worn threadbare in places, and beside the bed right into a hole. Notices displayed in prominent positions explain that a comprehensive redecoration and modernization is in progress, for the inconvenience of which the understanding of the amiable clientele is requested; but the notices themselves are suspiciously grubby, and there is not a paint-pot or a carpenter to be seen anywhere.

MONDAY, OCTOBER 6TH

I am here for the music; but to visit Barcelona and ignore Gaudí would be like going to Milan to sell ball-bearings and coming back well satisfied with the results but without seeing the 'Last Supper'. Gaudí is in architecture what in biology and zoology is called a sport: he came, stylistically speaking, from nowhere, and went nowhere, founding no school and leaving no lasting influence. Moreover, his fame rests on an astonishingly small output; Barcelona, his home and the centre of his work, contains only a handful of completed buildings, and his unfinished and unfinishable masterpiece, the Temple of the Holy Family. (It was in Barcelona, too, that he achieved the distinction of his death; Gaudí must be the only famous man to have died after being run over by a tram.)

First, to the Paseo de Gracia, where it is still warm enough, even this late in the year, to precede the expedition by sipping a cup of coffee at a pavement café: at No. 43 stands the Casa Battló, and at No. 92 the Casa Milà. 'Stands' is the wrong word; 'wavers' would be more appropriate, for there is scarcely a straight line to be seen in either building, and the crazy skyline of the Casa Battló in particular, with chimney-pots leaning in every direction like a convocation of drunkards, looks like something out of *The Cabinet of Dr Caligari*. And indeed of much worse films; there is a cinematic cliché in the representation of a dream, in which, just before the sleeper awakes, everything begins to shiver and ripple, like a sequence shot under water. That is brought to mind even more vividly here.

I have not been inside a Gaudí building, and there may be

drawbacks; are the interior walls and ceilings as irregular as the outside? And if so, would it be possible to live undisturbed there? The Casa Battló is a block of flats, so there must be an answer; I did once hear, from a mutual friend, of a man who lived in a Gaudí flat, but the only item reported – piquant enough, to be sure – was that his lavatory was four feet wide and twenty-two feet long.

The colours in themselves are bizarre enough to stop the traffic, from which I am in any case in great peril, as the only vantage point for a photograph is in the middle of the road; weird blues and reds and yellows in a mixture that Disney would have thought extravagant. Gaudí's work is, literally, like nothing on earth, yet no one who looks at these buildings with an innocent eye, free of premeditated judgment informed by what architecture 'ought' to be, can fail to see that they are the work of a completely original genius, who built that way not to make himself notorious or *pour épater les bourgeois*, but because he was driven by a vision of what architecture might achieve. In that respect, he was doing exactly what the architects of Barcelona Cathedral were doing, driven as they were by their need to sing a hymn in stone to the greater glory of God.

But not only in that respect. Not long ago, there was a spirited newspaper correspondence in which a wondrous fool maintained that Bach's St Matthew Passion and B Minor Mass did not constitute evidence of Christian belief in the composer. The idea of Bach as a kind of musical barrister, willing to turn his hand to a bit of Christian liturgy without having any opinion of his own in the matter, and thus no less capable of knocking out an equally convincing chant for a muezzin or indeed a marching song for the National Secular Society, is a fine example of a particularly modern form of intellectual incapacity, and can be traced, as can so many modern aberrations, to the fundamental fear of feeling, and – even more acute – of *showing* feeling. It is easier to ward off the unfortunate consequences of feeling if that which gives rise to it can be intellectualized. But turning the B Minor into the equivalent of the more arid *jeux d'esprit* of Erik Satie is about the most extreme form of this defence I have yet encountered.

I wonder what that correspondent would make, or does make, of Gaudí's Holy Family, and indeed of its extraordinary fate. It lies north of the Diagonal, in an unfashionable quarter of the city; soon, as I walk towards it, I catch sight of one of its spires, with a glittering wheel on top, and the cliché comes to life even more vividly than it did on the Paseo de Gracia: I really could not believe my eyes. Then I turn the last corner, and it lies before me, in all its lunatic majesty. Four stupendous towers rear to the sky, honeycombed with apertures as though monster science-fiction moths have been at them, and each crowned with a similar wheel. Below, what may be the basis of the nave, though it is impossible to be sure what any part of this astounding structure is supposed to be, takes the form of another series of smaller towers, no less eccentric in shape. In the brilliant sunshine, the whole thing appears to be a dream, and as I look up to the arm of the giant crane that towers even above the spires themselves, and which seems so frail that a puff of wind might blow it over, the feeling is strengthened by the sight of tiny figures balanced on it, insects crawling out along the cross-bar.

On the ground, chaos is come again. Enormous piles of stone and rock lie ready to be put in place, just as soon as somebody decides what place they should be put in. Lesser cranes lift bits of wall or arch, apparently at random, and put them down no less haphazardly; it is as though God has been given a Meccano set for Christmas and cannot contain his impatience long enough to read the instructions before starting to play with it. But the trouble is that there *are* no instructions; there is a model of what the finished building is supposed to look like, though it is impossible to say how closely the work is following it, and equally impossible to say how closely it *should* be followed, for the plans left by Gaudí were incomplete and inadequate – some reports say there were no plans at all, though I cannot bring myself to believe that he really was making it up as he went along like Fellini directing a film – and whether the workmen on the site know what they are supposed to be doing, and whose supposition is involved anyway, are mysteries that themselves go far towards explaining why, though the work was restarted forty years ago (the site having been abandoned for fourteen years after Gaudí's death in 1926), it gives no sign of having made any progress in all that time. Perhaps there are rival groups of workmen, each directed by an overseer with his own view of what the building should look like, so that the pieces put down on the board by one group of players by day are removed to another place, or taken off the board entirely, by another group by night.

It will never be finished; if ever there was an example of Robert Louis Stevenson's assertion that it is better to travel hopefully than to arrive, it is here, in the determination of men with the faith of ordinary human vision to press on towards an ever-receding goal set by a man with a vision of the divine. Which is an excellent formula for the development of the soul, but not so good as a method of forwarding work on a building site.

I pay my few pesetas and enter the site. I can ascend one of the towers by a staircase, the other by a lift. I look up to the spire disappearing into the sky, and take the lift. Emerging, I am still at least sixty feet from the top; a spiral staircase leads upwards. Half-way up that, I step through one of the embrasures on to a flat buttress, and make the mistake of looking down; I am at once hit by an attack of vertigo so powerful that I am frozen to the stone in terror, though I could not fall off if I wanted to, as the buttress is guarded by substantial ledges on both sides. Years ago, in Bangkok, I climbed the Temple of the Emerald Buddha. The steps, on the outside of the building, are narrow – as I recall, no more than the width of a single brick – but because of the somewhat pyramidical shape of the building, the climber is thrown forward against its bulk, and its solidity seems to hold him in its reassuring grip. At the top, there is a platform, and after admiring the extensive view from it, I decided it was time to descend. At that moment, I realized that I *couldn't*; to step out, away from the safety of the building, on to those terrible ledges, which now seemed to have shrunk to the thickness of a razor blade, was impossible. I stepped back on to the platform and examined it for an easier descent. There was none; what goes up must come down, and the same way, too. There was a constant stream of ascending tourists appearing over the edge of the platform, and another stream vanishing over it in the other direction; I alone seemed doomed to spend the rest of my life up here. I could not ask for help, and could not see what help was possible anyway; nobody could carry me down, and although the Bangkok fire brigade could no doubt send a ladder, I was not sure how I could summon them, let alone explain my problem. Half a dozen times I approached the edge, only to be beaten back by dizzified terror. Then I realized that the light was fading from the sky, and the number of climbers coming up had fallen sharply, as had the number of those still on the platform admiring the view. It was now or never; offering a prayer to Buddha (who else?) I turned out my feet like Charlie Chaplin and stepped over the edge. Very slowly, shrinking back against the building every second, I walked down the terrible precipice, and live to tell the tale.

To tell it, that is, on a ledge at the top of Gaudí's masterpiece, from which the ground can scarcely be imagined, let alone seen:

> The crows and choughs that wing the midway air
> Show scarce so gross as beetles; half way down
> Hangs one that gathers samphire, dreadful trade!
> Methinks he seems no bigger than his head.
> The fishermen that walk upon the beach
> Appear like mice, and yond tall anchoring bark
> Almost too small for sight. The murmuring surge,
> That on the unnumbered idle pebbles chafes,

Cannot be heard so high. I'll look no more,
Lest my brain turn, and the deficient sight
Topple down headlong.

I inch my way back to safety, and descend by the lift. A last look round the site, and a vow: if it is another fourteen years before I return to Barcelona, I shall hurry, the morning after my arrival, to Gaudí's impossible dream, and try to spot the bits that have been added since 1980, if any. Meanwhile, the first concert awaits.

The Palau de la Musica Catalana is Barcelona's equivalent of the Albert Hall and the Sacré Cœur, and to my eye seems to be in a position to give both a long start and an easy beating. Beside it, the most extravagant conceits of Gaudí resemble the most ordered Ben Nicolson; inside and out, the structure of the Palau vanishes from sight and from mind beneath the almost incredible profusion of decoration.

The exterior is smothered in monstrous groups, like Victorian allegory-paintings turned to three-dimensional stone, or in mosaics depicting further symbolic episodes in the life of art and carried out in a profligate variety of colours so vivid and inharmonious that the authorities ought to issue warnings, akin to those put out on the B.B.C. at the time of an eclipse of the sun, pointing out the danger of looking at the thing with the naked eye, and the mortal danger of doing so through a telescope. Among the allegorical statues and the mosaic allegories and the gargoyles and stained-glass windows and heraldic devices and portrait busts, rows of columns run – gallop – round the building, which in so far as it can be seen at all beneath the decoration, is made of brick so red that, caught by the setting sun, it must have unwary strangers calling out the Barcelona fire-engines three times a week.

And that is only the outside. Inside, lunacy rules in an anarchy of colour, design and materials so extreme that the building looks as though it will fly apart into its constituent atoms at any moment. There is hardly a square inch of wall, or for that matter floor or ceiling, that is not decorated in the most high-fantastical style. The pillars are thick with encrusted decoration; the balusters are giant barley-sugar sticks; the roof of the entrance hall is smothered in a glittering mosaic pattern of hypnotic garishness; the very treads of the staircase are covered throughout their length with embossed tiles; the lamps are a riot of metal vine leaves, fruit and coloured glass; every flat stretch of wall bears a mural, not so much *trompe l'œil* as *casse l'œil*; and all this is to be found before the visitor enters the auditorium itself.

Out of the wall on one side of the proscenium arch grows a huge stone tree, amid the branches of which nestles a gigantic bust, looking remarkably like Elgar but said to be of a Spanish composer of popular music called Clavé. On the other side, surmounted by equally enormous stone horses, is another bust, said to be of Beethoven, but looking much more like Sir Harold Wilson crowned with laurels. Between the two, stretching right round the back of the stage, is a terrifying frieze, consisting of eighteen busts of women tapering into mosaic representations of eighteen different flowing dresses, looking like the final closing-down sale at Gorringe's. These ladies are said to be 'the eighteen muses of music', whoever those might be; most of them are playing a musical instrument, though one – the seventh from the left – appears to have in her hand nothing but a rock, which she is brandishing as though she is about to hurl it at the conductor. (Desmond Shawe-Taylor once wrote of the depressing effect, at Royal Philharmonic Society concerts in the Albert Hall, of the bust of Beethoven in the centre of the platform behind the orchestra, 'which one always feels is listening – or, worse still, not listening'.)

I hope she will not throw the rock at Rudolf Barshai, who is conducting the Israel Chamber Orchestra, though in truth there is nothing very impressive about the performances. Haydn, Shostakovich and Bach; the original programme offered the Third Brandenburg, that work so dear to my youth, but in the event they play two of the Contrapuncti from The Art of Fugue instead. The texture of the orchestration used, however, is far too thick; I remember a performance of the whole work in the Festival Hall by a nonet from the Berlin Philharmonic, and thought then that it offered the best balance I had yet heard in any version of the work, and one which came closest to offering a convincing solution to the mystery of what Bach intended it to sound like. Not much sparkle any-where else in the evening, either, though the concert does provide one fascinating extra-musical experience. It is a warm night; the hall is without air conditioning, and gets very stuffy. Many of the women in the audience (almost everybody is Spanish – I think I may be the only foreigner here) have brought fans, and ply these vigorously. The fanners are im-mediately divided into two groups; those who fan in time to the music, and those who strive not to, achieving instead a kind of syncopation. Both groups have a hypnotic effect on a watcher from the balcony, and it is interesting to observe that the *rate* of the fanning is the same for both groups, in both cases being dictated by the tempo of the music; it is only the *rhythm* which divides them. Apart from the fans, I must make do, for memories, with the building itself (of which, incidentally, the guide-book says, with judicious understatement, that: 'The fantastic decoration is not the most ideal for putting us into a suitable frame of mind for penetrating the world of music'), which I finally decide might have been designed by Ludwig of Bavaria after a nightmare induced by eating too many peacocks at dinner.

TUESDAY, OCTOBER 7TH

This must be the least well publicized festival in Europe. There is hardly a poster to be seen anywhere in the city, and it would be easy to stay in Barcelona for a week without knowing that a festival was toward. The only really prominent evidence is a banner, crudely painted and obviously not part of the official publicity, strung across the Ramblas, and advertising to-night's 'Banal Concert'. I spotted this in the programme brochure, and quietly consulted a Spanish dictionary to make sure that the Spanish *banal* means the same as the English: it does. But what *is* a banal concert – in any sense, that is, that would make it a matter of pride on the part of the promoters rather than of dismissive criticism on the part of the reviewers?

There is only one way to find out, so here I am, wedged into a heaving crowd trying to get into the venue, a night club called La Paloma. Alas, the banality is in evidence early; the evening consists of something like a lecture on the life and art of an actress and singer called Elsa de Gabrielli, illustrated with creaking film and dreadful singing and acting. To announce in advance that banality is to be the theme of the proceedings is certainly disarming; but not disarming enough to overcome the fact that the promise is all too handsomely kept, and I flee after less than an hour.

WEDNESDAY, OCTOBER 8TH

I think I have discovered an important new law of economics: in any industrialized country, the variety of banks increases in inverse ratio to the level of prosperity. Spain seems to be almost entirely composed of banks, whereas Germany seems to have far fewer, with Britain somewhere between. I have not yet thought of an explanation of this phenomenon.

To the Picasso Museum, particularly rich in his early work. Very early indeed, some of it, including a school grammar, the margins of which are decorated with rude sketches of teacher. On the way, I pass a cinema showing a horror film: '*Los ovni*', says the poster outside, '*invaden la tierra desde sus base de las Bahamas.*' I wonder they didn't stay there, particularly since it has now started to rain heavily.

Things are definitely looking up. Back at the hotel there is a message from Godfrey Smith; he and Mary have arrived by car from France. He is writing a travel article on Barcelona for the *Sunday Times*; I am expecting them, but he wasn't sure, before I left London, when they would be arriving. We arrange to dine together tomorrow night. This is good news; Godfrey is almost the traditional genial fat man, not only witty in himself but the cause that wit is in other men, and the paucity of Barcelona's musical fare suddenly ceases to matter.

In the evening to the Monastery of Pedralbes, far out along the Diagonal. The moment I enter the enormous basilica, reminiscent of that mysterious *cathédrale engloutie* on Torcello, I feel that things are shortly going to start looking up musically as well, and so it proves. A harpsichord recital in a building so vast (when the lights dim, the roof disappears altogether) is an improbable thought, but Kenneth Gilbert, though he adds to the improbability with the lightness of his touch, still manages to make the sound hover over the audience rather than vanish into the huge spaces above us. Besides, his programme is largely composed of Rameau and Couperin, and the freshness and vigour of this music, from the age of the Grand Monarque at its best, would have made even Beethoven seem clumsy, and the Romantics quite impossible. Sydney Smith described the sound of a harpsichord as that of 'a piano which has succeeded in getting out of its skin and sitting in its bones'. But why do all extended works for this instrument sound like sets of variations? And why do they always sound as though they are about to become the Harmonious Blacksmith?

The harpsichord stands directly before the High Altar, its shadow rearing up on the paintings behind; the side-chapels are used to accommodate the audience overflow, for the place is packed. Packed, moreover, largely with the young, which in turn accentuates the fact, noticeable from the start, that this is the most informally dressed festival of all. So far, there has not been a single dinner-jacket, and truth to tell not many ties; and here jeans predominate. It makes a pleasant contrast with the ubiquitous evening dress of Salzburg, though that, after all, makes a no less pleasant contrast with the informality of Barcelona.

THURSDAY, OCTOBER 9TH

The best is last; Mozart followed by Godfrey and Mary. The Mozart is provided in the Palau, which has not become any less amazing a building in the interim; more, if anything, for it now occurs to me that this is what it would be like to be cooked into a batch of marzipan. The pianist is Friedrich Gulda, who has aroused my suspicions in advance by refusing to announce his programme, saying that he will leave his selection of works to the inspiration of the moment. That is what Christa Ludwig did at Hohenems with her Schubert recital; but she was substituting at the last minute, whereas Gulda has been down to play from the start. Besides, inspiration is all very well, but what about rehearsal?

His appearance on the platform makes the heart sink, particularly as the lights, when he comes out, are turned up rather than down. He is dressed in baggy black velvet trousers, no jacket, an electric-blue shirt fastened at the neck with a silver brooch, and a khaki-coloured hat, roughly the shape of the old army forage-cap, decorated with beads; his hair hangs down, long and straggly, behind it. What kind of clown have we here?

Within a dozen bars, the answer is plain: *cucullus non facit monachum*, for Gulda's motley is the outer man only, and inside there is a devoted and deeply serious servant of Mozart, with a complete technical mastery and a fully Mozartian dash, crispness and sparkle, always conscious of the depth beneath the brilliance. The acoustics of the Palau are brutal for a piano, but he makes it sing to eternal harmonies, and I can detect a serenity, an understanding, that goes beyond his communion with the composer; in the C minor sonata, K. 457, it becomes almost explicit, touching levels of feeling and beauty that turn him into a servant not only of Mozart but of whatever it was that Mozart served. In the interval, he changes his shirt – for one of rainbow hue; but by now I can forgive him anything.

Dinner at the Quo Vadis, in the Calle Carmen; I suppose

there is a Carmen Street in every city in Spain (and two in Seville?). I always have to make a conscious effort to remember that the opera is by a Frenchman, and that he invented the word *toreador* for no better reason than that neither of the two correct words – *matador* and *torero* – would fit the rhythm. The Smiths are in fine form, having had a splendid time in France, and so is the chef; the grilled prawns have clearly come straight from the San José Market, and the live section of the fish display, too.

FRIDAY, OCTOBER 10TH

Buying a souvenir for Arianna at the airport, a pretty little inlaid box, I get a shining-new fifty-peseta piece in my change. 'Ah,' says the girl at the kiosk as she gives it to me, '*del Rey*.' *Del Rey?* It can only mean 'of the king', but what does *that* mean? I inspect the coin, and all is clear. 'Whose is this image and superscription?' Why, that of Juan Carlos; I conclude that the fifty-peseta piece has hitherto circulated only in the old issues with Franco's head, and that the new ones are now coming out, as the twenty-five-peseta ones have been for some time, with the king's. It is a pleasantly symbolic note on which to end a visit to the new, free Spain.

The homecoming is less pleasant; London is thirty degrees colder than Barcelona.

The Luck of the Irish

This must be the fourteenth time I have been to Wexford. The thirteenth? The fifteenth? Just as, at Wexford itself, the days and nights blur into each other with less distinction made between them than at any other place on earth with the exception of Las Vegas, so memories of my annual visits have become one extended memory. It is not just a matter of assigning particular moments to particular years, like Americans, back home after doing Europe in three weeks, unable to agree whether the place with the Eiffel Tower was Brussels or London; I have long since stopped trying to remember which was The Year of the Grape-Lady, The Year of the Police Raid, The Year of the Disastrous *Oberon*, The Year There Was No Boat.

But I can remember at once that 1979 was The Year of the Missing Lemon Juice. The Theatre Royal in Wexford holds 440; it was completely full that night, so there are, allowing for a few who have already died (it is not true, though it might well have been, that some died of laughter at the time), hardly more than four hundred people who now share, to the end of their lives, an experience from which the rest of the world, now and for ever, is excluded. When the last of us dies, the experience will die with us, for although it is already enshrined in legend, no one who was not an eye witness will ever really understand what we felt. Certainly I am aware that these words cannot convey more than the facts, and the facts, as so often and most particularly in this case, are only part, and a small part, too, of the whole truth. But I must try.

The opera that night was *La Vestale*, by Spontini. It has been described as 'a poor man's *Norma*', since it tells, in music and drama much inferior to Bellini's, of a vestal virgin who betrays her charge for love. It was revived for Maria Callas, but otherwise figures rarely in the repertoire of the world's leading opera houses. But it is part of Wexford's business to revive operas which other opera houses and festivals unjustly neglect, and I have been repeatedly surprised in a most pleasant manner to discover much of interest and pleasure in some of them; Lalo's *Le Roi d'Ys*, for instance, or Prokoviev's *The Gambler*, or Bizet's *Les Pêcheurs des Perles*. (The Year of the Disastrous *Oberon* was a notable exception, though even then mainly because of the terrible production rather than the opera itself. The Year of the Grape-Lady was the year I found myself lolling in an armchair after a gigantic lunch, while the most beautiful woman in Ireland dropped luscious black grapes, one by one, into my mouth. The Year There Was No Boat was the year in which Mr Fletcher, who runs the lunch-cruising excursion from nearby New Ross was refitting his vessel and therefore not operating the cruise. Of The Year of the Police Raid I shall speak in due course.)

Well, in 1979 it was *La Vestale*. The set for Act I of the opera consisted of a platform laid over the stage, raised about a foot at the back and sloping evenly to the footlights. This was meant to represent the interior of the Temple where burned the sacred flame, and had therefore to look like marble; the designer had achieved a convincing alternative by covering the raised stage in Formica. But the Formica was slippery; to avoid the risk of a performer taking a tumble, designer and stage manager had between them discovered that an ample sprinkling of lemon juice would make the surface sufficiently sticky to provide a secure foothold. The story now forks; down one road, there lies the belief that the member of the stage staff whose duty it was to sprinkle the lifesaving liquid, and who had done so without fail at rehearsal and at the earlier performances (this was the last one of the Festival), had simply forgotten. Down the other branch in the road is a much more attractive rumour: that the theatre charlady, inspecting the premises in the afternoon, had seen to her horror and indignation that the stage was covered in the remains of some spilt liquid, and, inspired by professional pride, had thereupon set to and given it a good scrub and polish all over.

The roads now join again, for apart from the superior charm of the second version, it makes no difference what the explanation was. What matters is what happened.

What happened began to happen very early. The hero of the opera strides on to the stage immediately after the curtain has gone up. The hero strode; and instantly fell flat on his back. There was a murmur of sympathy and concern from the audience for his embarrassment and for the possibility that he might have been hurt; it was the last such sound that was to be heard that night, and it was very soon to be replaced by sounds of a very different nature.

The hero got to his feet, with considerable difficulty, and, having slid some way down the stage in falling, proceeded to stride up-stage to where he should have been in the first place; he had, of course, gone on singing throughout, for the music had not stopped. Striding up-stage, however, was plainly more difficult than he had reckoned on, for every time he took a step and tried to follow it with another, the foot with which he had taken the first proceeded to slide down-stage again, swiftly followed by its companion; he may not have known it, but he was giving a perfect demonstration of what is called *marcher sur place*, a graceful manoeuvre normally used in mime, and seen at its best in the work of Marcel Marceau.

Finding progress uphill difficult, indeed impossible, the hero wisely decided to abandon the attempt and stay where he was, singing bravely on, no doubt calculating that, since the stage was brightly lit, the next character to enter would notice him and adjust his own movements accordingly. So it proved, in a sense at least, for the next character to enter was the hero's trusted friend and confidant, who, seeing his hero further down-stage than he was supposed to be, loyally decided to join him there. Truth to tell, he had little choice, for from the moment he had stepped on to the stage he had begun to slide downhill, arms semaphoring, like Scrooge's clerk on the way home to his Christmas dinner. His downhill progress was arrested by his fetching up against his friend with a thud; this, as it happened, was not altogether inappropriate, as the opera called for them to embrace in friendly greeting at that point. It did not, however, call for them, locked in each other's arms and propelled by the impetus of the friend's descent, to careen helplessly further down-stage with the evident intention of going straight into the orchestra pit with vocal accompaniment – for the hero's aria had, on the arrival of his companion, been transformed into a duet.

On the brink of ultimate disaster they managed to arrest their joint progress to destruction and, working their way along the edge of the stage like mountaineers seeking a route round an unbridgeable crevasse, most gallantly began, with infinite pain and by a form of progress most aptly described in the title of Lenin's famous pamphlet, *Four Steps Forward, Three Steps Back*, to climb up the terrible hill. It speedily became clear that this hazardous ascent was not being made simply from a desire to retain dramatic credibility; it had a much more practical object. The only structure breaking the otherwise all too smooth surface of the stage was a marble pillar, a yard or so high, on which there burned the sacred flame of the rite. This pillar was embedded firmly in the stage, and it had obviously occurred to both mountaineers at once that if they could only reach it it would provide a secure base for their subsequent operations, since if they held on to it for dear life they would at any rate be safe from any further danger of sliding downhill and/or breaking their necks.

It was soon borne in upon them that they had undertaken a labour of truly Sisyphean proportions, and would have been most heartily pardoned by the audience if they had abandoned the librettist's words at this point, and fitted to the music instead the old moral verse:

> The heights by great men reached and kept,
> Were not attained by sudden flight;
> But they, while their companions slept,
> Were toiling upwards in the night.

By this time the audience – all 440 of us – were in a state of such abandon with laughter that several of us felt that if this were to continue a moment longer we would be in danger of doing ourselves a serious internal mischief; little did we know that the fun was just beginning, for shortly after Mallory and Irvine reached their longed-for goal, the chorus entered, and instantly flung themselves *en masse* into a very freely choreographed version of *Les Patineurs*, albeit to the wrong music. The heroine herself, the priestess Giulia, with a survival instinct strong enough to suggest that she would be the one to get close to should any reader of these lines happen to be shipwrecked along with the Wexford opera company, skated into the wings and kicked her shoes off and then, finding on her return that this had hardly improved matters, skated back to the wings and removed her tights as well.

Now, however, the singing never having stopped for a moment, the chorus had come to the same conclusion as had the hero and his friend, namely that holding on to the holy pillar was the only way to remain upright and more or less immobile. The trouble with this conclusion was that there was only one such pillar on the stage, and it was a small one; as the cast crowded round it, it seemed that there would be some very unseemly brawling among those seeking a hand-hold, a foothold, even a bare finger-hold, on this tiny island of security in the terrible sea of impermanence. By an instinctive understanding of the principles of co-operation, however, they decided the matter without bloodshed; those nearest the pillar clutched it, those next nearest clutched the clutchers, those farther away still clutched those, and so on until, in a kind of daisy-chain that snaked across the stage, everybody was accommodated.

The condition of the audience was now one of fully extended hysteria, which was having the most extraordinary effect – itself intensifying the audience's condition – on the orchestra. At Wexford, the orchestra pit runs under the stage; only a single row of players – those at the edge of the pit nearest the audience, together, of course, with the conductor – could see what was happening on the stage. The rest realized that *something* out of the ordinary was going on up there, and would have been singularly dull of wit if they had not, for many members of the audience were now slumped on the floor weeping helplessly in the agony of their mirth, and although the orchestra at Wexford cannot see the stage, it can certainly see the auditorium.

Theologians tell us that the delights of the next world are eternal. Perhaps; but what is certain is that all earthly ones, alas, are temporary, and duly, after giving us a glimpse of the more enduring joy of Heaven that must have strengthened the devout in their faith and caused instant conversion among many of the unbelievers, the entertainment came to an end when the first act of the opera did so, amid such cheering as I had never before heard in an opera house, and can never hope to hear again. In the interval before Act II, a member of the production staff walked back and forth across the stage, sprinkling it with the precious nectar, and we knew that our happiness was at an end. But he who, after such happiness, would have demanded more, would be greedy indeed, and most of us were content to know that, for one crowded half-hour, we on honeydew had fed, and drunk the milk of Paradise.

Beside that, The Year of the Police Raid is small beer, but it was not without its own contribution to Wexford's happiness. When the theatre acquired a bar it was run on the very sensible principle of providing only champagne, red and white wine and – for the few teetotallers who would come to Wexford –

soft drinks. What had not, it transpired, been provided was a licence, and in the first interval that year, the Gardai arrived and began to take the names of the drinkers who were doing their drinking on uncanonical premises. I suddenly realized that if only I could ensure that I was among the booked, I might, with real luck, find myself being prosecuted on the almost incredible charge of drinking in Wexford.

In vain, however, did I station myself in front of the senior police officer present, taking ostentatious gulps at my contraband, and I soon discovered why; the Bishop, mindful of his representative role in the care of his flock, had insisted on taking on his own shoulders the burden of suffering, and the police, furnished with a real live Bishop booked for life imprisonment and a flogging, were hardly going to bother with me. Nothing more was heard of the business, of course, and by the following year the necessary licence had been acquired.

I should not have been surprised, for the drinking laws in Wexford have a life of their own; a good many Festivals before, I had been sipping a glass or two with an Irish Wexford-goer who had been born in the town, though he no longer lived there. After a time, he expressed himself bored with the hotel, and suggested we sallied forth in search of a fresh venue for our last nightcap. We did so, and he led the way – I had long since lost track of the hour – to a pub that was dark and shuttered, at the door of which he began, to my considerable alarm, a thunderous knocking. No response was forthcoming, which did not surprise me, but did him, for he abandoned the knocker and began, while my alarm turned to full-fledged terror, to rain a series of mighty kicks at the door instead. Eventually a light came on behind an upstairs window, which was thrown up, to disclose a head. I shrank into the shadows, for I could not but believe that the owner of the head was armed with a blunderbuss, which he would presently discharge in the direction of the noise, and certainly his first words – which were 'Who the hell's making that racket down there?' – did little to reassure me. My companion, however, merely replied, 'It's me, you old fool', whereat the publican put his nightcapped head right out of the window and peered. 'Oh, it's you, is it?' he said, in a slightly mollified tone. 'All right, wait there and I'll come and let you in.' The head vanished and the window was closed; feet could be heard descending the stairs. As they did so, my companion spoke what remain, a decade later, the most remarkable words I have ever heard in Wexford, or possibly anywhere: 'It's a fine thing', he said with genuine indignation in his voice, 'if a man can't get a drink in his native town *merely because it's half-past two in the morning.*'

Wexford can best be described as the place where that kind of thing can happen; and not only can happen, but does happen. It follows, therefore, that the frame of mind in which other festivals are approached will not do for Wexford; it demands a special attitude of its own, and I have just adopted the attitude in question, this Friday morning, as I set out on the first ritual of an annual expedition that is almost entirely composed of rituals.

The *second* ritual; the first has been going on for months – indeed, since the end of last year's Festival. I was introduced to Wexford by Alan Wood, a director of Guinness (Uncle Arthur provides one of the financial pillars that help to keep the roof on the enterprise, and the town at Festival-time is awash with the firm's personnel as well as its product), who was, and still is, in the habit of taking a party of friends there. Returning from my own first Wexford, in 1967, in a condition that was to be summed up years later, after *his* first visit, by Anthony Lewis, as 'groggy with joy', I began to spread the word that there are three days of unparalleled delight to be had in the bottom right-hand corner of Ireland every year in the late autumn. Before long, I had interested several of my friends sufficiently for them to want to come; in no time I, too, had gathered a group together, and in 1968 we went as a party to match Alan's. Alan's secretary instantly dubbed the two groups 'Woodtours' and 'Levintours' respectively, and ever since Alan and I have vied with each other like real travel agents to provide more and more facilities for our clients. Alan was a hard man to beat at the beginning, for he had the use of the Guinness private plane to carry Woodtours across.

As Levintours has grown over the years, so has the transport problem; even a Daimler will not accommodate us all now, and dawn sees me climbing into a minibus to collect the party of nine from all over London for conveyance to the airport. Protests and groans die away as the sky brightens and the bus fills up; there are four newcomers on the trip this year, their appetites whetted by months of hints, anecdote and instructions. The whetted appetites are slaked early, at any rate in the literal sense, for we combine with Woodtours for lunch at the Royal Hibernian Hotel in Dublin – the first joint meal of the Festival, but by no means the last. Volunteers to drive the minibus from Dublin to Wexford have already been accepted and briefed; the briefing consists only of an appeal to drink no more champagne before lunch than is compatible with their awful responsibility after. (Is it true – it is certainly *ben trovato* – that the breathalyzer limit in the Irish Republic is exactly twice what it is in Britain? Perhaps it only seems that way.)

The Hibernian has now been the scene of many a merriment of this kind, finest of which was the occasion on which the Guinness plane developed a technical hitch and Woodtours turned up three hours late. By the time they arrived, we were all in a distinctly Sardanapalian condition, made the more agreeable by the thought that the other lot would be lucky if there was anything for them but a few digestive biscuits. But this is Ireland, not Margate or Wolverhampton, and the Hibernian staff proceeded to serve them a lunch as elaborate as the one we were just finishing.

The Dublin lunch is a time for reunions; for many of us, Wexford is the only time we meet during the year, and the send-off lunch is the time for catching up. And also for reminding ourselves of the extraordinary nature, origins and quality of the Festival we are about to embark upon.

For a start, why Wexford? This town, of not many more than 10,000 inhabitants, has nothing in the way of a musical tradition, and not much reason for anybody to have heard of it in any connection. Cromwell slept here when he was in the Irish massacre business; John Redmond was born here; the mother of Thomas (*Lalla Rookh*) Moore lived here. And that was about all until Dr Tom Walsh woke up one day at the end of the 1940s and decided that the derelict Theatre Royal should be bought, smartened up and equipped with an annual international opera festival. I have never asked Tom what happened when he began to broach the idea in the town, and even if I did the kindly man would not tell me, claiming that he had forgotten. But I dare say many of those whose interest he tried to arouse backed nervously away from him, plainly terrified that he might bite them in the leg, with hideous consequences in the form of hydrophobia. That was certainly the experience of John Christie of Glyndebourne, another man who dreamed of founding an internationally famous opera festival, and woke to find it true, and I cannot believe that Wexford was any easier to convince. But these inspired madmen are the people who keep the world turning when the rest of its population want to give up and make it stop to let them off, and Tom Walsh, who had taken the precaution of biting himself in the leg before setting out to do the same to his town, saw his dream come true in 1951. He has watched it come true, year after year, ever since. There was an estrangement, the cause of which none can discover, between Tom and the Festival after he gave up the post of Director; but the gulf has long since been bridged, and every year for many years now Tom has presided benignly over the revels, his place in the front row of the balcony automatically reserved, and his smile as warm as a rainbow. He is greeted on every corner, as he goes about the town, though that is true, in a sense, of most of us, for Wexford is a place in which the regular festival-goer cannot walk a hundred yards without meeting an old friend or making a new one.

Meanwhile, we are still in Dublin, and there is the drive

south ahead of us. Woodtours pile into their cars and we into our green minibus, and we set off, with Tom Blumenau, one of the first-time Wexfordians, uncomplainingly at the wheel. If we get the timing right (and by now, after fourteen years, it is not difficult to do so) we should arrive in Wexford in time to change in a fairly leisurely manner and broach a bottle or two before setting off for the opera. The question that hangs over this part of the trip, though, is: what will the weather be like? We have had Wexfords drowned in monsoon rains from be-ginning to end, and Wexfords bathed likewise in pre-monsoon sunshine, and every variation and combination in between, even including, on one occasion, flurries of snow. (The worst monsoon version moved me to describe the opera-goers struggling along Main Street towards the opera house in the downpour as looking like salmon going up a leap, and at the end of the opera on the worst night of that year's visit Sydney Kentridge and I contemplated taking all our clothes off and *swimming* back to the car park and the minibus, while the rest of the party waited in the foyer for rescue.)

The sky is clear as we leave Dublin; it is clear all along the route; and when, out of the darkness, there appear the lights of Wexford, signalled by the harbour bridge, which is fairy-lit from end to end during the Festival, we can reasonably hope that it is going to stay clear until Monday.

The Talbot Hotel, which stands sentinel at the far end of the town as White's does at the hither end, and which is presided over by the genial Liam Lynch, as White's by the jovial John Small, is our headquarters this year as every year, and Paddy the head porter is, as ever, there to welcome us across the threshold and sort out the baggage. As ever, also, the hotel resembles a dangerously overcrowded madhouse, the foyers looking like the approach to Wembley Stadium at Cup Final time, and the harassed staff coping with astonishing aplomb but none the less looking likely to need a real madhouse by the time the Festival is over.

Wexford at Festival-time is an exceptionally attractive blend of the formal and the relaxed. I don't know why, when or how the tradition of evening dress for the opera grew up; it certainly could not have been there from the start, for the Wexford Festival did not begin to attract visitors from overseas in any numbers for some years, and in 1951, when the Festival was launched with Balfe's *The Rose of Castile*, there cannot have been a dozen dinner-jackets in the town. Today, evening dress is *de rigueur*, but the obligation is entirely self-imposed; obviously, no one would be turned away for breaking the imaginary sumptuary regulations, but there is not even a hint, as there is in, for instance, the Glyndebourne programme, that evening dress would be welcome, and I have yet to meet anyone connected with the administration of the Festival who has a view on the matter. Yet instinct, which has already told us that Wexford is not so much a festival as a party, tells us that we should salute the party spirit as well as the immense effort that goes into making this the most enjoyable Festival in Europe, and dress in our best party clothes.

The ladies of Levintours are therefore earnestly requested to bring three long dresses, one for each of the three evenings we spend at the opera, and are no less emphatically besought to ensure that each of the three is more beautiful than the other two, a requirement which, whatever Euclid and Aristotle might have had to say about its logic, has invariably been met by all those so instructed.

We gather in the lounge, looking like the famous description of the opening night of Beerbohm Tree's new theatre in the Haymarket, Her Majesty's: 'a scene of brilliancy, tempered by ladies'. It is at this point that I produce my collapsible opera-hat, which is, or at any rate soon will be, the last example in Europe of this useful device. I wear it only at Wexford, which is only right, as it was Wexford which gave it to me, some years ago, in return for the unremitting campaign I have waged, publicly and privately, ever since I returned from my first visit, to spread the news of the Festival and the joy it offers. But what with the hat, and my opera-cloak, I enjoy again, every time we pass beneath a street lamp on the way to the music, the sight of my silhouette going on before me like the opening of a film melodrama – a feeling much reinforced on this occasion when one of the occupants of a passing car, spotting me emerging from the shadows with my hat a-top and my cloak billowing behind me, emits a scream of 'It's Jack the Ripper!'

We march along Main Street in a body, and it is clear at once, as we pass the brightly lit shops, all dressed to kill for the Festival competition for the best window, that in the year just passed there has been another modest but measurable improvement in the standard of life in this brave little town. When I first started to come to Wexford, it was bitterly poor, and it is not exactly Eldorado even today, but every year now the townsfolk look smarter, the shops are brighter and better stocked, more new buildings have gone up and more old ones been repainted. Main Street itself boasts a brand new supermarket; let others sneer at supermarket shopping, for he who does so forgets, or more likely never knew, that the rise of the supermarket reflects an unprecedented kind of mass affluence. This can be seen in, apart from anything else, the lessening attraction of shop-service as a means of earning a living, and the fact that that affluence (hardly luxury, after all) has now reached Wexford is surely no more than what is due to Wexford's generosity in so devotedly supporting a Festival for which, supermarkets or no supermarkets, most of the inhabitants still cannot afford the tickets. Wexford builds and paints the scenery; acts as ushers and usherettes; staffs the administrative offices; raises money; provides most of the chorus. Without these unpaid efforts the Festival could not exist, and why the townspeople should bother is one of the many mysteries of the Wexford Festival, even more intractable of solution than the question of just how many public-houses there are in Main Street, a thoroughfare some 400 yards long: a question which had never been satisfactorily answered because all those who had set out to solve the problem had felt it incumbent upon them to take a drink in each one counted, so that no one had ever succeeded in reaching the end – until, that is, I went out one Festival very early on a Sunday morning, when even in Wexford the pubs are shut, and came back with the official census: there are nineteen hostelries in Main Street, eleven of them on the west side and eight on the east.

Well, the pubs in Main Street, as elsewhere in Wexford, are tonight alive to the sound of music, for just as the shops have their window-dressing contest, so the pubs have theirs for the best singing, and the judges can often be seen weaving their way from one to the next, to lend an ear to the customers' music and to take a glass to encourage them in their efforts. I suppose I make Wexford at Festival-time sound, on the part of both the visitors and the inhabitants, like a convocation of lapsed alcoholics. Such a conclusion would be unfair; the number of people I have actually seen drunk in the town is extraordinarily small, and I have never seen even one of these obstreperous with drink taken, which is a lot more than I have ever been able to say on my visits to Scottish Opera's performances in the Theatre Royal, Glasgow.

We turn left at the Pearl, the nearest pub to the opera house and therefore used, before the opera house acquired a bar of its own, for a drink in the intervals. But in those days it was called Des Corish's, from the name of the host, who was the brother of the Leader of the Irish Labour Party, Brendan Corish; he, a regular festival-goer and an affectionately fraternal man, would lend his brother a hand behind the bar in the rush-hour. It is not many people in Britain, I think who can say that they have drunk a pint pulled by the Leader of the Opposition.

First surprise for the new Wexfordians: the entrance to the opera house. The Theatre Royal is set in a little street of little houses, and is nothing but a little house itself; indeed, until the little house next door was acquired, it had no room for a foyer or a bar, and an absent-minded visitor could easily walk past the front of it. Even now, the tiny auditorium has none of the pillars or porticoes of grander opera theatres. Second surprise: the orchestra pit is so small that the conductor cannot get to his place from backstage, and round grow the eyes of the first-timers as he marches down the centre aisle of the stalls, opens a little wicket-gate in the orchestra-pit rail, steps through it, shuts it neatly behind him as though the musicians might otherwise escape and trample down a neighbour's field, and takes his place.

All performances at Wexford start with The Soldier's Song, the Irish Republic's national anthem; it is one of the most stirring of all, almost as thrilling as the Marseillaise itself (though I have sometimes wondered, listening to its martial strains, how we are to take seriously a country in which the words of the national anthem were written by Brendan Behan's uncle) and gave rise a few years ago to a charming dilemma. I was having lunch with the then Director of the Wexford Festival, Thomson Smillie, in London and months from Festival-time, when he said he had a problem. What was it? Well, he said, as I knew, one of the operas in the forthcoming Festival was to be Cavalli's *Eritrea* (it proved to be one of the very few unmitigated musical disasters in the history of Wexford, but that was a different problem altogether). Now the orchestral scoring of that recondite work, he explained, was – at any rate in the realization he was using – for six violins, four 'cellos, a sprinkling of the lighter woodwind, a *viol d'amore* and a *cembalo*. But wherein, I enquired, lay the problem? 'Well,' said Thomson, 'how do you arrange The Soldier's Song for a combo like that?' I had, instantaneously, a glorious aural vision: no brass, no drums, no cymbals, no bassoons, no oboes even. The rousing fervour of Ireland's marching tribute to her heroes would become a bloodless saunter, commemorating an epicene army which could scarcely have tackled Peter Rabbit, let alone the Black and Tans. 'What are you going to do?' I asked. 'I think', he said, 'that I'll have to use a record.' I assured him warmly that if he did, and thus deprived me of the pleasure of the weird sound that would otherwise be provided, I would never speak to him again, and the threat worked – at any rate The Soldier's Song came out as a high-pitched and scratchy wail from Hector's ghost.

But first there are old friends to be greeted in the foyer, starting with the Wexfordians themselves, Tom Walsh naturally chief among them, then the Guinness team, then the people who run the Festival, sit on its committees or help organize its fund-raising. Again, I wonder: why? Nobody makes a penny out of it, nobody is even going to get a C.B.E., for they don't have such things in Ireland. Why does it matter to these people that Wexford should remain a byword for music and happiness? It really is very mysterious.

Puccini's *Edgar* now opens the proceedings; it has a plot of exceptionally complete absurdity, like Verdi in the toils of his worst early librettists, and with very Verdian music, too. The heroine is called Fidelia and the villainess Tigrana (we know she is the villainess because she wears a red blouse and has one of those loops in the side of her skirt). But the music, though Puccini had not yet fully found his own voice in it, is passionate and lyrical, and this year's Wexford is off to a ripe start.

Rounder and rounder grow the newcomers' eyes; it is now well after midnight, for the opera at Wexford always starts at 8·30, but back at the hotel, where the distinction between night and day was lost years ago, the Pike Grill is happy to receive us and to serve bacon and eggs and more champagne to go with it; old-timers are excused while I tell the tenderfeet of the occasion when even by Wexford's standards it was too late for dinner (it was, as a matter of fact, well after 3 a.m.), and a number of the company expressed a desire for bacon and eggs. A few seconds' negotiation with the management, the kitchens were flung open, and I cooked bacon and eggs for all. Inevitably, the feat has grown more remarkable as the years have gone by; tonight, I insist that I cooked 640 *gross* of eggs, with similar supplies of bacon. I dare say it wasn't quite so many.

SATURDAY, NOVEMBER 1ST

Saturday is boat day. Lie-a-beds lie a-bed, but I go for a brisk walk, the sky still being clear, and crossing the harbour bridge, for Wexford stands right on the mouth of the River Slaney, and the open sea is just beyond, in the teeth of the east wind, tangy with salt, that is invariably blowing from offshore, I feel that unmistakable lift of the heart that tells me that Wexford's magic has worked once again, not only for me and the regulars, but for the newcomers too.

Along the front, the annual angling competition (what a competitive lot these Wexfordians are, to be sure) is taking place. Since no self-respecting fish would be seen bathing in the muddy waters on this side of the harbour, the catch in this fiercely fought encounter is never large, and the prize is usually won by a minnow slightly larger than the other minnows, though I am alone responsible for spreading the story that the judges weigh the contestants' fish on a letter-balance. But if a fisherman anywhere is a serene and contemplative figure, heedless of his failure to garner an entire shoal of whales, a Wexford fisherman is even more content to watch the world go by and eat meat for his dinner.

Back to the hotel, for The Team has been instructed to be on parade at 11 a.m., and it will not do for The Leader to be late. New Ross, seventeen miles away, is where The Boat starts from, the Fletchers' boat, which rides low in the water when we board it but draws much less by the time we have eaten and drunk our fill.

Woodtours and Levintours combine for this outing too, and the joint party, always augmented by extra friends who have come independently, now fills one complete side of the dining saloon. The meal is, if anything, better than ever; if Mr Fletcher were ever willing to swallow the anchor and set up a restaurant on dry land – preferably in London, which has great need of him, and especially of his home-baked bread – he would make his fortune. But maybe he makes his fortune anyway.

Back in Wexford, The Team is warned to be ready at 6 p.m., for the next treat. The next treat is the Guinness party, one of the most remarkable occasions of the year, let alone of the Wexford Festival. It is held at White's Hotel, in a vast barn at the back; along two gigantic tables, each quite forty feet long, there is spread a buffet that would have put to shame the catering at the Field of Cloth of Gold. Giant whole salmon lie in their jelly, gill to cheek with glazed boars' heads, monster turkeys rear up for slicing, rows of hams suggest that there is not a pig alive in Ireland this night, mounds of potatoes, hills of beet, Everests of salad swell from the surface of the tables. What is more, everything is duplicated, for the two tables are set as two sides of a square, and carry the same riches from the outer end to the corner where they meet. This is to obviate queueing, though clients of Levintours have all been instructed, should there none the less be a line of hungry mouths waiting to be fed, to follow Arianna closely, like intrepid motorists clinging to the tail of an ambulance through a traffic-jam, as she deploys that incomparable skill of charming a queue into thin air before her.

It is time to go to the opera, after the usual search for a Guinness to thank; they tend to vanish modestly into the throng. Handel's *Orlando*, based on Ariosto, is a typical Wexford revival. From the start, Wexford has recognized that it cannot compete with the wealthier and more old-established festivals for stars, and should not compete with them for repertoire. It solves the first problem by seeking and finding young singers of promise at the outset of their careers, and the second, as I have said, by choosing operas not often performed elsewhere.

I doubt if *Orlando* has ever been professionally performed in Ireland, or Britain for that matter, and it divides interval-opinion sharply, some finding it lifeless and prettified, more, including me, declaring it a revelation in the field of what may be termed Palladian opera. Of course it isn't as dramatic as opera was just about to become when it was written, but it can be acquitted of the usual charge levelled against Handel's operas: it is not just an oratorio in costume, for these characters, or some of them, have real blood in them. The sets are hideous, unfortunately; how can it have escaped the attention of the producer, even if it did that of the designer, that music of this kind demands classical vistas, pillars, bosky dells, little temples open to the sky, instead of the grim wire-mesh contraption over which the cast spends much of its time clambering? It's a strong cast, though, with a commanding performance by John Angelo Messana in the hellishly difficult counter-tenor role of Orlando, and a sensational young Wexford find in Lesley Garrett as the shepherdess Dorinda, a classic Despina in the making if I ever heard one.

I told the newcomers that, despite the Guinness party, they would be ready for bacon and eggs after the opera. They didn't believe me; but they do now.

SUNDAY, NOVEMBER 2ND

Anyway, hangovers are unknown at Wexford, though I go out for another walk in the still-clear air, just in case. (For years we have not needed to ask Paddy for the English papers, which are very hard to come by in Wexford, particularly on the Sunday, and he brings up a precious set the moment they arrive – I sometimes think he hijacks the train bearing them, just outside the town.) Before lunch, we gather at Tom Walsh's beautiful Georgian home, where he keeps open house at this time on the final day of the Festival each year: the last ritual for the newcomers to enjoy. Tom was widowed a few years ago, and I claim my annual kiss from his daughter Victoria, who presides over Tom's revels, looking as usual as though she has just floated in through the window, borne on a leaf; perhaps she has.

On now to White's, for the last joint gathering of Woodtours and Levintours – Alan's Sunday lunch. Arianna has gone on ahead; I suspect nothing, having forgotten what the reason must be, and after I have waited for ten minutes or so downstairs, a kindly passer-by says casually to me, 'She's in the boutique.' Well, of course she's in the boutique; with a scream of dismay, I rush up to the lobby, but once again I am too late; she has already bought half the clothes in the place, and is only awaiting my arrival with a cheque-book.

At lunch, Alan and Joan have given us all alliterative place-cards, and thereby hangs a tale of such horror that as the memory comes back to me I shudder with the pain of it. A few Wexfords ago, Hugh and Reta Casson came with Woodtours, and Hugh went to the extraordinary (well, not extraordinary for him) trouble of doing a little pen-and-ink thumbnail sketch for each place. We were all caught in some familiar guise or pose or doing something connected with our work or with some anecdote for which we were Wexfordianally known; I, for instance, was seen hurrying along the street in cloak and opera-hat, my shadow following close behind. Last year, the Cassons came again, and Hugh surpassed himself; he did for each of us, again on an individually relevant theme, a beautiful and delicate water-colour; this time I was depicted as Captain Levin of Levintours, peaked cap cocked at a nautical angle.

We each admired our own, and a brisk interchange went on, so that we could also each admire all the others. An idea took shape in my mind.

When will I learn to curb my tongue, to follow the advice of all those who tell us always to sleep on a new idea, not to post fraught letters until the following day, to count ten before opening our mouths on any subject more significant than stamp collecting? Never, I fear; at any rate I had not learned to do so on this occasion. A word in Hugh's ear, to get his benediction on my plan (why doesn't *he* learn to keep his mouth shut when lunatics like me are roaming around seeking whom they may devour?) and I rose to announce that if the company would lend me their precious pictures, I would explore the possibility of having them all printed, in colour, in a booklet, so that in addition to our own original Casson we could have the complete set of reproductions of everybody else's.

The idea was greeted with acclaim (why can't *anybody* learn discretion?); I collected up twenty-seven original paintings by the President of the Royal Academy; I took them to London and discovered that for technical reasons my plan was impossible except at prohibitive cost; and my brief-case containing them was stolen from me on the pavement outside Fortnum & Mason – which, just to make matters symbolically worse, is itself opposite the Royal Academy.

Life being what it is, I did not realize for two days, spent cursing the thief for the loss of letters, notes, and other papers of no monetary worth but incalculable nuisance-value when it came to remembering, restoring or reconstructing them, that Hugh's pictures were in it.

It is almost an examination question for a degree in moral philosophy, or possibly an after-dinner game in a rather morbid household: how do you tell a couple of dozen people that you have lost *all* their portraits by Sir Hugh Casson, P.R.A.? For the life of me, I could not think of any answer to that question, and crawled about for nearly a fortnight in a kind of anaesthetized despair. Then I thought I had better start by telling the artist, so I went to see Hugh. He clucked sympathetically, then said in an off-hand manner, 'Well, provided you don't need them by next Wednesday, I'll do them all again.' So I assured him I didn't need them by next Wednesday, and he did. He turned them out in batches, and every time I collected a batch I sent them off; I had finally written all the letters of horror, condolence and apology, with a happy ending in the form of an assurance that replacements would arrive in due course. Two pictures only have not been delivered, and these I now have with me, to be presented, with a scarcely discernible trembling of the hand, here on the very spot where the first act of the tragi-comedy took place. But until I die, anyone speaking ill of Hugh Casson in my presence will very speedily wish that he had not, and even after I die anyone doing so within earshot of my ghost will be no better off.

The Woods' lunch goes on, as usual, until tea-time, which means that there is not really time to do anything but snooze, bathe and make ready for the opera and the last night of this year's Wexford.

Wexford does not do much modern opera, but what opera house does? The Festival saw its first Britten, *Albert Herring*, in 1970 and its second, *The Turn of the Screw*, in 1976; its first Janacek, *Katya Kabanova*, perhaps the best production of any opera in my fourteen Wexfords, in 1972; its first Prokoviev, *The Gambler*, in 1973. This year there is an opera by a living composer, and an American one, too: Carlisle Floyd's *Of Mice and Men*, from the Steinbeck novel. This comes with an American reputation; apparently it has already had several productions – no small achievement for a new opera anywhere. In the event, it is easy to see why it has become popular. For one thing, the strong, stark story has been successfully adapted (by the composer) for its musical transmogrification; for another, the music is lyrical and passionate at once, and full of colour and strength. There is nothing meretricious or cunning, let alone vulgar, about the score; if it is not music of great profundity or originality, it is certainly honest, dramatic and fitting, and the cheers at the end are as loud as any I can remember hearing in this house.

But we old hands know that, be the cheers for the final opera never so loud, there is more to come before Wexford finishes. First, there is the announcement from the stage of next year's repertoire, which includes Verdi's only other comic opera, *Un Giorno di Regno*, and Mozart's early, incomplete and mostly unperformed miniature, *Zaide*; within minutes half Wexford is convinced that what has been announced is *Aida*. Then the orchestra, which has remained in its place, strikes up those familiar opening bars, and we all join hands and sing 'Auld Lang Syne'. On the last night of Wexford you can find yourself linking arms with a monk, the Bishop, or even Tom Walsh.

During the bacon and eggs and mutual self-congratulation on our extraordinary wisdom in coming to the Wexford Festival there is an almighty crash outside the front door of the hotel. Snug in the grill, we murmur perfunctory commiserations for the owner of whatever vehicle is, to judge by the noise, a complete write-off; our commiserations turn heartfelt when one of our number, who has gone out to investigate, returns with the news that it is our minibus that has copped it.

The situation proves less serious than feared, at any rate for the minibus; a car being driven rapidly along the road has slewed across it, cannoned into a Jaguar parked beside us, which has been driven violently against the side of the minibus, and veered back into the middle of the road again. The police have arrived, and the young man who was driving the missile is in their custody; something in his demeanour suggests strongly that among the charges to be preferred will be one of driving under the influence of strong liquor. The Jaguar is in a bad state, but the minibus has sustained only a serious dent and a few unserious scratches, and the dent is not so serious as to impair its fitness to take us back to Dublin in the morning.

MONDAY, NOVEMBER 3RD

Which it does, and after another bottle in the airport bar, we return to London, full of joy and music. Eva Blumenau describes the three days we have just had as 'the world's best children's party for adults', and she has seen into the heart of Wexford's mystery, for we are all children at Wexford, innocent and delighted, accepting joy as the natural order of the universe, as indeed it is, though away from Wexford, we find it more difficult to believe.

But this visit has restored that belief, which indeed every visit to Wexford does, and we feel like the banished Duke in the Forest of Arden; we 'fleet the time carelessly, as they did in the golden world'. Tom Walsh, thirty years ago, little knew what he was starting. Or perhaps he did; perhaps he understood that the world needs such happiness if it is not to perish utterly, and divined a way to bring it about. Well, he built the foundations soundly, and here in Wexford his monument stands, a festival of music and joy to refresh the spirits, brighten the sky and flavour the year, until, as the months come round, it is time once again for me to get into the minibus at dawn and start criss-crossing London to collect the esteemed patrons of Levintours for the drive to Heathrow.

Index

JAMES GALWAY

AN AUTOBIOGRAPHY

Whether it's a Mozart concerto, a rollicking Irish jig, or Annie's Song, the enchanting hit single that took him to the top of the charts – there's nothing quite like the musical fireworks of James Galway.

But despite his international fame, to his friends and family back in the streets of Belfast he's still plain Jimmy Galway – the kid who played the penny whistle.

Here then is the heart-warming story of music's most unconventional, most engaging star – from his apprenticeship in Uncle Joe's flute band to fame and fortune alongside some of the greatest names the world of music has ever known.

'Full of anecdotes and characteristic humour'
The Bookseller

Post·A·Book

A Royal Mail service in association with the Book Marketing Council & The Booksellers Association.
Post-A-Book is a Post Office trademark.

CLEMENT FREUD

FREUD ON FOOD

For the first time, Clement Freud has produced a full-length book containing the distillation of his many years' experience as cook, restaurateur and writer on food.

Recipes and anecdotes jostle each other for the reader's attention. The book is brimming with compulsive recipes for dishes as various as Billybi, Cider Duck, Boiled Leg of Lamb with Caper Sauce, and Strawberry Romanoff. And there are amusing suggestions for occasions as well — dinner parties, picnics, Sunday lunch and week-end breakfasts.

'The joy of this book is that you get the wit — and it's a funny book — with no more than armchair effort. His approach to food gives a real lift to the spirit.'

Prue Leith, *Books and Bookmen*

CORONET BOOKS

ALEXANDER WALKER

PETER SELLERS

What did Peter Sellers do on the last day of his life? Why were some of his marriages so unsuccessful and painful? What really was his relationship with his children? Above all, whence sprang the genius for comedy that made him a great and memorable star in movies like *I'm All Right, Jack, Dr Strangelove,* the *Pink Panthers* and *Being There*? Aided by hitherto highly confidential information, and revelations of the utmost candour by Lynne Frederick, Sellers' widow, Alexander Walker has compiled a discerning and compassionate, yet often shocking, study of the British cinema's greatest post-war star and the international screen's finest clown.

'Compulsive reading . . . critical and compassionate, it comes as close to the truth of the artist and man as is likely.'

Roy Boulting

CORONET BOOKS

JOHN COTTRELL

LAURENCE OLIVIER

He has been called the finest actor of the twentieth century. His performances in theatre and film are now part of history – from *Henry V, Richard III* and *Rebecca* to *Othello, A Long Day's Journey Into Night* and *Sleuth*. He was the director of the three greatest Shakespeare films; and was the guiding spirit behind the National Theatre.

Laurence Olivier – a legend in his own lifetime, but what of the man behind the actor's mask? This is the fascinating story of Olivier's progress from a gauche, stage-struck parson's son to the honoured doyen of contemporary theatre.

CORONET BOOKS

ALSO AVAILABLE FROM CORONET BOOKS